The Figure of the Musician in German Literature

UNC | COLLEGE OF ARTS AND SCIENCES
Germanic and Slavic Languages and Literatures

From 1949 to 2004, UNC Press and the UNC Department of Germanic & Slavic Languages and Literatures published the UNC Studies in the Germanic Languages and Literatures series. Monographs, anthologies, and critical editions in the series covered an array of topics including medieval and modern literature, theater, linguistics, philology, onomastics, and the history of ideas. Through the generous support of the National Endowment for the Humanities and the Andrew W. Mellon Foundation, books in the series have been reissued in new paperback and open access digital editions. For a complete list of books visit www.uncpress.org.

The Figure of the Musician in German Literature

GEORGE C. SCHOOLFIELD

UNC Studies in the Germanic Languages and Literatures
Number 19

Copyright © 1956

This work is licensed under a Creative Commons CC BY-NC-ND license. To view a copy of the license, visit http://creativecommons.org/licenses.

Suggested citation: Schoolfield, George C. *The Figure of the Musician in German Literature*. Chapel Hill: University of North Carolina Press, 1956. DOI: https://doi.org/10.5149/9781469658315_Schoolfield

Library of Congress Cataloging-in-Publication Data
Names: Schoolfield, George C.
Title: The figure of the musician in German literature / by George C. Schoolfield.
Other titles: University of North Carolina Studies in the Germanic Languages and Literatures ; no. 19.
Description: Chapel Hill : University of North Carolina Press, [1956] Series: University of North Carolina Studies in the Germanic Languages and Literatures. | Includes bibliographical references.
Identifiers: LCCN 56063563 | ISBN 978-0-8078-8019-7 (pbk: alk. paper) | ISBN 978-1-4696-5831-5 (ebook)
Subjects: Musicians in literature. | German literature — History and criticism.
Classification: LCC PD25 .N6 NO. 19 | DCC 830/ .9

Table of Contents

	Page
Preface	xiii

Introduction: The Musician in German Literature before Romanticism

König Rother	1
Gottfried von Strassburg, *Tristan*	1
Kudrunslied:	1
Horant	1
Nibelungenlied:	1
Volker	1
Wittenweiler, *Der Ring*	1
Grimmelshausen, *Simplicius Simplicissimus; Der seltsame Springinsfeld*	2
Beer, *Simplicianischer Welt-Kucker oder abenteuerlicher Jan Rebhu*	2
Printz, *Musicus vexatus; Musicus curiosus; Musicus magnanimus:* Cotala, Battalus, Pancalus	2
Kuhnau, *Der musikalische Quacksalber:*	2
Teueraffe-Caraffa	2
Knigge, *Die Reise nach Braunschweig:*	3
Dubois-Carino-Zarowsky-Leuthammer	3
Goethe, *Wilhelm Meisters Lehrjahre:*	3
The harpist	3
Schiller, *Kabale und Liebe:*	3
Stadtmusikant Miller	3
Moritz, *Anton Reiser:*	4
Goethe, *Unterhaltungen deutscher Ausgewanderten:*	4
Antonelli	4
Heinse, *Hildegard von Hohenthal*	4
Lockmann, Hildegard	4

I. Romanticism	10
Wackenroder, *Herzensergiessungen eines kunstliebenden Klosterbruders; Phantasien über die Kunst für Freunde der Kunst:*	10
Joseph Berglinger	10
Rochlitz, *Aus dem Leben eines Tonkünstlers:*	14
Ludolph, Franzesco, Laura	14
Rochlitz, *Der Besuch im Irrenhause:*	15
Karl, Lottchen	15
Hoffmann, *Kreisleriana, Kater Murr:*	17
Johannes Kreisler, Julia	17
Hoffmann, *Das Sanctus:*	25
Bettina, Zulema	25
Kleist, *Die heilige Caecilie*	26
Hoffmann, *Ritter Gluck*	28
Hoffmann, *Don Juan:*	28
"Donna Anna"	28

Table of Contents

	Page
Tieck, *Musikalische Leiden und Freuden:*	30
Alten, Julie	30
Hauff, *Die Sängerin:*	31
Bolnau-Bolani, Giuseppa Fiametti	31
Hoffmann, *Rat Krespel:*	33
Krespel, Antonie	33
Hoffmann, *Die Automate:*	34
Professor X.	34
Hoffmann, *Kater Murr:*	35
Meister Abraham	35
Tieck, *Musikalische Leiden und Freuden:*	36
Hortensio, Julie	36
Hauff, *Die Sängerin:*	37
Chevalier de Planto, Giuseppa Fiametti	37
Heine, *Florentinische Nächte:*	39
Bellini	39
Paganini	40
Hoffmann, *Die Fermate:*	43
Lauretta, Teresina, Demoiselle Meibel, Theodor	44
Tieck, *Musikalische Leiden und Freuden:*	44
The Italian musician	45
Brentano, *Die mehreren Wehmüller und ungarischen Nationalgesichter:*	46
Michaly	46
Arnim, *Fürst Ganzgott und Sänger Halbgott*	47
Eichendorff, *Aus dem Leben eines Taugenichts*	48
Eichendorff, *Die Freier:*	50
Schlender, Fleder	50
Eichendorff, *Die Glücksritter:*	50
Siglhupfer-Klarinett	50
Eichendorff, *Das Marmorbild:*	51
Florio, Fortunato	51
Eichendorff, *Dichter und ihre Gesellen:*	51
Dryander	51
Müller, *Gedichte aus den hinterlassenen Papieren eines reisenden Waldhornisten:*	54
The Prague musician, the miller	54
Brentano, "Die lustigen Musikanten"	55
II. Biedermeier and Poetic Realism	56
Hoffmann, *Der Baron von B.*	56
Hoffmann, *Der Musikfeind*	57
Tieck, *Musikalische Leiden und Freuden:*	58
The "Musikfeind"	58
Grillparzer, *Der arme Spielmann*	59
Mundt, *Das Duett:*	64
Adelaide, Fanchon, Eduard, Freudenberg	64
Gutzkow, *Die Singekränzchen:*	66
Herr Weber	66

Table of Contents

	Page
Gutzkow, *Die Königin der Nacht:*	66
Lodoiska	66
Kürnberger, *Giovanna:*	67
Edgar von Lauenfels	67
Kinkel, *Der Musikant, eine rheinische Bürgergeschichte:*	68
Franz	68
Kinkel, *Aus dem Tagebuch eines Komponisten*	68
Kinkel, *Musikalische Orthodoxie:*	69
Ida Fernhofer, Sohling	69
Kinkel, *Hans Ibeles in London: ein Familienbild aus dem Flüchtlingsleben*	69
Meissner, *Enthusiasten:*	71
Baron Stein, Bleivogel	72
Stifter, *Zwei Schwestern:*	73
Camilla	73
Stifter, *Der Nachsommer:*	75
Heinrich Drendorf, the huntsman, the master zither maker	75
Storm, *Eine Halligfahrt:*	77
"Der Vetter"	77
Storm, *Ein stiller Musikant:*	78
Christian	78
Storm, *Es waren zwei Königskinder*	80
Marx	80
Lenau, *Faust*	81
Mephistopheles	82
Lenau, *Mischka*	83
Keller, *Romeo und Julia auf dem Dorfe*	84
"Der schwarze Geiger"	84
Keller, *Hadlaub*	87
Keller, *Das Tanzlegendchen*	87
Musa	87
Hoffmann, *Der Kampf der Sänger*	89
Heinrich von Ofterdingen, Wolfram von Eschenbach	89
Wagner, *Tannhäuser*	89
Scheffel, *Der Trompeter von Säkkingen*	91
Jung Werner	91
Wagner, *Die Meistersinger von Nürnberg*	91
Walther von Stolzing	91
Brachvogel, *Narziss*	92
Raabe, *Das Horn von Wanza*	94
Sophie Grünhage's Father	94
Brachvogel, *Friedemann Bach*	95
Mörike, *Mozart auf der Reise nach Prag*	96
Kürnberger, *Der Dichter des Don Juan:*	103
Lorenzo da Ponte	103
Nietzsche, *Die Geburt der Tragödie aus dem Geiste der Musik; Richard Wagner in Bayreuth; Der Fall Wagner; Nietzsche contra Wagner*	103

	Page
III. The Post-Wagnerian Age	107
Schubin, *Die Geschichte eines Genies:*	108
Alphonse de Sterny, Gesa van Zuylen	108
Wolzogen, *Der Kraft-Mayr:*	109
Florian Mayr, Antonin Prczewalski, Peter Gais, Franz Liszt	109
Strauss, *Freund Hein:*	111
Heiner	111
Huch, *Enzio:*	114
Enzio, the Kapellmeister, Richard	114
Bahr, *Der arme Narr:*	116
Hugo	117
Schaukal, *Kapellmeister Kreisler*	118
Schnitzler, *Zwischenspiel:*	119
Amadeus, Caecilie	119
Wassermann, *Das Gänsemännchen:*	120
Daniel Nothafft	120
Saar, *Die Geigerin:*	123
Anna, Mimi, Ludovica	123
Sudermann, *Heimat:*	124
Magda	124
Schnitzler, *Frau Berta Garlan:*	125
Berta Garlan, Emil	125
Bahr, *Die Andere:*	125
Lida, Amschl	125
Wedekind, *Musik:*	126
Klara Hühnerwadel, Josef Reissner	126
Dauthendey, *Josa Gerth*	127
Dauthendey, *Raubmenschen:*	128
Hanna	129
Hofmannsthal, *Der Abenteurer und die Sängerin:*	130
Vittoria	130
Heinrich Mann, *Die Branzilla*	131
Thomas Mann, *Tristan:*	133
Frau Klöterjahn	133
Halbe, *Die Tat des Dietrich Stobäus:*	133
Karola	133
Thomas Mann, *Das Wunderkind:*	135
Bibi Saccellaphylaccas	135
Hesse, *Gertrud:*	136
Heinrich Muoth	136
Zahn, *Der Geiger:*	137
Der Troger-Jakob	137
Sternheim, *Bürger Schippel*	137
Stern, *Ohne Ideale:*	138
Camillo Arsakoff	138
Wedekind, *Der Kammersänger:*	139
Gerardo	140

	Page
Bahr, *Das Konzert:*	141
Gustav Heink	141
Sternheim, *Schuhlin*	142
Sudermann, *Das hohe Lied:*	143
Kapellmeister Czepanek	143
Heinrich Mann, *Die kleine Stadt:*	144
Flora Garlinda, Itala Molesin, Nello Gennari, Gaddi, Cavaliere Giordano, Dorlenghi	145
Thomas Mann, *Buddenbrooks:*	146
Hanno Buddenbrook	146
Hesse, *Peter Camenzind:*	147
Richard	147
Hesse, *Gertrud*	148
Kuhn	149

IV. The Age of Musicology 151

Wassermann, *Laudin und die Seinen:*	151
Nikolaus Fraundorfer	151
Hauptmann, *Die Hochzeit auf Buchenhorst:*	151
Dietrich Kühnelle	151
Schäfer, *Der Cellospieler*	152
Schaeffer, *Fidelio:*	152
Peter Nehr	153
Borrmann, *Der Zwerg und das Grammophon:*	153
Hugo	153
Borrmann, *Venus mit dem Orgelspieler:*	154
Zebedäus	154
Alfred Neumann, *Rugge*	154
Winder, *Die jüdische Orgel:*	155
Etelka	155
Borrmann, *Der Don Juan der halben Dinge:*	155
Alice	155
Robert Neumann, *Karriere:*	155
Erna	155
Strauss, *Der Spiegel:*	155
Josef	155
Stehr, *Der Geigenmacher*	156
Hesse, *Der Steppenwolf:*	158
Pablo, Mozart	158
Brod, *Das grosse Wagnis:*	158
E. St.	158
Stoessl, *Sonnenmelodie:*	159
Johann Körrer	159
Schickele, *Symphonie für Jazz:*	161
John van Maray	161
Muschler, *Ivola:*	162
Abel Kühn	163
Kluge, *Die Zaubergeige:*	164
Andreas	
Schaffner, *Kampf und Reife:*	164

Table of Contents

	Page
Johannes Schattenhold	164
Ziesel, *Verwandlung der Herzen:*	165
Dietrich Vorwerk	165
Thomas Mann, *Betrachtungen eines Unpolitischen:*	166
Palestrina	166
Thomas Mann, *Leiden und Grösse Richard Wagners*	167
Werfel, *Verdi*	168
Verdi, Margherita Dezorzi, Fischböck	168
Thomas Mann, *Doktor Faustus:*	171
Adrian Leverkühn	172
Wendell Kretzschmar	185
Rudi Schwerdtfeger	186
Saul Fitelberg	188
Hesse, *Das Glasperlenspiel:*	190
Josef Knecht, the "magister musicae," Carlo Ferromonte	192
Conclusion	194
Notes	197
Index	201

PREFACE

The following study is meant to offer a picture of the musician as a figure in German creative literature during the years from the birth of Wackenroder's Joseph Berglinger to the publication of Thomas Mann's *Doktor Faustus*. A similar investigation has not been attempted heretofore. The theme would seem by its very nature to defeat itself; even the superficial reader of German literature will have been struck by the frequency with which the musician appears, not a surprising phenomenon, of course, in a culture so shot through with music as the German. From the first the most difficult problem was not the collection of material but its assortment and choice. In order to produce a survey of a practicable size, and to avoid the danger of mere cataloguing, it was found necessary to omit a consideration of works frequently interesting and sometimes possessing artistic worth. The centuries prior to the beginning of Romanticism have been given what may appear to be cavalier treatment; but the musically talented heroes of the Middle Ages are not musicians in the modern sense—music is but one of their many skills, having but little bearing upon their character. The lack of truly creative literature in the decline of the medieval world and during that age called frequently, and loosely, "Reformation and Renaissance," precludes a treatment of these periods, at least in a study which hopes to do justice to the later "Golden Age" of musical literature. Aided by the development of the novel, the Baroque and the eighteenth century alike present fascinating examples of the musician who is just that, not a noble adventurer in disguise, more devoted to the sword than to the harp. Since the musical novel from Grimmelshausen to Heinse has been described by H. F. Menck in his *Der Musiker im Roman*, however, the present writer believed that his hands were free to begin his intensive study with the inception of Romanticism.

Even in the nineteenth and twentieth centuries not every figure deserving consideration could be included; and the writer's dilemma frequently resembled that of the anthologist who strives to find a balance between the artistically distinguished and the representative. Authors like Lyser and Fouqué had to be dropped from the consideration of the Romantic musician, Wilhelm Riehl from that of the musician of Biedermeier and Poetic Realism; while in more recent days a host of musical novelists, by their failure to offer a new insight into the musician's soul, fell prey to the requirement of "Übersichtlichkeit." Not that any major work has been ignored; indeed, the relatively thorough interpretation of a *Mozart auf der Reise nach Prag* or a *Doktor Faustus* was thought to outweigh the mention, with scanty comment, of any number of lesser works. On the other hand, representative but literarily unsatisfying productions, such as the *Hans Ibeles* of Johanna Kinkel or Friederich Huch's *Enzio*, required lengthy discussion because of their historical value. Even bad literature could on occasion be adduced to illustrate the musician's literary decline; witness the tasteless musical portraits of the nineteen-twenties. Thus the writer has tried to give the great works and the representative works their due, and at the same time to describe the rising and falling curve of the musician's fortunes in literature, a curve which can and should be connected with the musician's fortunes in actual life.

The attempt to achieve conciseness has meant that the study must be concentrated upon the twin forms of the novel and the novella, where the musician can be examined most closely and at greatest length. Yet again, the musician of the lyric, the verse-epic, and the drama has not been excluded when his presence may illuminate a point or exemplify a type. The virtuoso in German literature could not very well be described if Wedekind's *Kammersänger* were sacrificed to an artificial limitation of the study to the prose narrative.

The nature of the material has also forced the writer to take certain expedients which are perhaps not congruent with the purest of critical standards. In an apparently rough-hewn fashion the book has been divided into four periods, Romanticism, Biedermeier and Poetic Realism, The Post-Wagnerian Age, and The Age of Musicology. The writer is well aware that the first chapter heading has a literary and musical connotation, the second is literary alone, while the last two have to do with music. The mixture of art forms and classifications has been necessary because of the peculiar relation between literature and music in Germany. Literary and musical Romanticism are much alike in form and expression, but in the eighteen-twenties literature assumes a character more and more opposed to Romanticism, in whose spirit however music continues. Since the problem at hand is basically literary, the second chapter employs those categories with which literary history, when speaking of the decades following the decline of Romanticism, has so often dealt. In the latter part of the century, literature, increasingly concerned with the abnormal personality and standing in the shadow of Richard Wagner, found itself closer to contemporary music—or, at any event to the contemporary musician—once more; and so the title "The Post-Wagnerian Era" was chosen for the age ending approximately with the First World War and the evaporation of Wagner's influence upon the literary man. In the final period, "The Age of Musicology," literature's chief representatives become infected with the idea that music can be regarded scientifically, as something to be studied rather than felt, and as a mode of artistic expression which has passed its zenith.

In dealing with the musician in literature, it is difficult and foolhardy to work with literary concepts alone; it is impossible to cut literature to fit a musical pattern. A tolerant and presumably careful judgment should be the author's means, a presentation of the whole picture his aim, rather than the pursuance of a scheme rigidly bound either to literary or musical history. The motto of the laborer in the two fields of art should not be a Kierkegaardian "Either-Or" but a Strindbergian "Both-And." Pater Melchior in *To Damascus* remarks: "Do not say 'Either-Or' but rather 'Both-And.' With a word, or two: 'Humanity!' and 'Resignation.'" The student of musical literature may not know more of humanity when he has finished his work, but he surely will have learned something of resignation.

The study is based upon a doctoral dissertation presented at Princeton University in 1949. A Fulbright Research Fellowship to Austria in 1952-53 made possible the collection of considerable additional material. The writer's special thanks are due to Professor Walter Silz who suggested and directed the original dissertation, and, what is still more important, encouraged the completion of the undertaking in ways too numerous to be mentioned here. Nor should the writer's gratitude to his wife and to his friends, Byron Koekkock and Gerard Schmidt, be forgotten.

GEORGE C. SCHOOLFIELD

Lund, Sweden
Spring, 1956

INTRODUCTION:

THE MUSICIAN IN GERMAN LITERATURE BEFORE ROMANTICISM

The musician as an imaginary figure in German creative literature makes his debut with the Middle High German epic, where he appears as the Spielmann, feigned or real. The disguise of the wandering musician is a favorite one of the epic hero. In *König Rother* (c. 1150-1160) the young monarch sails to Constantinople, and there, as the harper Dietrich, frees his imprisoned envoys and kidnaps the emperor's daughter. In Gottfried von Strassburg's Tristan epic (c. 1210) King Mark's nephew likewise assumes the garb of the Spielmann during his first visit to Ireland: as "Tantris" he becomes the tutor of his future love. The Spielmann of the folk-epic, here not a masquerading hero but an actual musician, assumes a more important role. Horant is a major figure in the sea-epic, the *Kudrunslied* (c. 1240); through his song Hilde of Ireland is persuaded to hear the suit of Hetel—the musician of the middle ages is often the venturesome wooer, for himself or someone else. The description of Horant's song in the sixth book of the epic is justly one of the more famous passages in medieval German literature and a worthy ancestor of Hoffmann's or Mörike's portrayal of the *Don Juan* music: the poet of the thirteenth century handily solves the vexatious problem of how music is to be reproduced in words. Horant has a more heroic counterpart in the *Nibelungenlied's* Volker (c. 1200), a brilliant fiddler as well as one of the doughtiest warriors in the Burgundian host. Volker, who with his fiddling prefigures the demonic violinists of nineteenth century literature, represents an apotheosis of the medieval Spielmann, combining all of that figure's positive qualities, his talent, his wit, and his daring.

Courtly culture declines, and with it the musician as a narrative figure; in a poem such as Heinrich Wittenweiler's *Der Ring* (c. 1400) we find the musician as a wretched entertainer at village dances. During the Reformation German music, producing a Hassler and a Praetorious, begins its victorious career, but it is not until the age of the Baroque, with its flourishing novel (the best vehicle, of course, for the depiction of the musician's life), that the musician returns to literature as a fully developed entity. Not that the musician has reached even the importance of the poet in the eyes of Baroque society: he is still the entertainer or, at best, the artisan. Grimmelshausen indicates in two of his leading characters that the musician is little better than an outlaw. The titular hero of *Simplicius Simplicissimus* (1668), having made his way to Paris, attracts attention by means of his excellent voice (not to mention his handsome person), and wins a position at the opera. The "Beau Alman," playing the role of Orpheus, arouses such enthusiasm among the ladies of the court that he is kidnapped and kept as a lover. Momentarily Simplicissimus becomes the seventeenth century equivalent of the virtuoso in modern literature, of Wedekind's Gerardo or Bahr's Heink; his real charms are sexual, not musical. In *Der seltsame Springinsfeld* (1670) Grimmelshausen offers an even more degraded example of the musician. Trained in childhood both as musician and juggler, a significant combination of skills, Springinsfeld has music as a livelihood now and again throughout his adventurous life; he marries a girl musician, the daughter of a blind beggar and a far baser individual than her husband. Shortly before his death, having lost his leg and his health, Springinsfeld ekes out an existence by begging and playing the fiddle in village inns.

In Baroque literature of a secondary rank the musician leads a more respectable life and deservedly so, since he takes his role as musician more seriously. Johann Beer's *Simplicianischer Welt-Kucker oder abenteuerlicher Jan Rebhu* (1679) shows a hero still perilously close to the ambiguous Parisian occupations of Simplicissimus.[1] Yet Rebhu has chosen the musician's life and follows it as closely as the picaresque novel, with its exorbitant demands for manifold adventure, will allow him. In the novels of Wolfgang Caspar Printz, *Musicus vexatus* (1690), *Musicus curiosus* and *Musicus magnanimus* (both 1691), the musician, although still submitted to a plethora of hazards, has as his constant aim the winning of a permanent position and a wife: Printz's Cotala becomes a Kapellmeister, his Battalus wins an organist's post. (His Pancalus, less successful, ends as a schoolteacher.) Bach's predecessor as Thomaskantor, Johann Kuhnau, has left an amusing description of the half-artisan, half-picaresque musician of the late Baroque in *Der musikalische Quacksalber* (1700), in which the boastful and dishonest "Caraffa" (the hero's Italianization of his German name, Teueraffe), purified by misfortunes, resolves to become a solid master of his art rather than a wandering rogue.

The amusical age of the Enlightenment produces no literary musicians, but in the last two decades of the eighteenth century the figure begins to appear more frequently, now as the Spielmann, now as the artisan, now, astonishingly, as the composer. The Spielmann has gained a new presumptiousness or a new affliction, the artisan has become vaguely dissatisfied with his lot. Romanticism is in preparation. Adolf Knigge, in *Die Reise nach Braunschweig* (1792), gives a cruel but meaningful vignette of the wandering flute virtuoso, called variously Monsieur Dubois in St. Petersburg, Signor Carino in Berlin, Herr Zarowsky in Hamburg, and Herr Leuthammer in Vienna. In the author's words he is "ein Erz-Taugenichts, der von den Schwächen anderer Leute lebte," a seducer, an embezzler, a thief.[2] However, Knigge's flautist is no mere rogue. One of his severest critics admits that "der Kerl spielt wie ein Engel," adding that the musician believes he is entitled to special privileges because of his genius: "Solche Pfeifer und Geiger glauben, dass sie die wichtigsten Leute im Staate sind . . ." (26). The rogue musician is beginning to assume the airs of the "genius": Knigge's Dubois-Carino, in his shameful way, predicts the battles to be waged by Hoffmann's Kreisler. Goethe's harper in *Wilhelm Meisters Lehrjahre* (1795-96) could be interpreted as a transitional figure between the ambitious wanderer of Knigge and the full-fledged Romantic artist, a noble and tragic example of the Spielmann, and certainly, in his combination of music and madness, he indicates a favorite Romantic theme. However, the complicated history which has brought about the harper's madness (and his entry into the musician's life) would remove him from the group of actual musicians. Music is neither his profession, nor his central passion, nor the cause of his insanity.

The artisan-musician receives more sympathetic attention than does his wandering colleague in Knigge's comical novel. Schiller's Stadtmusikant Miller in *Kabale und Liebe* (1783) is a classical representative of the type: completely pedestrian in his views on art, regarding it as a kind of trade, he is a stable member of the lower middle class, honest and hard-working. In his quality of musician he does not ask to be recognized as an equal by the petty nobility (as the Romantic musician was very shortly to do), nor does he wish to be regarded as an exceptional man—but he does make a brief rebellion against the despot. Miller has a younger and more discontented colleague in K. P. Moritz's *Anton Reiser* (1785-1790). Anton, in order to support himself, becomes a choirboy; to his regret he learns that, instead of serving a noble art, he has entered into a humiliating dependency upon his patrons—a kind of slavery which leaves its victims "am Ende niederträchtig gesinnt." Like Miller, Anton is a citizen, not a Spielmann; yet, despite his nominal membership in respectability, he detests his occupation and himself. Goethe's *Unterhaltungen deutscher Ausgewanderten* (1795) has a feminine counterpart of the artisan-musician. The singer Antonelli stands closer to the boundary between normal society and the demimonde than does Miller or Reiser; it is taken for granted that the woman musician is immoral—an outlook still common in German literature a hundred years later. Goethe's singer is powerful enough to choose and dispose of her lovers as she will; nonetheless she makes an attempt, and a successful one, to lead what she considers to be a quiet and well-ordered—in short, a "respectable" life.

Germany produced a prodigious number of outstanding creative musicians during the eighteenth century, but the composer in his single pre-Romantic appearance remains somewhat in the shadow of his calling's peculiar social position. Like his real fellows, he still has something of the servant about him, although his obvious abilities make an ever stronger claim upon special treatment. Lockmann, in Wilhelm Heinse's *Hildegard von Hohenthal* (1796), is assuredly an exceptional young man. From the very beginning of his life music has been a dominating passion with him, and he commands a brilliant array of talents: he composes an opera that sways Rome's fickle operatic public, he conducts the musicians at a petty court so skillfully that the listeners are reminded of Vienna, he sings with the voice of an angel—and, to boot, he is incomparably handsome. Nor is he unique, for Hildegard has his astonishing gifts translated into the feminine: of a beauty that drives men to insane deeds, she possesses a voice that puts experienced professionals to shame. At her first appearance she takes Rome by storm, and this despite the fact that in her disguise as a castrato she cannot give her physical charms full play. (Unbeknown to the public, Hildegard is the first woman to appear on the Roman stage.) Yet Hildegard is an amateur, Lockmann a professional; Hildegard is of noble birth, Lockmann a poor Kapellmeister. Heinse's plot depends upon this second difference; Lockmann cannot overcome Hildegard's hesitation to breach the social conventions of the day for the sake of love. The heroine marries an English lord, and the hero, recovering from his pain with surprising quickness, weds a Roman beauty.

Lockmann is not a Romantic; his social, erotic, and religious attitudes keep him a man of the eighteenth century. He has dimly realized from the outset that his love for Hildegard is hopeless, although he occasionally takes desperate measures to win her. The Romantic musician of Hoffmann will oppose all those noblemen (and patricians) who refuse to respect the creative musician as an equal. Lockmann receives infinitely more humane treatment at the hands of his high-born acquaintances than does Kreisler; but keeps the insulting gift of money which Hildegard sends him, and begins to persuade himself that he must forsake his love with the thought: "ihr Stand [wird] dir in jeder Rücksicht Händel verursachen."[3] His acquiescence to Hildegard's marriage is not out of keeping with the respectful obedience he grants his prince, against whose wishes it never occurs to him to rebel. (The prince, to be sure, is no Archbishop Colloredo nor even an Esterházy.)

Kreisler, fighting to preserve his adored Julia's physical honor from lustful noblemen, will also turn her into a musical ideal. Lockmann, on the other hand, has always entertained notions of a most fleshly nature about Hildegard; while admiring Hildegard's musical ability, he makes repeated attempts to seduce her. Insofar as the erotic drive is concerned, Lockmann has the overweaning passion of a Romantic; it even compels him to forget the limitations of his standing. But in the Romantic musician eroticism is channeled into musical inspiration; Lockmann begins his great opera, *Achilles in Scyros*, before he knows Hildegard, and for him music and his passion exist side by side, the latter encouraging but not inspiring his compositions: "Hildegard und Musik beschäftigten ihn auch so, dass er für Niemand und für nichts anders Musse hatte" (V, 222). And Hildegard's person can make Lockmann forget music altogether, a distinctly unRomantic happening. As Hildegard sings to Lockmann's accompaniment, her dress comes undone, and Lockmann becomes "ganz lüsternes Auge" (V, 124).

If Hildegard and her divine voice are not the mainspring of

Lockmann's music, no more is he the prey of the religious passion which seizes and inspires certain Romantic musicians. Lockmann and the prince's troupe take part in a Marian festival at a cloister. While Lockmann accomplishes his musical task worthily, he is so little moved by the piety of the place or the event that he undertakes a brief flirtation with a handsome nun. Heinse recounts the incident without a trace of blame for Lockmann: both author and hero are full of pity for the unhappy prisoner of the cloister's walls. (Heinse's flippancy in religious matters is further indicated by the ludicrous scene atop Saint Peter's dome, where the English lord, convinced that Hildegard is not a eunuch, proceeds to disrobe her.) The aversion of Lockmann and Heinse to the church does not only find expression in lubricity. Lockmann considers the composition of church music an easier task than music for the theater: "Die Kirchenmusik ist viel allgemeiner, als die Musik der Oper, welche weit mehr ein Werk des Genies ist . . ." (V, 109). The statement, made in introduction to the *Armida* of Iomelli, would seem to rank that forgotten composer higher than a Bach. A year after *Hildegard* a book would be published in which the youthful Wilhelm Wackenroder presented a different type of composer, consumed by his religious passion. For the musician who believes himself in contact with the transcendental, the composition of church music is a task of great difficulty and even greater responsibility. The musician who, like Lockmann, lacks religious inspiration but possesses what Lockmann calls "Kunst"—technical skill—should not find the writing of music for an ostensibly religious purpose difficult. To Lockmann's credit it must be said that he does not compose church music.

What then is Lockmann's inspiration? He cannot wish to prove himself the equal of Hildegard, since he so readily accepts her dictum that "Albernes Uebel und Weh begegnet uns auf jedem Schritte, wenn wir über unsere angebornen Verhältnisse hinauswollen" (VI, 164). He can write music without Hildegarde; he has done so before meeting her and, we presume, continues after he loses her. Religion has no meaning for him. Heinse's composer is essentially a man without problems, who in the last analysis is content with himself, his situation, and his spiritual condition. Music is not for him the way of contact with another world, or of venting his personal spleen against the present one, or of solving life's riddles. Music is the language he knows best, and therefore he speaks in it. He is not conscious of standing outside the fixed order of the world because of his gifts; he is a part of that world, and the word "genius" does not connote estrangement in his vocabulary. Lockmann realizes that he is simply a musician with greater ability than his fellow craftsmen—whom however he respects: his treatment of the players in the prince's orchestra is exemplary (in contrast to the Romantic genius for whom the work-a-day musician is frequently music's worst enemy). When he speaks of music, as he often does (the greater part of the novel is made up of Lockmann's disquisitions on the musical art), his words are less those of the passionate enthusiast than of the craftsman so full of knowledge that he is dull.

Lockmann's musical idols are the Neapolitan operatic composers Iomelli, Traetta, and Majo, and perhaps less beloved, Händel and Gluck. Bach is ignored, and Haydn and Mozart, while mentioned, are not subjected to the intensive scrutiny that the Italians and Gluck in particular receive. These heroes of Lockmann are figures who at the latest flourished in the seventies, some twenty years before the composition of the novel. Likewise Lockmann's favorite form is the (by the nineties) rather antiquated Italian opera seria, in which the dramatic effect takes second place to the chain of da capo arias; however, in his conversations with Hildegard Lockmann is able to do ample justice to those works of Gluck in which the opera is led toward a more dramatic spirit. Heinse is no more behind his times than Rochlitz, with his Händelian preference or Hoffmann, the celebrator of Gluck and Mozart. But a distinction must be made between the author of *Hildegard* and the later musical writers. Heinse gives his full attention to an interpretation of the musical value of a single work of a composer, regarding that work objectively and without relation to the plot of his novel. Rochlitz and Hoffmann, while likewise presenting fascinating musical interpretations, connect their discussions with their fictional characters, having Händel change a composer's life or a singer die after performing Mozart. Heinse is but vaguely conscious or not at all of the "demonic" powers in music, which in his eyes is a sublime amusement; the Romantics are keenly sensitive to those forces within the art which can lift the musician to the peaks of inspiration or cast him into despair and destruction.

Lockmann, who knows well the victory which harmony has won over the polyphonic style, is perceptive enough to note the emotional possibilities inherent in chord and key, and in this respect is a forerunner of the Romantic theory of music. It is Lockmann's opinion (says Hildegard) "dass jeder Accord seinen besonderen Ausdruck habe, und dass man etwas Besonderes dabei empfinde, auch ohne dass Worte es bezeichnen" (VI, 38); and, speaking for himself Lockmann remarks: "F dur ist, wenn ich mich so ausdrücken darf, schon un einen Grad besonener als das junge frohe Leben im C dur. B dur hat gleichsam die Würde von Magistratspersonen; und Es dur geht in das Feierliche der Priesterschaft. As dur ist Majestät von König und Königin. Des dur geht in den Schauder über vor verborgnen Persischen Sultanen, oder Dämonen" (V, 58). Hoffmann would not have apologized for his comparison by "wenn ich mich so ausdrücken darf," nor would he have used the "demons" as a supplement to Persian sultans. For Hoffmann the emotional possibilities of the harmonic system are but part of a larger scheme to bring music closer to the definite expression of the word; in Heinse the passages just quoted are reflections incidental to Lockmann's critical discussion of the important early eighteenth century question of tempered tuning, of "die gleichschwebende Temperatur"—a matter which by Hoffmann's day was hardly current. (Heinse is himself more than a little precious in his animosity toward a system which, long since generally accepted, had made the harmonic developments of the eighteenth century possible: "[Der gleichschwebenden Temperatur] fehlt . . . die vollkommene Schönheit, und der mannigfaltige Ausdruck," V, 56.) Another favorite Romantic theme, the ideal unity of operatic composer and poet in a single person, is skirted by Reinhold, Lockmann's elderly friend ("Poesie und Musik waren ursprünglich eins," V, 236) and Hildegard ("Welche Wunder würde Gluck nicht getan haben, wenn er wie ein Sophokles erzogen worden wäre," V, 320); and the favorite Romantic device of tone-painting is praised by Lockmann, who finds it in the works of his admired Iomelli. Heinse's characters are more Romantic in their musical theory than in their personal lives, but for all his anticipations of Romantic thought, Heinse is not the truly Romantic thinker he often seems to be: he is too much concerned with the technique of art and too little with the spark of genius. This last word is defined as an ability: "Der Meister muss sich in den

Charakter seiner Personen und deren Leidenschaften versetzen können, und dies mit Tönen ausdrücken" (V, 46). For the Romantic mind, genius is that inner entity which enables the artist to do the seemingly impossible; here it is a skill which might be acquired with practice.

If nonetheless we should grant that Heinse is the first of the Romantic thinkers on music—and the temptation is often strong—he is not the creator of the Romantic musical novel. Heinse's figures are bursting with physical vitality, high spirits, and sheer pleasure at their abilities; theirs is a world without shadows. Heinse does not realize, or will not admit, that the musical artist must pay a price for his talents, a price in happiness, in self-esteem, in mental health. At the close of the novel Reinhold dies and is found "aufgerichtet ... in einer vergnügten Gebärde" (VI, 168). Thus, we presume, Heinse's musicians will some day end, as ever unaware that their art is fraught with terrible dangers for its practitioners. The Spielmann and the artisan, insensitive as they are to the true nature of music, have been forced by the circumstances of their existence to take dim cognizance of the tragedy associated with this most ambiguous of the arts, which enobles and debases, saves and destroys. Lockmann, an unsuspecting "Kind des Glücks" like Hildegard, sees only the light. He sees it steadily, but not with that rare intensity vouchsafed the Romantic hero in the midst of his darkness.

CHAPTER I

ROMANTICISM

The first important musical figure in German Romanticism is Joseph Berglinger, a creation of Wilhelm Wackenroder. A dilettante in the arts, Wackenroder himself had modest ambitions as a composer. In a letter to Tieck he says: "... es bleibt aber noch immer mein Verlangen, einmal in der praktischen Komposition noch weiter zu kommen, dann würd' ich weit reichere Quellen des Räsonements [sic] darüber haben."[1] The little passage reveals much about Wackenroder's relationship to music: if he possessed a more thorough knowledge of music's practical side, he might have richer sources upon which to draw for his conversation, an indication of his purely amateur attitude toward the art. But the desire to compose, betrayed here and still more expressly a little further on (he wanted to set Tieck's Singspiel, *Das Lamm*, to music), is more important: Joseph Berglinger is an embodiment of Wackenroder's wish to become a composer.

Berglinger corresponds closely to Wackenroder: he is more enthusiast than professional, more dreamer than artisan. It is interesting to compare Wackenroder with J. N. Forkel, the biographer of Bach.[2] When Forkel states that Bach is a great performer and composer, he supports his claim by a discussion of Bach's fingering, by the quotation of musical passages. Wackenroder's approach is the opposite; it would seem that Berglinger has no knowledge of technique, that he in fact despises it. Wackenroder's attitude to Berglinger is not different from that which he adopts toward the painters eulogized in his *Herzensergiessungen eines kunstliebenden Klosterbruders* (1797). What we learn of Raphael's ethereality, Michelangelo's grandeur, or Dürer's honesty is not the result of analysis but of uncritical empathy. Yet in the essays on painting there is more solid detail than in the Berglinger narrations, since Wackenroder makes use in the former case of the *Vite* of Giorgio Vasari. Idealizing the musician, Wackenroder does not take recourse to a work like Johann Mattheson's *Grundlagen einer musikalischen Ehrenpforte* (1740) for details on musicians' lives;[3] Forkel's life of Bach, which with its strong religious element might have inspired Wackenroder to a Bach portrait, appeared in 1802, four years after Wackenroder's death. Wackenroder is daring in his decision to draw the musician freehand. Painters and poets were more acceptable subjects for creative literary treatment than musicians, who still lingered, together with actors, in the class of entertainers. Even the Romanticists, with their strong musical tendencies, selected painters instead of musicians as the heroes of their Künstlerromane (Tieck's *Sternbald*, Mörike's *Nolten*). Only a professional musician, such as Hoffmann, elected to give a lengthy picture of the musical artist.

Wackenroder's painters are historical figures, his Berglinger a product of his imagination and the most completely developed artist in the *Herzensergiessungen*. Why did Wackenroder choose the contemporary German musician for his original portrait of the artist? The Dürer essay proves Wackenroder's preference for the honest quality of German art, and not surprisingly he wanted to make his musician a German rather than an Italian. All Wackenroder's Italian artists stem from the period of the Renaissance; Wackenroder regarded contemporary Italian artists as mere charlatans. However, he did not wish to choose a German musician contemporary with Dürer; the *Herzensergiessungen*, despite its concern with the art of the Renaissance and the Reformation, is primarily a book for moderns. Its purpose is to persuade German artists of the late eighteenth century to return to the piety of earlier ages. In the essays on Dürer, Wackenroder says: "Weh muss ich rufen über unser Zeitalter, dass es die Kunst so bloss als ein leichtsinniges Spielwerk der Sinne übt, da sie doch wahrlich etwas sehr Ernsthaftes und Erhabenes ist" (I, 55). A long accusation follows against the "modern" painter, be he German or Italian. Nowhere in Wackenroder is blame laid at the feet of the musician. Wackenroder feels that the musician—in particular, the German musician—still possesses the simplicity of heart which the painter has lost.

Joseph Berglinger is the son of a physician, whose search for new facts about the human body has become an obsession; poverty has gnawed at the father's kindly nature until he ignores his children. Joseph, like so many of his descendants in German musical literature, comes from an unhappy home; however he soon discovers consolation in church music, during the performance of which he often kneels, overcome by reverence. Everyday life disillusions him, and he knows the typical Romantic urge toward solitude. Berglinger's existence is rent by the contrast between ideal and life: "Diese bittere Misshelligkeit zwischen seinem angeborenen ätherischen Enthusiasmus und dem irdischen Anteil an dem Leben eines jeden Menschen, der jeden täglich aus seinen Schwärmereien mit Gewalt herabzieht, quälte ihn sein ganzes Leben hindurch" (I, 131). His father attempts to force him into medicine; forbidden to hear music, the boy becomes physically ill, another trait of the musician in German literature noticeable even in the twentieth century (Emil Strauss's *Freund Hein*). After days of prayer, Joseph decides that God has destined him to become an outstanding artist in the eyes of heaven and earth (I, 137). In this respect Berglinger is again the prototype of the creative musician in German literature; the typical composer believes that he is the bearer of a "mission," one of the divine elect. Firm in his conviction Joseph runs away from home and becomes a famous Kapellmeister, only to grow dissatisfied both with himself and his public. Like Hoffmann's Kreisler he realizes that his audiences have lost their reverence for art, just as he loses his own reverence by playing before them. Berglinger in his despair believes that he alone knows the true nature of art: he arrives at the problem of subjective validity so much discussed in later Romanticism and Biedermeier, and revived during the modern period, where the question, becoming of crucial importance to music itself, is reflected in musical literature. Berglinger decides that the artist must exist only for himself and those few people who understand him (I, 147). Called to his father's deathbed, the terrible scene causes Berglinger to think that he cannot complete his *Passionsmusik*; suddenly heavenly inspiration fills him while he prays, and he finishes his masterwork, dying shortly thereafter.

Religious enthusiasm has played a most important role in Joseph's life, just as it did in the lives of his predecessors, Bach and Händel. The story of his last composition is not much different from the legend told about Händel's composition of *The Messiah*. But Berglinger's febrile religious attitude is unlike the steady faith of his non-fictional predecessors. He is a Catholic, and we think of the customary Romantic distinction between "coldly intellectual" Protestantism and "warmly emotional" Catholicism. He surely does not possess that combination of humility and grandeur to be found in Bach's character. If he is humble, it is not a peaceful humbleness, but rather a state of abject contrition; nor does he possess grandeur, being much too hysterical for that. Forkel believes that the composer must mold the public's taste through the splendor of his example; Berglinger turns his back on the public, having become overly conscious of the suffering his genius causes him. His estrangement from life indirectly brings about his father's demise, since, repelled by the unhappy conditions prevailing in his home, Berglinger has refused to visit it for many years. Berglinger's eldest sister, wasting the money sent her, has allowed the father and the younger children (those who did not fall into immorality) to starve. Wackenroder himself illuminates the contrast between Berglinger and the earlier artists (such as Dürer) who brought forth noble works in defiance of life's misery, and even toys with the thought that perhaps these artists were greater than Berglinger by their very ability to combine life and art. Yet his sympathy remains with Berglinger. A new type of artist, the Romantic artist, has been born.

In the second work of Wackenroder, *Phantasien über die Kunst für Freunde der Kunst* (1799), completed by Ludwig Tieck, Berglinger's views on music itself are expressed. These essays are precisely what we should expect from Wackenroder, impressionistic, enthusiastic, and generalizing. In the first of them, the *Märchen von einem nackten Heiligen,* "der verirrte Genius" of a tormented saint is transfigured through the power of song. The second section, *Die Wunder der Tonkunst*, concerns other miracles wrought by music in the present-day world: music is a beautiful remnant of that innocence which was the original state of man. The third essay, a discussion of the genres of church music, indicates once more that music is religion and its creator a priest. The fragment of a letter by Berglinger, where art is called the single constant factor in an otherwise chaotic world, forms a transition to the last essay, *Das eigentümliche innere Wesen der Tonkunst und die Seelenlehre der heutigen Instrumentalmusik*. Half the essay consists of an attack on those musicians who regard the art as a matter of mathematics and not of feeling. Wackenroder's attack—or the spirit of Romanticism?—was very effective here; until Hesse's Knecht and Mann's Leverkühn the composer in literature is distinctly unmathematical. The second part of the essay catalogues the emotions which can be evoked by music; the list is a forerunner, albeit inexplicit, of the program for Romantic music offered in *Kreislers musikalisch-poetischer Klub*. Wackenroder is ideally suited to describe the psyche of the new Romantic musician, but apart from the *Wesen der Tonkunst,* the nature of Berglinger's compositions remain a mystery. Music for Wackenroder's composer is the art of innocence, and to hear it is a childlike joy. Can the art of innocence be taught?

Friedrich Rochlitz, the longtime editor of Leipzig's *Allgemeine musikalische Zeitung,* had a far more intimate contact with musical reality than did Wackenroder. Nonetheless, the heroes of *Aus dem Leben eines Tonkünstlers* (1802) and *Der Besuch im Irrenhause* (1804) possess a childlike innocence which in the former tale involves the artist in intrigues he cannot understand (nor can the reader), and in the latter brings the musician to a madhouse. *Aus dem Leben eines Tokünstlers* consists of the letters of Ludolph, a student of composition, to his friend Anton. Ludolph realizes that he would be a satisfactory artisan-composer if he had not undergone an inspirational experience in his boyhood: "Ja ich würde keine Ahnung für [Religion und Kunst] in mir finden, sondern mich, wie die Andern, in meinem Handwerk festsetzen und in bequemer Selbstgefälligkeit vegetieren, wenn ich jene Ahnung nicht aus den Jahren meiner Kindheit hervortreten liess . . ."[4]

Ludolph's experiences with professional musicians confirm him in his suspicion that only the artisan can survive in the musical world. A music director, H., tells him that true music was composed by Hasse and Graun, not by Mozart, Gluck, and their like. These last are Romantics to H., who decries "das Stürmen und Wüten der Mozart und wie sie weiter heissen" (V, 334). Ludolph, momentarily encouraged by the music of Händel, in which he perceives that religious inspiration he regards as the source of his own art, falls in with Franzesco, the music master of an elderly princess. Franzesco finds fault with Ludolph's lofty approach to music; angered, Ludolph retorts, as he writes to Anton, that "ich sei bereit für [die Musik] zu leben und zu sterben, wenn [Franzesco] auch darin Recht habe, dass ich in ihr nur eine Idee vergöttere und eben darum etwas wahrhaft Schönes und Dauerndes zu schaffen mich unfähig mache..." (V, 356). Ludolph feels strangely attracted to Franzesco, this "Mephistopheles" whose "verhexten Kreis" he cannot leave; Franzesco is an early example of those musical mentors, both helpful and harmful to their pupils, that appear so often in German literature. Not only Franzesco's satanic personality holds Ludolph entranced. The Italian is able to give his young friend a thorough grounding in church music; furthermore he has a beautiful daughter, Laura, with whom Ludolph falls in love after he hears her performance in *The Messiah*, a musical passion beginning like that of Kreisler for his "ombra adorata."

The remainder of the fragment is swathed in mystification. Rochlitz hints that Ludolph and Laura are brother and sister, that Ludolph has had some connection with Franzesco's dead son. The story breaks off after Franzesco and Laura suddenly depart from the city; Laura leaves Ludolph a copy of *Nathan der Weise* with the lines underlined in red:

Ich deines Bluts!—So waren jene Träume,
Womit man meine Kindheit wiegte, doch—
Doch mehr als Träume!

The relationships of the characters would promise to be as complicated as those in Hoffmann's *Die Elixiere des Teufels*. The author's original intention, the portrayal of a serious and innocent young musician in collision with the hard facts of artistic life, is lost in Gothic intricacies.

Karl, the hero of *Der Besuch im Irrenhause*, shows the same early inclination to music and religion as Berglinger and Ludolph, but is thwarted more cruelly than they. At his first communion he experiences an ecstasy at once musical and religious: "Diese tiefe Bewegung wurde unterhalten . . . durch Haydns Worte Christi am Kreuz . . . Es war nicht nur die erste Kirchenmusik, sondern die erste bedeutende Musik überhaupt, die Karl hörte: 'Mein Gott rief mir zu von seinem heiligen Himmel!' war sein Ausdruck darüber" (VI, 20). He begs his father for music lessons, but instead is sent away to learn the merchant's trade. Returning home in a state of nervous collapse, he is confined to his room (where he reads the Bible constantly) until one day a servant takes him for a walk. Overwhelmed by the lovely landscape, he has his second mystical experience: "ich hörte auch die Sprache aller Lebendigen, die keine Worte hat, sondern nur Töne . . ." (VI, 31). Karl's musical fortunes improve ever so slightly: his mother gives him a piano, which he teaches himself to play; he hears Lottchen, an orphan girl, singing to the accompaniment of a guitar, and his musical ideal takes human shape. (The scene is strangely like the passage in Grillparzer's *Der arme Spielmann* where Jakob hears Barbara's simple tune.) Frustrated in his efforts to see Lottchen, Karl's love of music turns to hatred, and his parents, disturbed at last, engage a psychiatrist.

The physician takes Karl to the hill from which he had beheld the beauties of nature. Karl hears music from a nearby church, and "Da bemerkte man eine heftige Erschütterung aller seiner Glieder, und in demselben Augenblicke wurde sein Geist, auf Fittigen der Begeisterung, zu himmlischer Freude erhoben. . . . Lob und Preis war der Inhalt seines Gebets" (VI, 46).

In a sounder personality (or one whose musical development had not been so neglected) the experience might have inspired a religious composition; in Karl it marks another step along the way to mental destruction. Much too late, Karl is offered musical instruction, which he refuses; he returns to his incessant piano playing and his Bible. In letters addressed to the monarchs of Europe he discusses the relationship between music and religion. To Friedrich Wilhelm of Prussia he writes that God has given us music in order that we may praise Him; music is the language of the angels and will make us blessed in the next world. In harmony, the letter goes on, can be perceived the symbols of divinity: "es kann auch nicht anders sein, indem ein Ton, mit den dazu gehörigen Wohllauten, auf alles hindeutet, was über den irdischen Sinn hinausgeht . . . So deuten Grundton, Terz und Quinte, welche drei sind und doch nur Eins, auf den dreieinigen Gott, den wir anbeten" (VI, 51-52). Karl's theories form a transition between the musical religiosity of Berglinger and the ability of Hoffmnan's Kreisler to see not religious symbols but special emotions in the various musical keys.

Karl is admitted to the insane asylum where the narrator learns the case history composing the main part of *Der Besuch im Irrenhause*. At the asylum the narrator observes Karl's peculiar fashion of making music: "Karl schlug einige leise Töne, und dann Akkorde an, ohne Zusammenhang, ohne Zeitmass, ohne alle regelmässige Folge, liess jeden ganz austönen, und schien sich besonders zu freuen, wenn nun, beim Ausklingen der Saiten, die Töne des Akkords ganz in einen zu zerfliessen schienen" (VI, 9). Karl's performance prefigures the inclination of so many musicians in German literature toward a dream world of harmony, in which the performer, having lost all contact with reality, becomes completely subjective in his musical values. Actually Karl indulges in the basic process of Romantic musical creation, a ranging of the imagination through the manifold possibilities of the realm of harmony. And Karl is Romantic, too, although negatively so, in another aspect of his musical madness. He cannot endure the human voice in song, a residue of that bitter experience which robbed him of his human musical ideal. Music is not a solace to him when incorporated into that form which Lottchen gave it. The music which Karl performs is melancholy ("Es schien die Musik eines Todkranken, der eben seiner Auflösung entgegensieht," VI, 10); shortly after the interview with the narrator Karl dies, destroyed by his impossible search for the perfect expression of his spiritual experiences.

The musicians of Rochlitz, for all the faults of their literary dress, are not to be ignored in the history of the musician. It is likely that E. T. A. Hoffmann knew these works of his editor-to-be, just as it is likely that he was acquainted with the production of Wackenroder. However, Hoffmann would have created Johannes Kreisler even if Wackenroder had never conceived his Berglinger or Rochlitz his Ludolph and Karl. Kreisler is the sharply outlined figure of a musical genius, while Ludolph is the shadowy musical aspirant and Karl, in actual fact, not a musician at all. Berglinger and Kreisler resemble one another most in their reverent attitude toward music and their consciousness of the division between art and life. By nature not so inclined to ecstasies as his predecessor, Hoffmann had the opportunity to mature which Wackenroder did not. Hoffmann also possessed a more thorough musical training than any other important literary man of his day, and was active as a practical composer and man of the theatre; Wackenroder was an amateur in the arts. The creator of Peter Schönfeld had a strong bent toward mocking humor; Wackenroder's portrait of Berglinger loses by its unrelieved seriousness. The amorous vicissitudes of Hoffmann find poignant expression in the love of Kreisler for Julia, whose original of course is Julia Marc, Hoffmann's Bamberg idol. Wackenroder knew no such passion in his own life, and Berglinger exists without love. Wackenroder's Berglinger remains of necessity a spiritual portrait, since it can reflect no experiences from the author's exterior life. Hoffmann's personal adventures invite incorporation into the life of Kreisler.

What we know of Johannes Kreisler we have in a fragmentary form. The first of the *Kreisleriana, Kreislers musikalische Leiden*, appeared in September 1810; *Kater Murr*, the last of the works concerning the musician, saw the publication of its second volume in 1821. Into the period between the publication of the *Leiden* and *Kreislers Lehrbrief* (1814) fall the *Kreisleriana* proper together with some other musical stories; in 1816 and 1817 Hoffmann composed other tales (such as *Das Sanctus*) which cast light upon the character of the musician. *Murr* was begun in 1819. Hoffmann was therefore occupied with the figure of Kreisler throughout most of his literary career, but the picture of the musician is by no means complete. The *Kreisleriana* are a series of illuminating sketches on music which say perhaps too little about the man himself. *Kater Murr* tells us of Kreisler's childhood, of his life at a petty court, and of his relationship to Catholicism; it remains comparatively silent about Kreisler the musician. A tale from 1813, *Die neuesten Schicksale des Hundes Berganza*, gives some details concerning Kreisler's love affair with Caecilie (an early name for the Julia-figure). Two fragments from the winter of 1812 tell us of Kreisler's madness, a theme subduel in *Kater Murr*. *Der Freund* presents a terrifying picture of one "J. K.," insane and confined at a friend's country home, *Lichte Stunden eines wahnsinnigen Musikers* is a sketch for an unwritten novel about a mad musician, undoubtedly Kreisler. Whoever wishes to know Kreisler must piece together his information from a number of sources. A tendency on the part of German scholars has been to fill the gaps with information from Hoffmann's own life. It should be remembered that Kreisler is not a thinly disguised attempt at autobiography but the literary portrayal of the Romantic musician par excellence, and the outstanding musical hero in German literature.

Hoffmann created the inner Kreisler first and then gave him outward form, surrounding him with friends and enemies. Yet even in the *Kreisleriana* the themes of the composer's battle with society and of his passion for Julia are briefly presented. The prelude to the *Kreisleriana, Musikalische Leiden,* shows the wretched Kreisler at a party in Councilor Röderlein's home. While the elderly people play cards, the young ladies of the house are ordered to sing by their mother, and Kreisler must accompany them. Their errors and the absurd remarks of the guests drive Kreisler to despair. The only consolation for Kreisler is Amalia, the niece of Röderlein, "die mich mit Banden an dies Haus fesselt, welche die Kunst geknüpft hat."[5] She can essay such roles as Gluck's Armida or Mozart's Donna Anna. The niece is Julia Marc, and the society that of Bamberg; the piece was originally intended as a satire on musical life in the Franconian city. Beneath the satire we detect Hoffmann's eternal quarrel with society, which is to take various forms; he struggles both to be accepted as a musician by the general public and as a human being (and an equal) by his social "betters." And Hoffmann's search for the ideal is revealed in the figure of the niece, who embodies all that Hoffmann reveres in music. These two tendencies may be considered as the most important features of Kreisler's relationships with others, and accordingly we shall discuss them before proceeding to Kreisler's musical character.

Berglinger was conscious of "being apart" from his fellows; however his creator ignored the precarious and often humiliating position of the musician in late eighteenth and early nineteenth century society. Berglinger, plagued even by the connections he is forced to maintain with his family, will not involve himself in a mundane affair like the search for equal rights. Such was not always the case with actual composers of the period: how many stories, apocryphal or not, are told of the rebelliousness of young Mozart or Beethoven? The composer was no longer an artisan and a servant, but a "genius" and—in his own mind, at least—a privileged member of society. Hoffmann's own experience with the Seconda opera troupe may have taught him more about the degrading position of the professional musician that he had learned in Bamberg, where his conversational abilities made him acceptable even in the most proper homes. It would be too much to say that Hoffmann himself suffered excessively from the slights dealt the musician; his education, his social background, and his membership in one of the professions prevent us from placing him together with those geniuses who were musicians and no more. But Hoffmann realized all too well the abuses to which the musician was subjected, and accordingly he launched a series of attacks against the upper levels of society.

These attacks, written both from the standpoint of the musician and of the protester against social injustice, make up a great part of *Kater Murr*. The Kreisler portion of the novel takes place at the court of Prince Irenäus, whose minute state has been swallowed up by a neighboring grand duchy. Prince Irenäus has retained his empty title, surrounded by his little group of functionaries. The Prince himself is none too intelligent, and his son Ignatius is an imbecile. The Prince's former mistress, the Rätin Benzon, is present at the court; she intends to sacrifice her daughter, Julia, in a marriage with Ignatius. Julia is also pursued by Prince Hector, the fiancé of Princess Hedwiga, the willful daughter of Irenäus. Kreisler has been introduced into this sordid tangle by Meister Abraham, an old organ builder and formerly Kreisler's teacher, who now is the scheming Benzon's chief opponent at the court. Becoming Kapellmeister at the princely residence, Kreisler is immediately caught up by the currents of intrigue. Both Julia and Hedwiga are attracted to him, although frightened by his strange nature; he in turn grows deeply attached to Julia.

In this milieu Kreisler wages a losing fight to save music from prostitution. The humiliations to which Kreisler is subjected are most affectingly catalogued in a conversation with Rätin Benzon (V, 87ff.). The Rätin, becoming spokeswoman for the less articulate philistines of the court, wounds the musician by telling him that he takes music too seriously, although he has just stated that music alone keeps him from madness. Resorting to irony, Kreisler tells of the profits he reaped while serving the Grand Duke, an experience repeated on a smaller and more comical scale at Sieghartsweiler. He has learned to listen calmly while conducting *Don Juan* and *Armida*, to nod encouragement as a soprano spoils a cadenza through her vocal acrobatics, to smile pleasantly when a Lord Chamberlain tells him Haydn's *Seasons* is boring. He has even learned to be patient when a member of the court, stating that Mozart and Beethoven know nothing of music, suggests that Rossini and Pucitta are the real masters of opera. The climax of his diatribe is reached in the outcry: "Erlassen Sie mir die Schilderung, wie ich durch fade Spielerei mit der heiligen Kunst, zu der ich notgedrungen die Hand bieten musste, durch die Albernheiten seelenloser Kunstpfuscher, abgeschmackter Dilettanten, durch das ganze tolle Treiben einer Welt voll Kunstgliederpuppen immer mehr und mehr dahin gebracht wurde, die erbärmliche Nichtswürdigkeit meiner Existenz einzusehen" (V, 89). Kreisler has fled this servitude, to meet a more distressing situation in the miniature kingdom of Irenäus. He is insulted by the functionaries and by such visitors as Prince Hector, who demands that the "lackey" show him proper respect; he sees the final degradation of music in the aftermath to a performance given by Julia and himself before the Prince. Crying that he is overcome by the music, the Prince rushes forward and attempts to kiss Julia.

(Only once, in a moment of the highest musical inspiration, has Kreisler allowed himself to call Julia "du".) Kreisler drives him away, but as far as we know, Julia later is married off to Prince Ignatius and so falls prey to the brutal aristocracy after all. Music and the musician are debased in every way, and Kreisler is powerless to act. His only defense is his scurrilous humor.

Hoffmann's darts are not directed solely against the aristocratic foes of music. Granted that Prince Irenäus and his fellows are members of the aristocracy, they nonetheless stand for the philistine world as a whole. Not only do the aristocrats closely resemble the middle-class circles of the *Kreisleriana* and such stories as *Die Fermate*; the Julia-figure is sacrificed to aristocracy and bourgeoisie alike. The tale *Berganza* indicates clearly that Hoffmann makes general war on the philistine. Caecilie is wedded to George: Hoffmann gives us an agonizing description of the bridegroom's entrance into the nuptial chamber. George, afflicted with disease as the result of excesses, attacks the almost unconscious Caecilie; the brave dog Berganza attempts to kill him. The imbecility of Ignatius and the lustfulness of Hector are combined in George's person, and Berganza's defense of Caecilie is but a ludicrous version of the scene where Kreisler drives Hector away from Julia. Much has been made of the fact that the origin of these unpleasant scenes was the union between Julia Marc and the merchant Gröpel, yet most critics have overlooked the fact that Hoffmann was too fine an artist to repeat the theme again and again simply to vent his personal feelings. Hoffmann has given an extremely pessimistic meaning to the defilement of the Julia-figure; it is characteristic of his attitude toward music that he mentions the sufferings of Julia far more often than he does his own. He remains the servant of music, Julia is music itself.

Hoffmann's eulogies of the feminine voice are among his least ironic creations, an indication of his deep feeling. Written over a period of years, they still bear a close resemblance to one another; Hoffmann cannot vary his description of absolute musical beauty. Whatever the name of the heroine may be, Amalie, Ombra adorata, Caecilie, or Julia Benzon, the essentials of her song and her character remain the same. Other feminine singers not connected with Kreisler bear similar features: Antonie in *Rat Krespel* and "Donna Anna" in *Don Juan*. In each case the most important (and at times the only) feature of the ideal is her heavenly voice, which frees the musician from the trammels of life. The portion of the *Kreisleriana* entitled *Ombra adorata* is perhaps the purest example of Hoffmann's cult of the female voice. The *Ombra adorata* is tacitly dedicated to Julia Marc; her name is never mentioned. The voice remains unidentified and unattached to any human form; we know it as the guide which leads the composer into the dream world of art. Later the voice takes the form of Caecilie and Julia Benzon; but even after Julia appears fully developed in *Kater Murr*, she remains an ethereal figure. Hoffmann provides a detailed account of her musical abilities; otherwise she is still the "adored shadow" who neither knows sensual feeling for Kreisler nor arouses this feeling in him. The sensual function is assumed by the Princess Hedwiga, in her humors a feminine counterpart of Kreisler. That Julia arouses the lust of Hector detracts nothing from her essentially spiritual nature; here Hoffmann indicates, as we have said, the debasement of art by the non-artist. In the conversation with Rätin Benzon, Kreisler carefully points out the difference between the love of the "bad musicians" and the "good musicians." The "bad musicians" are enamored of a pair of beautiful eyes and generally wed their possessor, leading her home into the prison of marriage; the "good musicians" see transported to earth the image of the angel which had secretly rested in their breast: "Und nun lodert auf in reinem Himmelsfeuer, das nur leuchtet und wärmt, ohne mit verderblichen Flammen zu vernichten, alles Entzücken, alle namenlose Wonne des höheren, aus dem Innersten emporkeimenden Lebens" (V, 193). Kreisler modestly says "die guten Musikanten;" he means the creative musicians like himself who are able to appreciate the nature of the ideal and therefore do not wish to disturb it.

We have as yet said nothing of Hoffmann's technical thoughts on music; in the passages on the Julia-figure Hoffmann does not concern himself with the details of music as an art, although he does cite the texts which his heroines sing. Sometimes these are works by Hoffmann himself, sometimes arias from Mozart and Gluck, and more often songs by now forgotten Italian composers of the eighteenth century; Hoffmann was always an ardent admirer of Italian music before Rossini, believing that in Italy the composition of melody had reached unparalleled heights. At no time does one of his heroines sing a work by a composer whom music history classifies as a Romantic; a possible exception would be "Donna Anna" in *Don Juan*, where Mozart receives Hoffmann's "Romantic" interpretation. (Hoffmann's own compositions are remarkably "classical.") Nevertheless, the *Kreisleriana* provide conclusive proof that Kreisler is a Romantic musician in his technical thought as well as in his attitude towards life and art.

In the *Kreisleriana* and their paralipomena Hoffmann attempts to erase the division between musician and poet. Hoffmann, himself both literary man and composer, saw no reason why one art could not assume certain of the functions of the other—why language could not become more musical and music closer to the word. This idea is first given complete expression in the dialogue, *Der Dichter und der Komponist* (1813), and is already hinted at in *Don Juan* (1812), where the opera is thought of as a music drama. In the course of the dialogue Ludwig, the musician, defends the Romantic opera as the single true opera, for only in the land of Romanticism is music at home: ". . . nun soll die Musik ganz ins Leben treten, sie soll seine Erscheinungen ergreifen und Wort und Tat schmückend von den bestimmten Leidenschaften und Handlungen sprechen" (XIII, 107). Poet and musician must be in complete harmony, an anticipation of Wagner's ideal of the Gesamtkunstwerk; music must win new means of expression closer to those of literature. Hoffmann develops his theory in that section of the *Kreisleriana* called *Kreislers musikalisch-poetischer Klub*. At the club's present meeting Kreisler decides to improvise at the piano; putting on the famous Kreislerian costume, the red cap and the Chinese dressing gown, he begins to play. What follows is a series of chords, played one after another, each specifically designated as to key and dynamics. To every chord is assigned a particular picture, in every case an emotion, in most cases a figure or a color. A soft A flat major chord calls forth a picture of spirits with golden wings, the A flat minor carries the musician into the realm of eternal yearning. The A minor causes a beautiful girl to appear; her lover embraces her in heroic F major. The next series of chords concerns nature; from this point on Kreisler thinks orchestrally, indicating the instruments best suited to the chord. Flutes and oboes play a B major chord which paints the springtime. The E flat major chord depicts the forest in the green tone of the horns, full of joy and pain. Now the mood begins to darken; C major calls forth a gruesome picture of the devil dancing in a graveyard to the accompaniment of trumpets and tympani. The passage ends with the C minor chord, in which madness is hiding. "Siehst du es lauern, das bleiche Gespenst mit den rot funkelnden Augen—die krallichten Knochenfäuste aus dem zerrissenen Mantel nach dir ausstreckend?—die Strohkrone auf dem kahlen glatten Schädel schüttelnd! Es ist der Wahnsinn . . ." (I, 93). The passage indicates unmistakably what path Hoffmann's musical thought has taken. Music is no longer an interweaving of melodies, of polyphony; it is essentially a matter of tonal combinations and their modulations. The musician is not to confine himself to the intellectual task of polyphonic construction; he can make use of the emotional effects inherent in harmony. Each chord is assigned a definite emotional connotation; the exactitude of the connotation is increased through the use of instruments, and to a degree through the mingling of color and sound. Ludwig Tieck applies the same synaesthetic device in his early poetry, but there it is not based upon musical knowledge; Hoffmann has laid the groundwork for a manual of Romantic compositional technique.

Hoffmann's Kreisler, like Thomas Mann's Leverkühn in *Doktor Faustus*, reveals much of his character in his thoughts on music; in both cases it is difficult to say which is the product of the other, character or musical thought. In the *Klub* Kreisler shows his extreme changeability; within a few moments he runs the gamut from reverence to eroticism, from charming landscapes to macabre graveyard scenes, from heroic confidence to fear of madness. The figures which surround Kreisler are represented in the chords. The beautiful girl, the musical ideal, is to be found in them, as well as the foe of music: "als Freijäger — Konzertmeister — Wurmdoktor — ricco mercante — er schmeisst mit Lichtscheren in die Saiten, damit ich nur nicht spielen soll . . ." (I, 93). Even madness, music's opponent, may take musical form, literally the most fruitful thought presented in the *Klub*. Music is usually the most noble of the arts; yet Hoffmann suspects that a dangerous power exists in music— that music may be the destroyer as well as the savior. While this thought does not entirely disappear in the last works, it is most clearly expressed in the *Kreisleriana*, in particular in *Der Freund*, where Kreisler's insanity is depicted. The friend attempts to heal the madman through musical therapy, as it were; Kreisler listens attentively at first, but soon falls into such a rage that the friend ceases to play. The friend then places a small piano and a guitar in Kreisler's room, and the musician involuntarily touches the strings of the latter instrument. At the sound of the C major chord (that chord associated with the devil in the *Klub*) Kreisler smashes the instrument. Hoffmann recognizes that evil lies hidden in music's beneficence. The theme of music's danger is later given a one-sided development by such writers as Lenau, for whom music becomes almost entirely harmful in its influence. Hoffmann transforms the factor of evil, making his musician a demonic figure whose life is possessed by music. The strength of this possession may drive him to destruction or prove to be his salvation.

Wackenroder has already defined the musician as a chosen person, a priest. Being elect destroys Berglinger as far as earthly life is concerned; we must presume that his spiritual rewards are great. Kreisler too regards himself as chosen, although he makes a distinct dichotomy between himself and the art, incorporating the latter in the figure of the beloved. In Wackenroder, on the other hand, it is almost as if Berglinger regarded himself as an embodiment of the art. We are prevented from this assumption only by Berglinger's extremely religious nature, an element not so strongly emphasized in Kreisler but compensated for by the Julia-cult. Hoffmann does not deny music a religious power; he himself composed a large amount of music for the church during his residence in Poland, and religious music appears frequently in his works, especially those with semi-ecclesiastical backgrounds such as *Die Elixiere des Teufels*. Religious music is the sole theme of *Das Sanctus* (1816), and forms an important part of *Kater Murr*. In both tale and novel it is connected with the figure of the female singer. *Das Sanctus* is a study of piety and the artist, correlating music and religion. The problem is presented in a Rahmenerzählung. The outer tale is that of a soprano, Bettina, who leaves the choir loft during the Sanctus of a Haydn Mass and loses her voice as a result of her impiety. She recovers it only after having heard a parallel tale of a Moorish singer. Zulema, captured by the Spaniards during the siege of Granada, is converted and given the name Julia. Her splendid voice enhances the choir of nuns which sings before Queen Isabella, but during the performance of the Sanctus

Julia is lured away by the tones of a zither. Soon the city falls, and Julia, repentant, leads a band of Moors to the altar where they embrace Christianity. Julia, who has intoned the Sanctus throughout the march to the altar, falls dead before the cross.

While the outer story of *Das Sanctus* is based on an incident which took place during the rehearsals of Hoffmann's *Undine*, the influence of Kleist's *Die heilige Cäcilie* cannot be mistaken.[6] In this tale a group of ruffians, intent upon wrecking a Catholic church, is put into a religious trance by the music which emerges from the choir loft. The Gloria which charmed the young men has been conducted by Saint Cäcilie herself; the usual musical director lay ill during the performance. In both *Das Sanctus* and *Die heilige Cäcilie* music is credited with a supernatural power; Kleist however concerns himself with the association of music and Catholicism, while Hoffmann takes the impiety of the artist as his principal theme. Hoffmann himself was not a religious man in the formal sense; and his tale is given a lighter air than Kleist's by the outer story of the Rahmenerzählung and by the comical interjections of the Kapellmeister during the doctor's narration of the Moorish singer's tale. Yet Hoffmann's theme is basically as serious as Kleist's; the musician must remember that he is engaged in a religious duty whenever he performs. Kreisler is often reproached for the extreme earnestness of his approach to music; in *Kreisler und Baron Wallborn* he replies that without music he cannot live.

Hoffmann's attitude toward the Catholic Church may well be identified with the author's attitude toward religious music, since the writer's association with Lutheranism had no influence upon his musical thought. During much of his life Hoffmann resided in Roman Catholic communities (Plock, Warsaw, Bamberg) and often busied himself with musical performances in Catholic churches; his church music was composed exclusively for Catholic use. Yet he never became a Catholic nor does he allow his Kreisler (who seems immune to the religious ecstasies of a Berglinger) to do so. *Kater Murr* is the best source for information on Kreisler and Catholicism. Kreisler's religious music is mentioned several times before his retreat to the Benedictine monastery at Kanzheim; one of the most effective scenes in *Murr's* first part is that where Julia and Hedwiga, kneeling in a chapel, listen to the evening litany. The choir begins with an *Ave maris stella*. which Kreisler has composed: "Leise beginnend, brauste der Gesang stärker und mächtiger auf in dem dei mater alma, bis die Töne, in dem felix coeli porta dahinsterbend, fortschwebten auf den Fittichen des Abendwindes" (V, 243). As elsewhere the Church and its music are treated with utmost reverence. In the essay *Alte und Neue Kirchenmusik* (1814) Hoffmann says that the composer, before beginning to write for the Church, must ask himself if the spirit of truth and piety compels him to praise God and to speak of the wonders of the heavenly kingdom in the miraculous tones of music (XII, 51). Otherwise the composer commits an act of irreverence, like the German singer or her Moorish counterpart in *Das Sanctus*.

In the second half of *Murr* Kreisler finds shelter in the monastery at Kanzheim. The monastery needs the music which Kreisler can provide; he is received with a respect unknown to him in the outside world. The abbot of Kanzheim prefers to combine gentility with reverence, a union so attractive to Kreisler that he dons the robes of the Benedictines and seriously considers enrolling in the order, believing that in the cloister he will experience the quiet necessary for him to serve music best. The theme has become especially popular in recent years, both Hesse and Thomas Mann treating it in their musical novels. But, unlike Mann's Leverkühn, Kreisler rejects the peace of the cloister. Realizing that the monk may give only a one-sided service to music, he is driven back into life by his musical demon. The interview in which the Abbot approaches Kreisler concerning his conversion is one of the most masterly portions of *Murr*, a novel abounding in subtle conversational battles. Kreisler mentions the renunciation necessary to become a member of the order, and the Abbot answers him with a reference to the peace in which he could create new works of art. Kreisler falls back into his protective shell of irony, claiming that many an excellent family would be glad to have him as a son-in-law; then a vision of Julia arises before him and the surprised Abbot has difficulty in arousing him from his dream. Kreisler realizes that he must return to life in order to save music from those who would misuse it. The service of the Church through music is a noble mission, to be sure, but the true musician has made music his religion.

Essentially humble in his attitude towards music, Kreisler has the arrogance of the "genius" toward those who serve music poorly or only one-sidedly. Kreisler is so possessed by his art that during his literary debut it can make a madman of him; in *Kater Murr* he considers flight from the dangerous aspects of music, for at Kanzheim he finds not only peace from the philistines but also from his visions of madness. The musician destroyed by his art is not unknown to Hoffmann, and two of his earlier stories, *Ritter Gluck* and *Don Juan*, center around such figures. In *Ritter Gluck* (1809) the narrator meets an old man in a café and is astonished by his pregnant remarks on Gluck's *Iphigenie*. Later he comes upon the old man again at a performance of Gluck's *Armida*; invited to the old fellow's room the narrator hears him play the overture of the opera, but in a distorted form and from a score consisting of empty staves. The pianist tells the narrator that he is Gluck. The composer died in 1787; the story takes place in the year of its writing. The old musician has been driven mad by his devotion to another's music; he has made this music his creation, and has lost his own personality in the process.

In the famous tale *Don Juan*, written four years later, we have an even more extreme example of musical destruction; a singer becomes so devoted to her role that she dies as a result. One evening the narrator attends a performance of Mozart's *Don Juan* in a theater adjoining his inn. During the latter half of the first act the "Donna Anna" comes to his loge in order to watch the stage until her next appearance. She and the "enthusiast" hold a long conversation on Mozart's opera. At the end of the performance he returns to his room where he writes a letter to his friend Theodor interpreting the opera. Suddenly he believes that he hears "Donna Anna" singing her great aria, "Non mi dir, bell' idol mio!" The next morning he learns that the singer has died during the night. Over and beyond Hoffmann's interpretation of the opera as a battle between the heavenly powers (Donna Anna) and the demonic powers (Don Juan) lies a more important distinction. "Donna Anna," like Berglinger and like Zulema-Julia, succumbs after her moment of inspiration; the human musician will fall prey to the excessive demands the ideal makes upon him. The Don himself, likewise yearning for perfection, is as much inspired as "Donna Anna;" "Ein kräftiger, herrlicher Körper, eine Bildung, woraus der Funke hervorstrahlt, der, die Ahnungen des Höchsten entzündend, in die Brust fiel; ein tiefes Gemüt, ein schnell ergreifender Verstand— Aber das ist die entsetzliche Folge des Sündenfalls, dass der

Feind die Macht behielt, dem Menschen aufzulauern und ihm selbst in dem Streben nach dem Höchsten, worin er seine göttliche Natur ausspricht, böse Fallstricke zu legen" (I, 150-151). We cannot be sure that "Donna Anna's" real death has been more blessed than the stage death of the Don; extreme devotion to any cause—and Hoffmann in the *Klub* has already expatiated upon the evil inherent in music—can carry the seeds of madness or destruction within itself. "Donna Anna" and Don Juan alike are the prey of a "demon," which may take a multitude of shapes, and by the same token it may be supposed that Kreisler could have found such an end. The conclusion of *Kater Murr* is unknown, and the sketches for the initial Kreisler novel point unmistakably to the madness of the musician. Kreisler is not the first demonic musician; that title must belong to Berglinger, whose demon takes the form of religious inspiration. In Kreisler the demonic begins to assume a more evil aspect, although music is still regarded by and large as beneficent. After Kreisler, musical characters appear who themselves have become evil, a perversion of Hoffmann's thought. Thomas Mann borrows from Hoffmann in this respect too: his hero, himself a good man, is forced to enter a pact with evil as a necessary concomitant of his genius.

Hoffmann's Kreisler figure produced certain offspring in Romantic literature; these other examples of the creative musician appear in the works either of less inspired literary men or of artists not primarily writers but rather composers. The fact that Hoffmann alone among the writers of Romanticism has produced a full length portrait of the composer is not astonishing when we remember that he is simply describing that phase of life and artistic effort which he knows best. Neither Tieck nor Wilhelm Hauff, two Romanticists who have also treated the composer, possessed the necessary technical knowledge—or indeed the interest in the art—to stay the course; the *Davidsbündler*-series of Robert Schumann, a third follower of Hoffmann's tradition, remains the work of a talented amateur.[7]

Ludwig Tieck in his attitude toward music as toward the other arts, was a brilliant dilettante, capable of facile discussion but unable to achieve depth. From his earliest manhood he had lived in an atmosphere conducive to the development of interest in music. The composer Reichardt treated him as an adopted son, but he learned more Goethe than music in Reichardt's home.

Tieck was acquainted with a larger number of great musicians than any other literary man in German history, since his long life ran almost contemporary with the Golden Age of music in Germany. Yet he did not achieve any real appreciation of the art. Mozart—because he was "ironic"—was the composer he admired most.

Tieck's novella on music and musicians, *Musikalische Leiden und Freuden* (1822), is a series of discussions, its plot being a rickety skeleton on which to hang Tieck's opinions. A number of its characters are interesting however: the young Romantic composer, the old charlatan-musician from Italy, the music-hating layman, and a Svengali-like individual, Hortensio (who, as it turns out, is more inclined to good than evil). The Romantic composer had been the most important musical character in Hoffmann's works; Tieck busies himself more with his bizarre creations. Indeed the young Count Alten, probably modeled on Hoffmann's Kreisler, does not compose professionally; this task is left to an individual briefly called "Der Komponist." Likewise the Count does not perform; the duties of the musical director, such a torment to Kreisler, are given to a talkative Kapellmeister, who acts as a representative of practicality in art as opposed to Alten's idealism. Alten's resemblance to Kreisler is a matter of temperament. Like Kreisler nervous in the extreme, he cannot hear any musical composition from beginning to end without becoming disturbed. Nothing excites him but music; he hurries from one city to another in order to hear new singers, new compositions. Possessing a taste that seems to be as capricious as it is limited, Alten is seldom pleased with a work of art or its performance; he is "wie von bösen und guten Geistern geplagt und verfolgt,"[8] a description which could be applied with equal precision to Kreisler.

Alten shares another Kreislerian feature: he is guided in his musical life by the womanly ideal, whose name is Julie. Having heard her sing only once, Alten searches all the concert halls of Europe in the hope of repeating the experience. Julie's father, Hortensio, has forbidden her ever to perform in public (a resemblance to the situation of Hoffmann's *Rat Krespel*); however Alten finally rediscovers her and marries her with her father's blessing. Freed from her vow by Hortensio she sings the principal role in the Kapellmeister's opera, makes a success of it, and retires with Alten to his estates, where they live happily ever after. As soon as Alten has achieved the object of his search he becomes a normal individual and settles down to a peaceful married life. The emphasis on a single feature of the young man's character, a passion for a voice of unearthly beauty ("Dieser reine, himmlische Discant war Liebe, Hoheit, zarte Kraft und Fülle der edelsten, der überirdischen Empfindung," XVII, 314) gives a certain superficiality to Tieck's conception; yet herein also lies the primary feature of Kreisler's musical character. The difference between Kreisler and Alten is that Kreisler's ideal is an embodiment of his conception of music, into which no sensual element may enter; Alten's musical enthusiasms are really a result of his passion for the singer. When Alten first hears Julie he is quite as impressed by her physical charms as by her voice; he beholds the singer's "Nacken, dessen blendende Weisse von einem wunderlich gekräuselten braunen Löckchen erhöht wurde, so wie einen Teil des feingerundeten Ohres . . ." (XVII, 314). Unlike Kreisler, whose love for music nothing can dampen, Alten says feebly that he often curses the social position which keeps him from being a practicing artist. When he has won Julie, he retains music as a mere amusement. Tieck is unable to create a true Romantic musician. His Alten is at bottom as much a philistine as any of the "Halunken" whom Kreisler so thoroughly despises.

Another Romantic composer based on Kreisler is to be found in Wilhelm Hauff's story, *Die Sängerin* (1827). Hauff began to write just at the time of Hoffmann's greatest popularity, and Hoffmann's influence is discernible everywhere in the younger writer's work. In *Die Sängerin* Hauff has taken the theme of parental opposition to a musical career (perhaps from Wackenroder's *Herzensergiessungen* or Tieck's *Musikalische Leiden und Freuden,* where Alten's father commands him to become a diplomat), and superimposed upon the composer certain traits of Kreisler. Kommerzienrat Bolnau has tried to make a merchant of his offspring: "Der Sohn aber lebte und webte nur im Reich der Töne, die Musik war ihm alles, der Handel und Kommerz des Vaters war ihm zu gemein und niedrig."[9] The son disappears, returning to his home city some years later disguised as "Carlo Bolani," an Italian Kapellmeister. Bolani, a brilliant conversationalist and excellent musician, is inclined to moodiness. He despises the female voice while speaking enraptured of the masculine. When the old doctor visits him in an attempt to reconcile him with the singer Fiametti (for she is the cause of his hatred of all sopranos), he runs to the piano and plays: "Hören Sie dieses Weiche, Schmelzende, Anschmiegende? Aber bemerken Sie nicht in diesen Übergängen das unzuverlässige, flüchtige, charakterlose Wesen dieser Geschöpfe?" (V, 239). Bolnau was once in love with Fiametti; upon learning that she had been the inmate of a house of prostitution, he developed an insane hatred of the female voice. As in the case of Kreisler and Alten, the beloved has been identified with her musical talents. This is not the only Kreislerian feature which Bolnau betrays: his use of certain chords to characterize human beings suggests Kreisler's use of tone-painting. Like Kreisler he feels himself superior to the philistine; his mood, like Kreisler's, changes constantly: he can be both calmed and excited by music. Bolnau shows a marked contrast to Alten in his attitude toward music; he lives and breathes the art, and when we first see him, it is as if we saw Kreisler himself. Scores, guitars, violins, strings lie strewn about his room, and in the midst of this wreckage there stands the Kapellmeister in a wide black lounging robe, a red cap on his head and a role of music in his hand (V, 238). The picture of Bolnau is, however, a limited one; actually he is but one character in a kind of detective story, and must share our interest not only with the fiendish de Planto and the persecuted Giuseppa but also with the plot itself, the unraveling of the mystery which surrounds an attempt on Giuseppa's life. *Die Sängerin*, intended to be entertainment literature, does not purpose to picture a musician's life; it is doubtful that the work would ever have been written, or at least supplied with musical characters, had Hauff not been under the influence of Hoffmann.

The demonic musician does not appear in Hoffmann simply in the form of Kreisler; he also manifests himself in the individual whose talent is devoted to the control of other musicians rather than to a furthering of itself. This type we might call the "mentor-virtuoso" for he, in addition to his urge toward personal power, possesses great ability in the field of music and is often concerned with the mechanical advancement of the art. Only the entrepreneur in Hauff's *Sängerin*, who represents the mentor in his most debased form, fails to demonstrate a certain amount of devotion to music; Hoffmann's Krespel and Tieck's Hortensio are musicians of no mean sort. The mentor-virtuoso is not necessarily evil, but he frequently misuses his power, a fault even of Meister Abraham, the friend of Kreisler and owner of the tomcat Murr.

Rat Krespel and Meister Abraham were conceived after the composition of the last of the *Kreisleriana*; they are products of that later Hoffmann who concerns himself less with music and more with the problems of the personality. Krespel is a retired jurist and diplomat who astonishes his fellow citizens by his mad tricks, such as building a house without windows or making toys on a miniature lathe for the children at a banquet. Mechanical skill is characteristic both of him and of Abraham, and in both cases it takes a musical turn, since Abraham is an instrument maker by profession while Krespel is a master violin maker. In pursuit of his hobby Krespel has assembled a large collection of violins. The violin maker believes that a secret, inherent in the structure of each violin constructed by a master, can be discovered by dissecting the instrument. One of his violins has not been taken apart, however, since Krespel imagines, although he will not admit it to himself, that the violin has a life of its own: "... es war mir, da ich zum ersten Male darauf spielte, als wär' ich nur der Magnetiseur, der sie Somnambule zu erregen vermag, dass sie selbsttätig ihre innere Anschauung in Worten verkündet" (I, 240). Having made this unusual confession to Theodor, the teller of the story, he adds that Antonie, presumably his ward, has developed a love for the instrument and often wishes to hear it.

Antonie is actually his daughter, not his ward. The girl possesses an exquisite voice; she cannot use it, for if she sings she will die. Krespel will not allow her to marry the young composer with whom she is in love, fearing that he will give her his melodies to sing. Antonie succumbs to her father's will, and in some uncanny way associates her voice with that of the precious Cremona violin. This violin shatters on the night of Antonie's death, which is surrounded by strange circumstances, and in these circumstances the importance of the story lies. Apparently not so devoted an artist as Berglinger or Kreisler, Krespel does not want his daughter to die as a sacrifice to her art: Berglinger perishes after an outburst of inspiration and Kreisler goes mad. One night Krespel hears Antonie singing a song of the young composer, and can do nothing to prevent it: "... unbegreiflich sei der Zustand gewesen, in dem er sich befunden, denn eine entsetzliche Angst habe sich gepaart mit nie gefühlter Wonne"

(I, 258). When he succeeds in arousing himself, Antonie is dead. His desire to keep his daughter alive has been conquered in a moment of crisis by his love for music. Does Krespel show a tendency to an evil use of his power over Antonie? We cannot be sure that purely humane motives have prompted him to keep his daughter alive. There is an element of the Svengali in Krespel: possibly he guards Antonie because he desires to have a creature completely under his control. Antonie has really been a substitute for another of his creatures, a favorite violin long ago destroyed by his Italian wife Angela in a fit of rage. In revenge Krespel seized Angela, who was pregnant, and threw her from a window; immediately thereafter he left Italy, to discover some months later than Angela had borne a child, Antonie. We have already seen that Krespel regards his violins as his slaves, and Antonie must serve the same purpose. That she is identified with the Cremona violin (which sings with a life of its own) is indicative of a certain resistance to Krespel's will; yet he remains the mesmerizer, she the somnambulist. At the end of the tale Antonie comes momentarily under the power of another, the young composer, and dies as a result of her singing. Krespel is overcome by the beauty of her voice; his will is broken. In this way he is partially redeemed in our eyes, for he proves himself to be as true a servant of music as Kreisler.

Another and paler example of the Krespel type in Hoffmann is Professor X., the maker of *Die Automate*. Written in 1814, the little story is a preparatory study for the tale just discussed. Its thin plot concerns a "talking Turk" created by the mysterious Professor. Are the Professor's mechanical figures intended to serve evil ends or the musical art? An episode with a mechanical orchestra would lead us to the former possibility. Ludwig, a musician, is enraged after hearing the Professor's orchestra, not because music has been debased through artificial tricks but because the most human of the arts has been united with figures merely imitating the human in form and motion: "... die Maschinenmusik ist für mich etwas Heilloses und Greuliches..." (I, 185). Yet on the basis of the garden scene at the end of the story, in which the Professor entices such lovely tones from the trees and the bushes, it would seem that the old man has offered his talents up to the improvement of music. This opinion is substantiated by the statement of a friend, made after the Professor's disappearance, that his mechanical figures were a subordinate hobby, ". . . und dass tiefes Forschen, tiefes Eindringen in alle Teile der Naturwissenschaft eigentlich der unausgesetzte Zweck alles seines Strebens sei" (I, 194). Professor X. remains too undeveloped a figure for us to decide whether he will fall into the category of Krespel or not; if he is not devoted to music as an art, at least he probes into the secrets of nature for new acoustical principles.

Meister Abraham is a more difficult figure than Krespel, since we know too little about him. Abraham Liscov is a master organ builder who, while instructing Kreisler in the elements of music, also taught him his special "Kreislerian" humor. The organ builder was wont to pull the piano bench out from under the boy as he played or to give him apples that broke into a thousand pieces. Kreisler did not become completely the creature of Abraham, for his nobler nature revolted against the organ builder's maliciousness. No one could deny Abraham a piercing and vivacious intelligence, Hoffmann writes, but a talent for the bizarre and the cruel often overshadowed his finer qualities. A Krespel-like desire to control another human being appears in Abraham from the very first, a desire inevitably bringing with it the connotation of evil.

In later life Kreisler learns the secret of Abraham's existence. After leaving Göniönesmühl, Kreisler's home city, the organ maker fell in with Severino, an Italian magician of the diabolical type often to be met with in Hoffmann's works (Doctor Trabacchio, Doctor Dapertutto, and Spalanzani). Severino is the owner of "das unsichtbare Mädchen," a little gypsy girl, Chiara, whose voice is projected by ventriloquism from a crystal ball. After Severino's death Chiara becomes the property of Abraham, who eventually marries her. Chiara continues to play the role of the "invisible maiden," until she is spirited away and Abraham sees her no more—one of the many loose ends left by the fragmentary form of *Kater Murr*. The relationship of Abraham to Chiara is a more tender one than that of Krespel to Antonie, yet Chiara remains the creature of Abraham. He willingly continues to employ her as the "invisible maiden," regarding her more as a possession than as a wife.

The relationships of Abraham to the boy Kreisler and to Chiara should not be construed to mean that Abraham is evil through and through. It is by Abraham's efforts that Kreisler is brought to the court of Prince Irenäus, and the organ builder never hesitates to use his knowledge of other people's secrets to aid Kreisler's career. Yet even here the old man demonstrates a certain unscrupulousness which fits the character of one who has tormented an impressionable child. Meister Abraham does not possess the demonic depth of Krespel. He is a talented instrument maker, but we learn little of his art; he desires to control others through the force of personality, but his wish never leads to tragedy as in Krespel's case. Nothing is said of his attitude toward music itself and little of what influence he has had on the formation of Kreisler's musical character. The later Hoffmann is more interested in the personality than in the special problems of the musician. Abraham remains nothing more than one of the catalytic agents at work on Kreisler's soul.

It is likely that Tieck borrowed many features of Hoffmann's Krespel for the figure of the old composer Hortensio in *Musikalische Leiden und Freuden*. Hortensio has forced his daughter, Julie, to promise that she will never sing without his permission. The similarity between Hoffmann and Tieck is enhanced by the fact that Count Alten has apparently fallen in love with Julie's voice; Hortensio is determined to prevent him or anyone else from hearing his daughter sing. His motives are not precisely the same as Krespel's. Discovering that her voice was disappearing, Hortensio's wife "sang sich zu Tode" (XVII, 352) not long after her daughter's birth. Hortensio set out to train Julie according to theories gained from a study of the masters of church music. The singer must become a sort of poetess, capable of a divine vision. Hortensio's child grows up to be precisely the type of singer he desires, but when he presents her to the public, a fiasco ensues. The old man receives the verdict that his daughter should have some training with a good singer in order to learn "method." The blow drives Hortensio half insane, and after he has extracted the promise of silence from his daughter, he retires with her to a small city, where he gives himself over to melancholy. Fortunately he changes his mind in time for Julie's performance to save the new opera, and he has the gratification of knowing that his method of vocal instruction has been justified.

Both Krespel and Hortensio regard their daughters as their possessions. Hortensio's outlook is tinged by materialism, to be sure, for he looks forward to a prosperous old age, once he has acquired a position as chamber singer for his daughter. As he says: "Ich glaubte, ein unschätzbares Kleinod in ihr zu besitzen" (XVII, 353). But it would be fair to presume that Hortensio's brooding is more a result of artistic than material disappointment. (Tieck contrasts his vocal method with that of an Italian musician: the German teaches singing from the "Gemüt," the Italian from the throat.) Here an attitude toward music quite different from Krespel's appears. Krespel kept Antonie silent through lack of devotion to music, Hortensio prevents Julie from singing on account of his love of music, at least of music as he sees it. The two fathers are equally egocentric: Krespel thinks of his daughter as one of his instruments, Hortensio wishes to keep the product of his theories from public humiliation. He suffers more from Julie's lack of success than she does herself; for she admits that on the evening of her first concert she was not up to her usual standard (XVII, 354). Tieck undoubtedly means us to believe that Hortensio represents the devoted artist. It is nevertheless questionable that Hortensio is the truer musician in the last analysis. Krespel's musical instincts prevail when he is overcome by the beauty of Antonie's song. Hortensio allows his daughter to marry Count Alten and retire from public life. The one singer completely trained in accordance with Hortensio's theories will henceforth be heard only by whatever guests are present at Alten's estate.

In Hauff's *Die Sängerin* there appears another representative of the Svengali-type, uninterested in music and completely evil. This is the diabolical Chevalier de Planto, into whose hands the singer Giuseppa Fiametti falls. Giuseppa is the daughter of a famous violinist and an opera singer who, like Hoffmann's Angela and the mother of Tieck's Julia, has lost her voice. After the violinist's death the mother is forced to marry a conductor, who plans to turn Giuseppa into a child prodigy. Upon the mother's death the stepfather sells the unfortunate orphan to the Chevalier; he in turn installs his charge in an elegant Parisian house of ill-fame. Giuseppa, warned as to the nature of the place, finds refuge with the ambassador of a little German court. She becomes a well-known singer; unfortunately de Planto discovers her, and when she refuses to give herself up to him, he tries to murder her. The attempt is not successful, and eventually the criminal is found dying from a wound received in the struggle with Giuseppa.

Hauff has given the entrepreneur all the superficial features of the diabolical villain as he appears in Hoffmann's works. Giuseppa and the other characters in the story make particular mention of his eyes, a hint at the hypnotic powers associated with the type: Krespel calls himself a mesmerizer (I, 240) and Kreisler refers to the icy cold which emanates from Abraham's piercing glance (V, 138). Even as a child Giuseppa had been frightened by de Planto's gaze; later she recognized this glance through de Planto's disguise, and on his death bed his "... graue stechende Augen [gaben] ihm noch etwas Leben und einen schrecklichen, grauenerregenden Ausdruck..." (V, 247). The Chevalier also possesses, in common with Krespel and Abraham, a hoarse and uncanny laugh. Apart from these superficial resemblances de Planto has little recalling Hoffmann's mentors; he makes a profession of selling talented girls to houses of prostitution, where their musical abilities are an added attraction. He demonstrates no conflict between devotion to music and personality, nor has he been a formative influence in the life of a genius. He is an evil man engaged in a sordid trade; and whatever diabolical traits Hauff gives him are surface trimmings. The Chevalier de Planto is important only insofar as he demonstrates the degeneration of a type. From the tragedy of Krespel the figure of the mentor with demonic powers has been reduced to a character more suited to Grand Guignol than to serious literature. It is not until the post-Wagnerian era that the evil impresario reappears, flourishing in works by Bahr and Wedekind.

Curiously, the true virtuoso is not represented in Romantic literature until he appears in the prose works of Heinrich Heine. Berglinger and Kreisler devote their energies to composition. Krespel and Abraham are virtuosi of a sort, in that they are both skilled instrument builders; however they do not perform publicly. They try to control individual human beings over a long period of time; the great virtuoso, likewise attempting to dominate his fellows by the personality, expresses this personality through the medium of performance and limits his rule to the period during which he plays. And he does not seek to control the individual but rather the entire audience; he is essentially more theatrical than the mentor. Heine, himself very close to the virtuoso, would be the most apt of the important Romantic writers to describe the type. Here and there throughout his journalistic works references to music and musicians are to be found; these passages, couched in brilliant language, often betray a disturbing lack of taste. A characteristic section is that concerning Rossinni and Meyerbeer, in *Über die französische Bühne* (1837). The tone of the discussion is hardly critical: Heine loves both composers, and refuses to praise one at the cost of the other.[10] Indeed he proves his impartiality by saying that Meyerbeer's religion is that of Mozart, Beethoven, and Gluck, that is, music itself, and in his conviction he is like these earlier musicians in depth, passion, and perseverance (VIII, 110-111). The "swan of Pesaro," Heine's personal favorite, is not slighted either: he demonstrates beauty in his every movement, the stars of heaven listen to him entranced (VIII, 103-104). On the other hand, when confronted with a genius of the first order, such as Berlioz, Heine can do little more than relate an anecdote about the composer's "monstrous, antediluvian hair;" he calls Berlioz's music fantastic, allied to sentimentality (VIII, 121). These samples of Heine's musical criticism will indicate that he was attracted more by the opportunity of juggling with words than of giving an accurate musical judgment.

More famous passages concerning musicians are to be found in the *Florentinische Nächte* (1836). The qualities noted above are again evident: an interest in personality rather than artistry, and an inclination toward the bizarre; but now these qualities are given a more polished form. The brief but striking characterization of the composer Bellini and the masterful depiction of Paganini's violin playing form portions of the tales which Maximilian, the hero of the two *Nächte*, tells his beloved Maria on her deathbed. Their conversation falls by chance upon the opera, and Maximilian relates how he loves to observe Italian women: they become beautiful only when music illuminates their faces. Italian music is feminine, Italian music is a product not of individuals but of an entire folk. Heine's appreciation of Bellini depends upon his understanding for the composer's weakness when confronted by the feminine, his appreciation of Paganini upon his immediate sympathy for the virtuoso struggling to overcome his audience. While Heinrich Mann and Werfel have since spoken more penetratingly upon the femininity and the mass aspects of Italian music, Heine deserves credit for being one of the rare nineteenth century authors to give a friendly interpretation to the Italian musician.

At first glance Heine's description of Bellini seems a cruel parody. Proceeding from physical appearances Heine notes that Bellini's features have something characterless about them, a little like milk; and in this "milk-face" there whirls sometimes an expression of pain, which substitutes for the missing intellect. Bellini's walk is maidenly, elegiac, ethereal, and "Der ganze Mensch sah aus wie ein Seufzer en escarpins" (VI, 402). Soon Heine reveals that beneath all this mocking talk there is admiration of Bellini's natural youthfulness. Despite the comical impression he makes upon Maximilian—who, as he himself says in the same passage, loves "das Totenhafte und das Marmorne" more than rosy colors—Bellini nevertheless possesses a soul untainted by any evil contact; he has that childlike quality never lacking in people of genius.

Heine does not leave matters at heavy scorn and faint praise. Shortly before Bellini's death, Heine sees him again in the salon of a Parisian belle. The poet rises to the bait of the death-consecrated artist. Having poured out melody upon melody at the piano, the exhausted composer sits down before the beauty and converses in his dreadful Sicilian-French. The lady, ignoring his words, takes his cane and musses his carefully combed hair, while a malicious smile plays round her lips. In this moment Maximilian feels a relationship to the composer, who is as if transformed: "Sein Gesicht erglänzte im Widerschein jenes Lächelns, es war vielleicht der blühendste Moment seines Lebens" (VI, 405). And Heine is careful to point out that the face which causes the transformation is also an Italian one, such as is to be found in the paintings of da Vinci. The Italian artist, seemingly so healthy, falls prey to his native sensuality (the belle) and to the claims of his audience (the melodies at the piano). Bellini died at thirty-three, exhausted by the intense demands the Italian operatic theater made upon him. There is something of the demonic about Bellini, after all, and something of the virtuoso. Bellini's special Italian demons destroy him; Heine brilliantly calls attention to his weaknesses by juxtaposing him with a stronger demonic virtuoso, Paganini.

Paganini is not destroyed by his art but uses it to overwhelm his audiences. That he makes a more immediate appeal to Maximilian than Bellini did is not surprising; the creative personality appears now not as the sacrificed but the sacrificer. Heine begins once more with a description of the musician's appearance; in Paganini's case, not caring to engage in persiflage, he proceeds directly to the demonic impression made by the violinist: "Nur in grell schwarzen, flüchtigen Strichen konnten jene fabelhaften Züge erfasst werden, die mehr dem scheflichten Schattenreich, als der sonnigen Lebenswelt zu gehören scheinen" (VI, 407). In order to become the greatest of violinists Paganini has sold his soul to the devil; when he wanders through Hamburg with his famulus the pair resembles Faust and Wagner strolling before the city gates. On the concert stage Paganini seems a figure ascended from the underworld, a vampire with a violin. The demonic musician has come to depend too much on gruesome trappings. The day of Kreisler's intrinsic demonism has passed, the day of theatrical demonism has begun.

Heine cannot resist introducing an element of the scurrilous into his description of Paganini's appearance: there is something comical about the violinist's wooden movements (VI, 410). As in Kreisler's case, we forget the absurd aspects of Paganini's personality as soon as he begins to perform; his playing conjures up various images, just as Kreisler's performance before his club did. The identification is not complete: Hoffmann thinks in terms of the composer, Heine in terms of the virtuoso. Hoffmann makes a chord call forth a particular mood; Kreisler's physical make-up remains essentially unchanged, however much the various chords may affect his spirit. Heine does not describe the melodies played by Paganini at all, but devotes his efforts to a depiction of the various images which they evoke in the listener. As Maximilian says to Maria, ". . . so kennen Sie ja mein musikalisches zweites Gesicht, meine Begabnis, bei jedem Tone, den ich erklingen höre, auch die adäquate Klangfigur zu sehen . . ." (VI, 410). The images excited by Paganini's playing surround the performer as he stands on the stage, and, what is most typical for Heine's description of the virtuoso, Paganini is transformed in accordance with their nature. The spectator sees him, young and handsome, accompanying a maiden's song. Or he stands enchained, surrounded by goat-like monsters; then he becomes a monk, playing beside a reddened sea. Finally he is a planet wandering through the cosmos, a group of white-robed pilgrims following him. All this Heine describes with the least possible reference to the music itself; only in the last section does he touch upon the musical effects employed, where the tones are said to unfold themselves calmly, like an organ chorale in a cathedral, a comparison paling beside those pictures painted in non-musical terms.

Heine, himself a literary virtuoso, treats music precisely in the manner of a Paganini. Neither cares for the music itself. Heine is interested in the flashing performance in words, not in the music performed; Paganini desires to call attention to his own performance of the music. It is immaterial what music is chosen by the virtuoso: Heine neglects to name the compositions played by the violinist. Not only has music been subordinated to the performer; the performer now employs music (as an expression of his personality) to achieve mass hypnosis, a feature of the virtuoso temperament not shared by Bellini. Heine's Paganini remains the primary portrait of the nineteenth-century virtuoso, a figure whose reasons for existence were not to be questioned until the turn of the century.

The itinerant musician, with his small talents and great impudence, is a virtuoso manqué. He does not possess the gifts necessary to be a great performer; his power to influence others is not so strong that he can become a mentor, either to good or evil ends. He can scarcely be called diabolical, although he does not shun the black arts in a petty form. In his ability to support himself by his wits he resembles the Spielmann of medieval literature; but he lacks the heroic qualities of a Volker or a Horant. He does not have the trusting simplicity characterizing the wandering musician of Eichendorff, nor does he arouse innocent laughter. His picaresque efforts to fit himself into society without accepting its responsibilities, or boastingly to justify his position as an outsider, result in an unaffectionate amusement on the reader's part.

For all his negative qualities the déclassé musician has perhaps more basis in fact than any of the other types represented in Romantic literature. The musical world of the eighteenth and early nineteenth centuries was made up in large part of the inhabitants of a demimonde, without social rights or duties. They filled the choruses and orchestras, or, in less fortunate circumstances, toured the provinces as "itinerant artists." Unsettled as they were, they seldom reached the level of the petty bourgeoisie; and a Stadtmusikant Miller would look down on them. Strangely enough, instrumental players of the first rank often appeared in this class, although they seldom became famous, not being performers on the major instruments such as the harpsichord or organ. Musicians like the clarinetist Anton Stadler and the hornist Ignaz Leutgeb were friends of Mozart, who not only composed masterpieces for them but also helped support them. Often, like Leutgeb, who operated a cheese shop in his spare time, they were forced to take up other occupations in addition to music. A true account of the sufferings of a wandering musician in the early nineteenth century can be found in that fascinating autobiography, *Die Irrfahrten des Daniel Elster*; while Karl Ditters von Dittersdorf, in his *Leben*, provides an instructive description of eighteenth-century musicians forced to sit below the salt.[11]

We are disappointed to find that there is no déclassé musician in any of Hoffmann's stories. Despite his vast interest in music Hoffmann has confined himself to the demonic musician possessing great talents, musical or otherwise. Even his mad musicians represent the other face of the coin of genius. We do not know if Hoffmann ever planned a detailed picture of the ordinary German orchestral musician of his day. Certain facts would be against it: his musicians are primarily products of the new nineteenth century way of thought, while the wandering orchestral musician is a figure more typical of the eighteenth century, and disappears in the Romantic Age. It is possible, too, that Hoffmann felt music to be too sacred an art for him to paint a life-size portrait of a musician who used it badly. Only the story, *Die Fermate*, contains musicians belonging to the itinerant class, and these are Italians.

There had long been a reaction in German musical circles against the popularity of the Italian musician, a reaction which can be seen in Kuhnau's *Der musikalische Quacksalber*, in Forkel's life of Bach, or in the popular legends concerning musical battles between German and Italian masters (such as Bach and Alessandro Scarlatti). By the end of the eighteenth century the Roman fad had run its course and the Italians were often forced to take to the outlying districts in order to earn their daily bread. *Die Fermate* (1815), based on an incident from Hoffmann's youth, is a picture of just such musicians, singers who take a small German town by storm. Hoffmann's account of musical life in the town before the arrival of the singers, Lauretta and Teresina, is surely the best description of amateur musicians in German, if not in world, literature. The most important of the grotesque figures described in it is Demoiselle Meibel, the vehicle for a parody of that instrument, the female voice, which Hoffmann otherwise regards as sacred. Theodor, the young hero of the tale, bored with the absurd musical life of his town, becomes a member of the Italian troupe, accompanying the sisters' performances and composing songs for them. When he learns that they make fun of him and his compositions, he leaves them for an independent musical career. Many years later, now a famous composer, Theodor chances upon the sisters in Rome; they attempt to persuade the German to compose for them but he refuses, having dedicated himself to a higher type of music. The first meeting with the sisters, however, had caused the youth to become a composer—once more the theme of ideal music incorporated in a female voice. Yet Hoffmann is chary of praise for the sisters in their inspirational role; they, or their art, simply spoke "das Schöpfungswort" that awoke Theodor's sleeping spirit. "Gewiss ist es, dass so angeregt alle Melodien, die aus dem Innern hervorgehen, uns nur der Sängerin zu gehören scheinen, die den ersten Funken in uns warf" (I, 223). Happy the composer who never again sees the initial inspiration of his inner music!

Hoffmann was always prepared to attack falsity in music, whether it be German or Italian. The first part of *Die Fermate* scathingly pillories the stuffiness of German amateurs alongside the empty virtuosity of Italian professionals; yet the Italians seem worse than the Germans, since they, more talented, have something nobler to betray. Teresina is more than willing to make fun of her sister's coloratura antics; in her opinion these unmeasured runs, these eternal trills are no better than the foolhardy leaps of the rope-dancer (I, 214). She herself uses flattery to obtain flowing canzonette from Theodor in order that she too may show off her "Kunststückchen." That the possessor of a lovely voice will debase it to serve her own egoistic ends, instead of consecrating herself completely to "der edlen Musika," completely disillusions the young composer. Italian music receives a backhanded compliment. But Hoffmann also poses a question beyond nationality: does the musician serve music or does he make it serve him?

In *Musikalische Leiden und Freuden* Tieck does not seem to

be quite sure what attitude he should take toward the itinerant musician, a result perhaps of that desire for a presentation of all sides of the argument which led him to become so fond of the dialogue form. When we first meet Tieck's old Italian musician, his account of his battle against "Aberwitz und deutsche Seelenmanier" moves us to sympathy. As a young man he accepted an engagement in Germany; here his wife, the possessor of a wonderful coloratura voice, fell in love with Hortensio, a German composer. She became Hortensio's pupil and attempted to learn to sing in the grand manner, no longer from the throat but rather from the "Gemüt," "eine extra deutsche Erfindung, die alle andern Natione (sic) gar nicht kennen" (XVII, 307). When Hortensio, who was already married, repulsed Isabelle's love, she returned to her old brilliant style, but the German method had ruined her voice. Having lost their position, the two Italian singers sank lower and lower; finally the wife began to go insane. Societies of angels, led by King David ("gewiss ein Kenner in Musiken"), appeared in their attic room—just as David appeared to Musa in Keller's *Tanzlegendchen*—and presently the husband joined the wife in her intercourse with the departed spirits. We begin to lose respect for the arguments presented in favor of Italian music, since we see that Tieck has placed them in the mouth of a madman. The Italian cannot be regarded as a tragic figure: he reproaches Hortensio for his failure to become his wife's lover, he makes a theatrical attempt at suicide, and finally he sets out to murder his former rival, but only succeeds in having himself arrested. At the end of the story he is ejected from the theater when he cries during Julie's performance: "taugt nix! gar nix! miserable Pfuscherei, kein Vortrag!" (XVII, 356). Tieck has sketched the most damaging picture of the Italian musician in German literature, meanwhile giving us a picture of the popular attitude toward the Italian musician in nineteenth century Germany. The Italian can no longer command the respect that he did even in Hoffmann's youth; he is now regarded as an immoral and addled fellow who reproaches the Germans for their morality. He is incapable of holding a position on the German musical stage, if for no other reason than his buffoonery: Tieck's singer tells how he once pinched his prima donna during a love duet. He is quite capable of attempting a crime; he lacks all self-respect, for he announces his suicide, and then changes his mind at the last minute. His attitude toward music is mechanical, and he thinks only of technique, never of "die seelische Manier." In short, he is a thoroughly disreputable fellow, and the music of his native country can be no better than he is.

The gypsy musician is given fairer treatment than the Italian, since he pretends to be no more than an entertainer. Like the Italian he is not averse to criminal activities and is still less conscious of social duties. The Italian musician is willing to take up a permanent position in order to further himself materially. The more primitive gypsy needs to be free of ties of any kind. The gypsy's attitude toward music is more natural, in the eyes of German literary men, than the Italian's. He is scarcely the Italian's technical equal, but he plays with a self-sacrificing love of the art to which no Italian musician can lay claim.

In Brentano's tale, *Die mehreren Wehmüller und ungarischen Nationalgesichter* (1817), the gypsy musician, vagabond and rogue, appears in all his shabby glory. Brentano was related by nature to the wandering musicians, and it is not strange that he includes the gypsy violinist among the polyglot individuals he collects in a quarantined village on Hungary's Croatian border. Michaly is the most famous member of the company. His performance on the fiddle has a magical effect on the local peasants. Nor can the more sophisticated members of the beleaguered party resist his playing. He is able to sadden or cheer them like a second Orpheus.[12] The violinist is so excited by his own rendition of an old gypsy battle song that he weeps, but soon he plays such joyous melodies that the whole company grows gay once more.

At the end of the story Michaly appears in a different light. That he is a carefree vagabond we may guess from his description of his sister Mitidika, whose motto is "He who has nothing has all" (III, 158). What he says of her applies in equal measure to himself. Such an attitude would seem to place Michaly almost in the class of the footloose miller's son in Eichendorff. However Michaly is a student of the black arts, and finds an opportunity to use his skill—although to a good end. When the "false Wehmüller" faints, Michaly and his sister revive him by very curious means, resorting to torture and vile threats in an effort to persuade the impostor to disclose his identity.

Brentano, like Tieck, destroys whatever favorable opinion we may have had of the wandering musician and reveals him as a villainous individual, not averse to any sort of unpleasant deed. His musical gift is more elemental, and seemingly greater, than that of Tieck's old Italian, yet his audience is usually one of drunken peasants; the better sort of company for which he plays in the hut has been made more receptive to his music by the uncanny situation. It is doubtful whether as a person he is more appealing than the old Italian; he succeeds in his petty villainy, while the Italian fails in his attempt at an actual crime.

Brentano's friend Arnim has also described a rogue musician in his tale *Fürst Ganzgott und Sänger Halbgott*, which appeared a year after *Die mehreren Wehmüller*. Its chief figure is a German opera singer forced (since he has lost his voice) to live by his wits. The unhappy singer makes his way to Karlsbad, where he hopes to be recognized by those royal judges of art who are his "equals." Thus Arnim touches lightly on Hoffmann's argument for the musician's social rights. At an inn Halbgott is mistaken for Prince Ganzgott, with whom he willingly changes roles. The Prince would like to be a singer, and the singer has no objection to becoming a prince. Halbgott is given one task in particular: he is to overcome the frigidity of Ganzgott's wife, the Princess; soon the singer is so captivated by her beauty that he forgets his duty to her husband. His voice returns and he performs the *Stabat Mater* of Pergolesi in order to win the favor of his "wife." The singer is ready to commit adultery when the Prince appears with the news that Halbgott is his half brother. At the end of the story Halbgott is appointed minister of state and sets out to rule the land in his carefree way.

The singer, like the Italian musician of Tieck, is not a vagabond by choice but rather by necessity. Similarly, we sympathize with him, until we learn that he will betray his benefactor without a moment's hesitation. Only the discovery of his royal blood, which removes him from the irresponsible class of the ordinary musicians, prevents him from taking advantage of the Princess. However, he continues to rule the state through his power of song, a second Orpheus, as the prince says.[13] Arnim has worked out a pretty compromise between Hoffmann and Eichendorff concerning the position of the musician in society. Hoffmann feels that his Kreisler is the superior of any prince, while Eichendorff, gently satirizing the Taugenichts, makes it more than plain that the musician cannot wed the noblewoman under any conditions. Arnim avoids the clash so evident in Hoffmann's works by making the singer half royal. Halbgott's mother, an Italian, is a former opera singer who betrayed her husband with Ganzgott's father. (Incidentally, Arnim's tale introduces the mother-son relationship which was to become so important in the German musical novel. Despite his dislike of his mother's activities, Halbgott is completely dominated by her; he is willing to accept his ministership only upon the stipulation that the evil old woman will become the official fortuneteller of the principality.)

Arnim's Halbgott is more attractive than his fellow wanderers in Hoffmann's *Fermate*, in Tieck, and in Brentanò, for he possesses a feature in common with Kreisler. Just as Kreisler thinks of music as a female voice, so Halbgott recovers his voice through his love, however sinful, for the Princess and sings as he has never sung before. (Thus Arnim, like Heinrich Mann with his Cavaliere Giordano of *Die kleine Stadt*, would also seem to connect musical ability with sexual prowess.) Halbgott stands higher artistically than any of the other rogue-musicians whom we have encountered; the effect of his song surpasses that of Michaly's fiddling, since he is able even to influence nature. As he sings, the fountain's jet spurts higher, glowworms surround his head like a wreath of stars (IV, 169).

Joseph von Eichendorff, the creator of the classic guileless wanderer in *Aus dem Leben eines Taugenichts* (1826), had a peculiarly simple relationship to music. His letters rarely mention the musicians of his time, and in his biographical sketch, *Halle und Heidelberg*, he devotes but a few sentences in his discussion of Romanticism to the music of the movement. Having defined Romanticism as the relationship of the "Diesseits" to a greater "Jenseits," he says briefly that the Romantic spirit has led music back from a mere excitation of the senses to the old Italian masters, and to Bach, Gluck, and Händel; "Derselbe ernstere Sinn . . . weckte auch in der Profanmusik das geheimnisvolle wunderbare Lied, das verborgen in allen Dingen schlummert, und Mozart, Beethoven, und Karl Maria von Weber sind echte Romantiker."[14] Eichendorff is thus taciturn on the most important of the Romantic arts; in his creative writings on the musician he is more voluble but often as unsatisfying. Everyone and no one in Eichendorff is a musician; his musical figures are amateurs, students and noblemen, always ready to seize a violin or a guitar, or wanderers of a lesser social station, for whom music is one of a number of occupations. As in other, non-musical connections, Eichendorff presages the attitude of the Biedermeier, where the amateur musician was preferred to the professional.

In the Taugenichts Berglinger's religious fervor and Kreisler's nervous energy have become sheer artlessness and random enthusiasm. Where Berglinger's piety results in the composition of the *Passionsmusik*, the Taugenichts' serenity of spirit is artistically unfruitful, unless we consider his songs as serious compositions. Kreisler knows an enthusiasm which reveals itself as musical inspiration or, when rejected, as mockery or despair; the Taugenichts' enthusiasm is uncritical. But the Taugenichts has an ability which Kreisler lacks; he can place himself in complete harmony with his surroundings, in particular with nature, while Kreisler, upon beholding a lovely scene in the castle park of Prince Irenäus, bursts into ridicule of all that is beautiful, conscious as he is of the terrible contrast between the park and the deeds performed there. The Taugenichts, blind to every possibility of harm, is the happier and more content of the two ("den lieben Gott lass ich nur walten");[15] the demonic musician, with his heightened sensitivity to the threats which life (and his own powers) offer his welfare and his sanity, has been replaced by a musician with a protective coating of trust. The Taugenichts, although he does not attain the blessed subjectivity of Grillparzer's Spielmann, still points to the Biedermeier figure in his construction of a private paradise, for which he has sacrificed much of the Romantic musician's former perceptivity.

In their social concepts of the musician, Hoffmann and Eichendorff are worlds apart, and again we see how an air of passive contentment steals over the musical scene. Eichendorff, himself a member of the nobility, regarded the musician as a member of a lower class, from that fluctuating segment of society which had the double purpose of self-preservation and amusement of its betters—and from which Eichendorff's musician does not wish to escape. The Taugenichts (who, a miller's son, is actually a cut above the vagabond musician) will eventually content himself with the quiet life. At no time does he attempt seriously to leave his class, and his love for the supposed "schönste, gnädigste Gräfin" is gently chided as one of the many misadventures of a simple soul.

Other musicians of Eichendorff must also be content to stick to their social last. In the play, *Die Freier* (1833), the musician Schlender is a true vagabond, a homeless ex-soldier who played the cymbals at the battle of Leipzig. The musician, an object for smiles in the *Taugenichts*, must now endure ridicule, although he is almost too foolish to care: Schlender is hired by a noble company to take part in a masquerade. Himself disguised as the "Countess Adele," he is told that the pompous Hofrat Fleder is the Countess in man's clothing. Still in his petticoats, Schlender flees from the castle and from the innkeeper to whom he owes a considerable bill. Eichendorff's picture of the amateur flautist Fleder can be contrasted to his Schlender; Fleder after all has the consolation of his position, but Schlender, without social standing, must continue as a clown. *Die Glücksritter*, appearing eight years after *Die Freier*, has in Siglhupfer-Klarinett a wandering musician of a less laughable sort than Schlender, but he too is aware of his social place. In his double capacity as clarinetist and soldier of fortune (the story takes place during the Thirty Years' War) Klarinett might seem to belong more to the category of the rogue musician than to the goodhearted class of the Taugenichts. Simple Klarinett is not; when he first met his friend, the student and hornist Suppius, he "schoss einen seltsamen scharfen Blick herüber, als wollt' er erst prüfen, wieviel er hier vertrauen dürfte" (II, 231), and he knows all the tricks of the experienced soldier. Appearances deceive; the anachronistically named Klarinett (the instrument was not invented until the eighteenth century) is a good fellow who has only the fault of wanderlust (". . . er fühlte sich auf einmal leicht in dem alten Wanderkleide und schaute in das stille Meer der Nacht . . ." II, 259). And Klarinett has the fate of Eichendorff's guileless musician. Suppius, from a higher social class, saves the castle of Count Gerold, wins his daughter, and makes his fortune, while Klarinett disappears forever into the forests, followed by his faithful sweetheart, Denkeli.

A clearly defined example of the creative musician is not a part of Eichendorff's battery of characters. We must content ourselves with Florio, the troubadour in *Das Marmorbild* (1819), who is not strictly a composer: "Ich habe mich wohl zuweilen in der fröhlichen Sangeskunst versucht" (II, 76). In some respects Florio resembles the Taugenichts; like the fiddler he is in harmony with nature, having an even better acquaintance with her subtler moods. However, Florio's life is not so uncomplicated as that of the Taugenichts, for he is tempted by the powers of sensuality represented by the mistress of the marble palace, a manifestation of Frau Venus. He is saved by the song of Fortunato, another troubadour, who brings the Wolfram von Eschenbach of Hoffmann's *Kampf der Sänger* and of Wagner's *Tannhäuser* to mind. The contrasted pair of artist friends appears frequently on the German musical-literary scene. The one, the Florio-type (or Heinrich von Ofterdingen or Tannhäuser) is tempted by and may even succumb to some sinister force; the other, the Fortunato or Wolfram, is the artist with unassailable moral faith, a humble practitioner of his art. On the morning following Florio's escape, Fortunato points to the ruins of a temple of Venus, standing on the site of the previous night's palace; then he recites his creed: "Glaubt mir, ein redlicher Dichter kann viel wagen, denn die Kunst, die ohne Stolz und Frevel, bespricht und bändigt die wilden Erdengeister, die aus der Tiefe nach uns langen" (II, 107). The contrast Florio-Fortunato can be found elsewhere in Romantic literature (Karl Maria von Weber, in his sketch for a novel, *Tonkünstlers Leben*, gives his composer a poet-friend, Diehl, to act as a counterbalance to the musician's enthusiasms);[16] but it flourishes most mightily in the twentieth century, with Strauss's *Freund Hein*, Hesse's *Peter Camenzind* and *Gertrud*, Friedrich Huch's *Enzio*, and, later, Mann's *Doktor Faustus*. Despite changes of emphasis, the formula remains the same: the artist susceptible to the supernatural, even though that taming may lead to lessthem. Eichendorff makes the stronger case for the taming of the demonic powers, even though that taming may lead to lessened productivity. But is Eichendorff Romanticist enough to be deeply concerned with the fate of the creative musician?

In the novel *Dichter und ihre Gesellen* (1834) a potentially demonic figure of the musician, Dryander, is kept within the limits of the grotesquely comic. When we first see Dryander at an inn, he has many of the appurtenances of the diabolical fiddler, like Heine's Paganini or the devil of Lenau's *Faust*: "ein . . . Männchen mit einem scharfen, geistreichen Gesichte, emsig in den wunderlichsten Läufern die Geige spielend, während seine Augen mit unverkennbarem Wohlbehagen die Tanzenden verfolgten. Vergebens riefen diese ihm zu, sich zu moderieren, der Unaufhaltsame drehte mit wahrem Virtuosen-Wahnsinn die Töne, wie einen Kreisel, immer schneller und dichter, die Tanzenden gerieten endlich ganz ausser Takt und Atem . . ." (III, 83). After further acquaintance Dryander begins to seem less a demonic musician than an energetic madman; he functions briefly as a magician, a court poet, as the would-be lover of a princess. In none of his roles is it possible to take him seriously; having nearly won the princess, he changes his mind when a moonbeam strikes the noble lady's forehead. When the princess leaves him in disgust, he immediately becomes enamoured of a nursemaid, calling her "heilige Jungfrau" and himself at once "Hund und Wild." He attempts to persuade her and her charges to fly with him "nach der blauen Ferne, bis in das stille Himmelreich" (III, 157)—only to learn that the children's mother is sick. Seized by a terrible fear of infection, he runs away.

For all his crazy transformations Dryander arouses our sympathy, and his song of the wandering Spielmann has genuinely tragic overtones hidden in the extravagance of its language:

Von Lüsten und Reue zerrissen die Brust,
Wie rasend in verzweifelter Lust,
Brech' ich im Fluge mir Blumen zum Strauss
Wird doch ein fröhlicher Kranz nicht daraus!

Wird aus dem Schrei doch nimmer Gesang,
Herz, o mein Herz, bist ein irrer Klang,
Den der Sturm in alle Lüfte verweht—
Lebt wohl, und fragt nicht, wohin es geht! (III, 212)

Yet Baron Manfred remarks of the poem's author that "Man sollte nicht wirklich denken, er sei durch und durch verzweifelt . . ." (III, 212). Manfred has just seen Dryander fighting unchivalrously with his wife Trudchen, whom he has been forced to wed as a result of his own concupiscence. Thinking Trudchen was a naiad, Dryander pursued her; he came face to face with Trudchen's father, who compelled a handy clergyman to marry the couple. Manfred's revulsion at Dryander's antics is increased after he finds the violinist posing as a hermit. (The religious disguise is a favorite of Dryander, and Manfred's friend Fortunat also comes upon the musician acting as a pilgrim on a Danube boat, or undergoing a mock "period of atonement" at the hermit's cell.) Eichendorff almost importunately reiterates that Dryander is not really a madman, as he claims to be in part ("ein tragischer, wahnsinniger König und ein Hanswurst, der ihm schnell ein Bein unterstellt, die hetzen und balgen sich Tag und Nacht in mir . . ." III, 211), but that he is at the most an addled clown, a spiritual jack-of-all-trades in the tradition of Hoffmann's Peter Schönfeld.

Dichter und ihre Gesellen has a measure of tragedy in the unhappy career and death of the poet Otto, and given Dryander's hopelessly unstable nature, it seems altogether logical that the musician should come to a tragic end, instead of continuing his pranks ad infinitum. Nevertheless, we last glimpse Dryander as the leader of a troupe of comedians. Both Eichendorff's strongly "humanistic" Catholicism and his position in literary history prevent him from expanding the demonic side of Dryander's character; from the religious point of view, Eichendorff can scarcely honor the demonic by giving it credence, and as a poet on the borderline between Romanticism and Biedermeier, he is prone to smile at the excesses, indeed at the normal features of the older period. Dryander might be interpreted as a parody (or succession of parodies) of the forms the Romantic musician sometimes takes: the virtuoso, the idealistic lover, the wandering Spielmann, the madman, the religiously inclined artist; and Eichendorff should be given credit for having formulated a critique of the Romantic musician. Unhappily, the structure of the novel is so helter-skelter that Eichendorff's parodistic intentions cannot be enjoyed to the full; Dryander, bobbing up here and there like a will-o'-the-wisp, is never regarded consistently or clearly. And what we, as readers, remember of him from these hasty glances is not his silliness, his lust, or his poltroonery; we recall those despairing moments in which Dryander realizes and rebels against the flaws of his nature. Eichendorff is enough of a Romanticist to have created in Dryander, intentionally or not, a distant relative of Kreisler and an ancestor to those musicians, rendered incapable of practicing their art by the faults of their personality, who are standard fixtures in the post-Wagnerian musical novel and play.

This study cannot include the many appearances of the vagabond musician in the Romantic lyric. One lyricist deserves mention, however, since his poem cycles offer a whole picture of the wanderer. Wilhelm Müller had the not unusual desire of the Romantic literary man to become a composer. Addressing himself to Johannes Kreisler in his diary, he writes: "Mit deinem Musikfeind habe ich manche Ähnlichkeit. Ich kann weder spielen noch singen und wenn ich dichte, so sing' ich doch und spiele auch. Wenn ich die Weisen von mir geben könnte, so würden meine Lieder besser gefallen, als jetzt."[17] He goes on to say that he consoles himself with the hope of finding a "gleichgestimmte Seele" who will hear the melody in his words —this was of course to be Franz Schubert. In the very title of Müller's *Gedichte aus den hinterlassenen Papieren eines reisenden Waldhornisten* (1821-24), he demonstrates his wish to be a musician; note that he aspires only to the rank of performer, not of composer, a sign of the growing modesty of literary claims on music. As in Eichendorff, Müller's vagabond musician is a member of a low class of society, accepted, like the gypsy, on the strength of his picturesqueness, but there is no condescension toward him. The nobleman is never contrasted to Müller's musician; the character set in opposition to the sentimental young man is from the same social milieu, the huntsman, for example, in *Die schöne Müllerin*. The musician of Müller loves a member of his own group; the Prague musician has a "Schätzel" in his home city. The tragedy in the life of the musical miller (he is a lute-player and singer) is that another member of his own class with a more colorful profession has won the lovely miller-lass.

In other respects the vagabond musicians of Eichendorff and Müller are much alike. Wanderlust is the most typical feature of Müller's musician, as it was of Eichendorff's. The fiancée of the Prague musician complains: "Ei, kommst denn nimmermehr zu Ruh', / Du Musikantenblut?"[18] The favorite haunt of Müller's wandering musician, as of the Taugenichts, is the forest, although forest-songs are fewer in Müller than in Eichendorff. Some of Müller's Prague musicians are sad at leaving their loves, yet they soon recover from their pain. The deserted girls however faithfully await the wanderers' return. That they do return, thus indicating their basic goodness of heart, is to be seen at the close of *Der Prager Musikant* where the vagabond waves his full purse before the window of his beloved:

> "All' ihr Prager Musikanten,
> Auf, heraus mit Horn und Bass,
> Spielt den schönsten Hochzeitreigen!
> Morgen leeren wir ein Fass." (42)

Thus Müller's wandering musician, like the Taugenichts, presumably marries, founds a family, and lives happily and quietly ever after. Another Romantic has vanished.

The literature of the late eighteenth century, with its "social consciousness" resulting from Storm and Stress, offers artisan-musicians whose lot was a wretched one: Moritz's sometime choirboy, Anton Reiser, and Schiller's famous Stadtmusikant Miller. These unhappy souls are still members of the bourgeoisie, and regarded as worthy handworkers by their neighbors. Romanticism is unwilling to peer into the lower depths of musical existence, if they are not sufficiently picturesque. Only Clemens Brentano, in a little song, "Die lustigen Musikanten," from the Singspiel of the same name (1803), illuminates the darkest corners of the musical world, and he does so with a poignancy we seek in vain even in the modern period. (It does not detract from the brilliance of Brentano's performance that the musical figures in the Singspiel itself are happier than their lyric equivalents. An entire Singspiel of social protest would have been unthinkable in Brentano's day—and what poet, including Brentano, would have written it?) Brentano's poem becomes all the more amazing when his group is compared with the typical nocturnal serenades of Romanticism, who seem to have no existence save that of wandering through the moonlit streets of some quaint old city. Brentano's musicians—bereaved girl, blind mother, ague-shaken brothers, crippled child—penetrate this illusion; young and old alike can never have enough of their songs, they bring joy to lovers, pretty maidens, drunken guests; yet, pariahs and mendicants, they are like the nightingales which sing only in the dark:

> Bei uns kann es nur fröhlich schallen,
> Wenn uns kein menschlich Auge sieht.[19]

Art and life cannot know a more bitter contrast.

CHAPTER II

BIEDERMEIER AND POETIC REALISM

Romanticism as a vital force died amidst the spiritual and economic exhaustion which came over Europe in the aftermath of the Napoleonic Wars, and the Romantic musician in literature vanished with the literary atmosphere that had produced him. The musician of real life, having found the Romantic milieu to his liking—flattering to himself and flattering to his art—did not give up so easily: he prospered and multiplied, reaching his culmination decades after Hoffmann's death in the person of Richard Wagner. In literature the demonic musician and his satellites made way for a less prepossessing (and less demanding) band of players, composed of incapable musicians, amateur musicians, domesticated musicians. Frequently Romanticism broke out afresh, but the author was quick to stamp it out. Pedagogy, a reigning interest of the Biedermeier, assumed a more important role than inspiration, and it came to be not the artist's productions but his moral character that counted. Even in the arch-Romantic Hoffmann, and in Tieck, somewhat less firm in the Romantic faith, there occurred in grotesque form the pedagogical concern which would soon envelop other musically minded literary men—and had not Wackenroder and Rochlitz already pondered the effect of bad training on the gifted child?

Hoffmann's *Der Baron von B.*, published in the *Allgemeine musikalische Zeitung* for March, 1819, is closely related to *Ritter Gluck*, but with an important difference; there the madness of the old musician is viewed as a demonic quality, perhaps equivalent to genius, here emphasis is laid on the illusions of the "violin teacher" as such. In Hoffmann's earlier works insanity was considered almost a prerequisite quality in the musician; Kreisler's madness no longer has a role in *Kater Murr*. For the later Hoffmann, madness has become a comical rather than an almost noble state. *Der Baron von B.* is an anecdote from the youth of a violin virtuoso. The young musician, after hearing much about the Baron, is finally presented to him. The Baron, a connoisseur of the violin and its literature, condescends, he says, to give lessons to the virtuosi of the day. The youth is surprised when he learns that the "greatest of all living violinists" cannot bring forth a tone: "Dicht am Stege rutschte er mit dem zitternden Bogen hinauf, schnarrend, pfeifend, quäkend, miauend . . ." (I, 274). The Baron pays the violinists to take lessons from him. A competent judge of music, he says much that inspires the young musician, all the while persisting in the delusion that he is a master performer. Hoffmann has transformed the theme of the mad artist into a parody. The artist with the highest ideals (which the Baron undoubtedly cherishes) may not be able to produce a note upon his instrument. A practical view toward the art had always been present in Hoffmann; in *Der Baron von B.* it has won the upper hand entirely. Considered from the later Hoffmann's standpoint, the dreamer Theodor in *Die Fermate* might have been a just object of scorn for the technically capable Italian singers. Hoffmann mocks the highly subjective state of mind in which his Kreisler has created his noble works; perhaps he even mocks himself, who possessed musical ideals of the highest order and lacked the technical ability to realize these ideals in music correspondingly great.

Hoffmann lays the blame for his own lack of "technisches Können" on his poor youthful training in the art. The professional, even dry, attitude toward music of his critical writings may be an exaggerated reaction against his faulty knowledge. Hoffmann's early musical education receives its most scathing denunciation in *Die Fermate*; another tale from the same period (1814-15), *Der Musikfeind,* also reflects his feelings in the matter. Everyone applauds when the future "Musikfeind's" father hammers and bangs, much to the child's bafflement; music for the boy is rather the wonderful voice of his aunt: ". . . kaum hatte die Tante einen Satz gesungen, so fing ich an, bitterlich zu weinen und wurde unter heftigen Scheltworten meines Vaters zum Saal hinausgebracht" (I, 70). The aunt believes that the boy is extremely sensitive to music; his father retorts that he howls like an anti-musical dog. When the boy begins to take music lessons he demonstrates considerable talent, for he discovers the art of transposition by himself. Given a presto in the difficult key of E major to learn for a family concert, he solves his musical problem by raising the number a half step into the easy key of F. His father, believing that he has played the trick maliciously, puts an end to his music lessons. As a grown man, the music-hater is frequently so excited by a performance that he must leave the hall before the number is finished; often he returns to an opera again and again because he wishes to understand it completely. For these reasons he arouses the mockery of his more brilliant friends who give him his hateful nickname; in truth he possesses far more talent than any of them.

When the music-hater was supposed to practice an exercise as a child, he began instead to experiment with chords, and so discovered the technique of transposition. It is interesting to compare this habit of "Akkordsuchen" with a similar one of Rochlitz's Karl, of Grillparzer's Spielmann, and Thomas Mann's Hanno Buddenbrook. Karl is carried away into a musico-religious world of his own; the ungifted Spielmann finds a solace in art from the cruelties of the world about him; little Hanno loves music because it satisfies the death-drive within him. Hoffmann's figure, more gifted than these, is genuinely fascinated by the technical possibilities of his discovery. Tragically his musical career is ruined by youthful influences which might not have touched a less sensitive individual; yet he can still know the essence of music. When the music-hater complains about his lack of musical talent, his friend Kreisler remarks that he is to be compared with the apprentice at the temple of Sais in Novalis's story, "der ungeschickt scheinend im Vergleich der andern Schüler doch den wunderbaren Stein fand, den die andern mit allem Fleiss vergeblich suchten" (I, 78).

The story of the "Musikfeind" in Tieck's *Musikalische Leiden und Freuden* has obviously been influenced by Hoffmann's tale. Just as Hortensio is a poorer imitation of Krespel, so tragic implications in Hoffmann's music-hater have been turned into mere comical whims in his successor. Tieck quite reasonably criticizes the harmful effect of poor early instruction, yet we wonder if his music-hater merits any better kind of teaching. Tieck's biographer, Köpke, relates that the poet's music-hater reflects certain sufferings from his boyhood, but Tieck, unlike Hoffmann, seems to have been completely lacking in talent. When he retells his experiences in the music-hater's guise, he offers excuses borrowed from his literary model for the sad outcome of his musical career. Thus Tieck's mingling of his childhood experiences with those of Hoffmann results in a figure which, like the other characters in Tieck's story, does not seem to know what standpoint it represents. Attempting to learn the violin, the incipient music-hater pays no attention to keys, tempos, or bars; his teacher never explains to him that some notes have longer duration than others. Without the intelligence of Hoffmann's hero, he does not discover these matters for himself. After seven years of instruction the boy is asked to play at a party; his repertoire is soon exhausted and he retires in disgrace. Shortly thereafter a new teacher (the composer Hortensio) tries in vain to undo the damage done, and as soon as the boy goes to the university his musical education ends. Later in life he can always excuse himself when bad singers appear, since he has the reputation of being completely unmusical, although Tieck's Kapellmeister hints that he uses his reputation to avoid poor performances. Tieck does not expand this last theme, and we are left in the dark as to what the author's intention with his music-hater may have been. Tieck talks of the danger of careless instruction, but how can the talentless performer be damaged? And is it possible to say whether the music-hater is a competent judge of music, or would have been one, had he not been discouraged in youth? The Kapellmeister's jest and the fact that the music-hater often visits the circle of music lovers indicate that he is essentially musical: perhaps his poor musical training has done damage after all. At any rate no tragedy has occurred; the narrator of the anecdote is quite happy to be regarded, pose or not, as a foe of the art.

Despite his stormy friendship with Beethoven, Franz Grillparzer formed his theory of musical aesthetics on the music of Mozart, in whom the poet honored that respect for measure he thought to be most characteristic of Austrian art. In the poem "Zu Mozarts Feier" (1842) Grillparzer says: "Was er getan und was er sich versagt / Wiegt gleich schwer in der Schale seines Ruhms."[1] The lines contain Grillparzer's theory of musical art in a nutshell; music that does not meet this austere criterion of "nothing in excess" is not good music. How narrow such a theory is can be shown by its application to the late Beethoven or Richard Wagner. Grillparzer's well-known aversion to Wagner's program-music is not surprising in view of his earlier attack on Weber and *Der Freischütz*. In his *Freischütz* essay Grillparzer defines music as the art which does not delineate something definite but which pleases through its inner construction and "die . . . dunklen Gefühle" which accompany it.

These feelings are the true province of music, and here poetry must grant it primary rank. Grillparzer concludes that the poet is a fool who wishes to emulate the musician in the sound of his verses, and that the musician (Weber) is a madman who desires to be the poet's equal in definiteness of expression—that Mozart is the greatest composer and that Weber is not the greatest (Abt. I, XIV, 35-36).

For Grillparzer, Beethoven is of more importance as personality than as artist; standing apart from the great artisan-composers of the eighteenth century, Beethoven is joined with Byron under the rubric of the gloomy Weltschmerzler. In the poem "Wanderszene" Grillparzer describes Beethoven as the "demonic" personality. A man with a hurried step goes through thicket and field; neither stream nor abyss can hinder his course. He stands at the goal as victor, "Nur hat er keinen Weg gebahnt" (Abt. I, X, 212). With "Wanderszene" Grillparzer allows himself his most outspoken public criticism of Beethoven: a massive genius who has left no path for others to follow. Beethoven's virtue is his daring, but what good is daring if it does not contribute to the development of the art as a whole?

How closely Beethoven's art and personality were associated in Grillparzer's mind with the problem of intelligibility can be seen in the private papers of the dramatist. Piety did not prevent the diarist from bitterly accusing the transgressor against Grillparzer's inflexible aesthetic code. Grillparzer cannot overcome the belief that Beethoven's influence in the musical world has been primarily a harmful one. In a sketch from the year 1834, entitled *Beethovens nachteilige Wirkungen auf die Kunstwelt, ungeachtet seines hohen, nicht genug zu schätzenden Wertes* (Abt. II, IX, 171), Grillparzer sets up a list of crimes Beethoven has committed against the art of music. His harmonies are too daring, he has removed the concepts of order and continuity in music, he has created an interest in the strong rather than the beautiful. Weber had sinned by attempting to make music a depictive art; Beethoven, by destroying form, has destroyed the very art of music. The classicism of Grillparzer's aesthetic attitude prevented him from understanding the music and the musician most typical of the nineteenth century; fond as he was of music as the pre-eminent art of the emotions, he did not wish the emotions to win the upper hand over form to the detriment of the music's intelligibility.

Grillparzer has left no portrait of the creative musician. His novella, *Der arme Spielmann,* contains however a treatment of the theme of subjective validity so important in his writing on Beethoven. The hero of the tale is thought to have been patterned after an old musician whose acquaintance Grillparzer had made in the inn where he took his meals. To this figure Grillparzer added features from his own life, as, for example, his strained relationship with his father. However valuable the story may be as autobiographical source, it should be remembered that Jakob, the Spielmann, bears certain outspoken resemblances to Hoffmann's and Tieck's music-haters, and to Hoffmann's Baron von B. Jakob, like Hoffmann's music-hater, has been the victim of a stern if well-meaning father; each child has been prevented from practicing music in his own way, each spends hours dreaming over his instrument. The young music-hater falls into improvisation whenever he begins to practice. The Spielmann is likewise a victim of the habit (as was Grillparzer himself); "Wenn ich abends im Zwielicht die Violine ergriff, um mich nach meiner Art ohne Noten zu vergnügen, nahmen sie mir das Instrument und sagten, das verdirbt die Applikatur, klagten über Ohrenfolter, und verwiesen mich auf die Lehrstunde . . ." (Abt. I, XIII, 51). (Tieck's music-hater has indulged in a less inventive variety of the same amusement, the repetition of sixteenth notes or the playing by ear of a favorite tune.) Hoffmann's hero and Grillparzer's resemble one another in their pureness of spirit, their shy sensitivity, and in their clumsiness. Their chief difference is one which points to the essence of Grillparzer's creation: the music-hater has originally possessed great musical talent, which Jakob totally lacks. Hoffmann is concerned with the problem of the artist while Grillparzer is not. Tieck's music-hater is a compromise figure: so far as we know he lacks the talent of Hoffmann's hero and the saintliness of Grillparzer's; however he too partakes in less measure of the innocence common to the others and certainly is as much plagued by shyness as they.

The violin performances of Hoffmann's Baron von B. and Jakob closely resemble one another. The Baron brings forth the most hideous sounds from his violin, meanwhile believing that these scratchings are magnificent music; the "Phantasieren" of old Jakob consists of long and painful notes played without sense of rhythm. Each of the "artists" is convinced of the validity and beauty of what he is playing; the old Baron forces this belief upon others, Jakob exists in a private world into which no one need follow him. The Baron's devotion to art is a double one, to art regarded objectively (that of others, which he judges brilliantly) and to his own subjective world of sound. The Spielmann, musically of a less complicated make-up than the Baron, is wholly given up to his curious mode of playing. An interesting sidelight on his character is that when the objective "sound-world" is able to enter his consciousness in the form of Barbara's song, he comprehends the melody and plays it correctly: "Er spielte, und zwar diesmal mit richtigem Ausdrucke, die Melodie eines gemütlichen, übrigens gar nicht ausgezeichneten Liedes . . ." (Abt. I, XIII, 54). Devotion to a fellow creature has been able to pierce the wall of his subjectivity, which would not occur in the case of the Baron: the Spielmann is a human being, the Baron an artist. When the Baron scratches away, he believes that he is demonstrating a technique new to the musical world of his day; in his mad fashion he is a musical progressive, a Kreisler gone wrong. Jakob has no such pretensions; his violin playing is a matter of sensuous enjoyment for him alone.

The element of enjoyment is repeatedly emphasized by Grillparzer. When the narrator first sees the Spielmann playing at the church festival, he notices that the old man performs with a self-applauding mien. Later the narrator hears long held tones coming from the Spielmann's room, "und zwar immer derselbe Ton mit einer Art genussreichem Daraufberuhen wiederholt" (Abt. I, XIII, 46). As he exercises he dwells on intervals that please his ear, while slighting those combinations, even though harmonically permissible, which he dislikes: "Der Alte genoss, indem er spielte" (Abt. I, XIII, 48). Jakob has become the representative of a principal tenet of Grillparzer's musical theories. In the Weber essay Grillparzer says that music is a putting together of tones which, without the intervention of the mind, brings about pleasant or unpleasant sensuous impressions. On this conception of music as a purely sensuous art Grillparzer bases his attack against the progressive Weber, who seeks to give music the intellectuality of words. At the end of his criticism Grillparzer introduces Mozart as the greatest of composers, whose appeal is almost purely sensuous, almost wholly unintellectual. Thus far the Spielmann's conception of music is exactly that of Grillparzer, although presented in exaggerated form.

Grillparzer adds a feature to the Spielmann's musical character which cannot be easily explained. One of the problems we have to deal with in Jakob's case is that of subjective validity. His method of making music is perfectly satisfactory to himself; in fact he views the music of others with a certain condescension and lives in the conviction that he has reached the true essence of music—a conviction which he is much too modest to force upon anyone else: "Obwohl mir das jeweilige Was der Musik mit Ausnahme jenes Lieds [the song of Barbara] immer ziemlich gleichgültig war und auch geblieben ist bis zum heutigen Tag. Sie spielen den Wolfgang Amadeus Mozart und den Sebastian Bach, aber den lieben Gott spielt Keiner" (Abt. I, XIII, 55). Grillparzer does not subscribe to this concept of music; despite the fact that it grows out of a theory identical with Grillparzer's own, it represents a violation of the principal tenet of the poet's general aesthetic theory, "nothing in excess." While Grillparzer's story is written in praise of the old man's naive spirit, which has produced this nonintellectual theory of music, he cannot subscribe to any exaggeration of the theory to the point of destroying form, which is precisely what the old man in his capriciousness has done. Grillparzer's attitude toward the Spielmann is in this respect identical with that toward the Beethoven of the later works. Beethoven, disregarding form, is inclined to follow his own will, without a thought for his listeners; the old man has committed the same error. Grillparzer's most outspoken criticisms of Beethoven stem from the years during which we presume Grillparzer was at work on the Spielmann, or when he at least was thinking of the matter. We cannot be sure of the exact dates of the tale: it appeared in the fall of 1847, but mentions the flood of 1830; most of the Beethoven criticisms are from the decade between 1834 and 1844.

It would nevertheless be absurd to see nothing but musical criticism in the figure of the Spielmann. The *Spielmann* is a treatment of the question of the validity of the inner or imaginary world as opposed to the real and practical world (that of the Spielmann's father and brothers). And music is only one side of what remains a treatment of a more general problem. The fact that the Spielmann is a musician, coupled with Grillparzer's almost obsessive critical pre-occupation with the question of intelligibility in music, has led the author to allow secondary musical problems at times to get the upper hand over the principal, human argument. Jakob is devoted to a strange and subjective form of "art," but this "art" is indicative of the nature of the whole man. He does not compel others to listen to him, although he feels that he "is playing God, not Mozart or Bach" on his violin. The bizarre nature of his musical passion notwithstanding, his unpretentious devotion to it discloses the same heroism in parvo which his final self-sacrifice reveals on a grander scale. In contrast to his father and brothers, who have been "successes" in the eyes of the world, he is a failure; as a human he has been almost a saint. His unhappiness as a child, his curious devotion to music, his love story reflect the character of a man whose life is a parable of faith and humbleness; they are intended to serve an ethical rather than a musical purpose. The Spielmann lacks talent for music as others think of it: music would have offered the same intensively subjective and joyful experience to him, no matter what training he had received, and he would have become as little the artist in the accepted sense of the word. The Spielmann is always at one with life, accepting his situation gladly. Jakob cannot be interpreted as one of the first attempts at a reconciliation between artist and life. The Spielmann is not an artist nor is there a division. We must turn to other authors of the Biedermeier for an attempt at such a reconciliation, and here too the musician is frequently more human than artist, the division more accepted than revolted against.

Two authors usually associated with Young Germany, Theodor Mundt and Karl Gutzkow, give evidence in their musical tales of how the human element ousts the artistic. Theodor Mundt's *Das Duett* (1831) describes the progress of young musicians from Romantic excesses to a more settled life, or failing that, to destruction. Eduard, a notary of vague artistic ambitions, falls in love with Adelaide Winter. Adelaide's home is as disturbed as Antonie Krespel's; her mother, a former actress, has compelled Professor Winter by threats of suicide to allow the girl to go on the operatic stage. In fact Frau Winter even plots her husband's murder; she leads her willing younger daughter, Fanchon, into an immoral life. (The difference between the Winter sisters can be detected in the music they sing: "Die leichte, graziöse Fanchon ist so ganz eigentlich die Sängerin Rossinis ... während ich dagegen unsere geistreiche Adelaide die Sängerin Glucks und Mozarts nennen möchte".[2]) While paying court to Adelaide at the opera house, Eduard comes to the attention of Freudenberg, an impresario, who insists that the young man become a singer. Eduard, perhaps remembering the dangers to which the Romantic musician has been exposed, hesitates to choose music as his profession, but the aesthetician Winter councils him with words that would have seemed strange to Wackenroder or Hoffmann. Music is a serene art, and "... am Ende die zeitgemässe Kunst, und es scheint mir wenigstens charakteristisch, dass in unseren Tagen alles künstlerische Talent, das hervortritt, sich immer mehr von der Innerlichkeit der Poesie entfernt, in der dem Deutschen allerdings von jeher mancher Wahnsinn gedroht hat" (191). Romanticism has passed, and music is the art of the new and calmer age!

Freudenberg arranges a party at his country estate; Mundt uses the ride to the Freudenberg mansion to indicate how times have changed: "Wenn vor einigen dreissig Jahren eine Gesellschaft gefühlvoller Damen und Herren durch einen Wald fuhr, horchten sie alle links und rechts, ob nicht irgendwo ein wundersames Waldhorn durch die andächtige Stille klinge" (155). At the party Eduard makes his debut with Adelaide: to the disappointment of the audience, which would have preferred an eighteenth century composer, they sing a love duet from Spohr's *Faust*. Mundt is forward-looking enough to regard such conservative listeners with irony; but even he can let the levelheaded Dr. Rosenschütz claim that "Die Tonkunst hat überhaupt ... weniger zu neuen Zielen in die Zukunft fortzustreben, als sich vielmehr annähernd wieder zurückzuwenden zu ihrem Kulminationspunkt, den sie in Mozart, Gluck, und Haydn schon erreicht hatte" (57).

Eduard, attaining musical success, marries Adelaide. They go on concert tours together and at the same time found a family, a reconciliation between art and life not so surprising when it is considered how harmless the art has become. The fates of Fanchon and Professor Winter are less happy. Fanchon, encouraged by her mother ("... sollte es auch eine Fürstin zur linken Hand sein, was tut das? Glanz ist Glanz . . .," 126), has been seduced by the prepossessing Albin, an embezzler in disguise. Just before their engagement is announced, Albin is killed in a duel. Fanchon dies in giving birth to Albin's child. Winter goes into a decline; his last hours are cheered by Adelaide's noble voice. Only those characters fit to exist in the Biedermeier world are left alive.

The death of Romanticism is celebrated less tragically in the musical stories of Gutzkow. In *Die Singekränzchen* (1834) music becomes an excuse for harmless flirtations. The narrator, hoping to meet a certain young lady, joins the "singing institute" of which she is a member. Herr Weber, the institute's president, has the deceiving appearance of a Kreisler or at least a Dryander; the narrator sees a "Spiel des Dämonischen und Schalkhaften um die zusammengekniffenen Mundwinkel," a "Vexiergeist auf den Augenbrauen," a "fixierten Blick, den sogenannten satanischen . . . bei unserem Direktor die Folge seiner Lehrstunden und der für sie notwendigen Gravität . . ."[3] Un-Romantically, Weber knows which side his bread is buttered on; he assures the narrator, who cannot sing a note, that he has a beautiful voice. At rehearsals the narrator notices how quickly the singers form pairs after the conductor has put down his baton. The tale ends with one of those pastoral promenades which are the "singing institute's" reward for a successful concert. In the country the musical pairs are free from parental surveillance.

Gutzkow's silly story affords a depressing measure of music's fall from the heights. His later musical tale, *Die Königin der Nacht* (1844), is more sensitive in its treatment of the transformation of musical thought. The soprano Lodoiska, a noted Mozart performer, has begun to lose her voice; she retires to a small principality, where she becomes the mistress of Max, its ruler. The Prince becomes engaged for political reasons to Princess Jucunde, with whom he soon falls deeply in love. For their wedding Lodoiska insists upon performing *Die Zauberflöte*, whose "Königin der Nacht" is her greatest role. In order to honor his bride, an amateur botanist, the Prince has the palace corridors decorated with her favorite plants; the chief surprise is to be a cactus grandiflorus, "die Königin der Nacht," which will bloom during the very hours of the performance. Lodoiska, learning of the plan, manages to spirit the plant into her rooms. Between the acts of *Die Zauberflöte* the Prince and his bride come to see the cactus; they find it gone, but the Princess traces it by its fragrance to Lodoiska's chambers. The singer confesses that she wanted a single memory of her Max; the clever Princess tells her a parable about the cactus, which blooms only once in a hundred years, and implies that Lodoiska by her immorality has been unworthy of her calling: "[die Königin der Nacht] ist die Fürstin der Blumen. Sie darf geliebt werden, aber, da sie Allen gehört, sich nie verschenken."[4]

Gutzkow uses a setting somewhat like that of *Don Juan,* and his Jucunde utters a concept of the artist lofty enough for a Hoffmann. Yet Jucunde, determined to found her domestic happiness, intends her subtly humiliating parable to get rid of her rival. Romanticism gives way to Biedermeier, the professional singer to the amateur botanist, and the Prince abandons his musical (and amorous) pursuits for cacti and the marriage bed. Lodoiska, in her defeat, is also infected by the atmosphere of the later period to the extent that she learns one of the noblest virtues of the Biedermeier musician, that of renunciation, both of the man she loves and, eventually, of her art. She never finishes her part in *Die Zauberflöte*. Leaving for the Rhineland, she devotes one more year of her life to Mozart: "in Don Giovanni lieber die Elvira, als Donna Anna, niemals aber mehr die Königin der Nacht" (198).

By the middle of the century even the composer argues for a clipping of the musician's wings. Ferdinand Kürnberger's *Giovanna* (1857) offers an example of the musical son misunderstood by his parents. Edgar von Lauenfels is destined by his mother to become a lawyer; his father, less determined, suggests that he work in a law office and at the same time devote himself to the composition of a great opera. Supposedly at the law office, Edgar instead goes to the country, where he meets a mysterious Italian girl, Giovanna. After much confusion Giovanna is discovered to be the illegitimate daughter of Lauenfels senior. The story's ramifications are tedious; its interest lies in the long conversation between Edgar and his father about music. The father is a Romantic, and out-of-date, when he suggests to his son that he compose an opera. Edgar, much more the Biedermeier man, is indignant: "Wer ein leidliches Lied setzen kann, der schreibt eine Oper, das heisst: ein Liederspiel, das er eine Oper nennt, und der versunkene Geschmack mit ihm.

Auf diesem rosenbekränzten Lotterbette könnte ich im besten Saft und Blut mich zur Ruhe legen ... Aber ich will's weiter bringen, und so lassen Sie mich immerhin die nächste Folgezeit noch an Quartetten arbeiten und studieren."[5] The Romantic musician, ready for any act of musical daring, would not have uttered such sentiments. Later in the conversation the two speakers exchange roles, Edgar complaining, like a Romantic, that he cannot work amidst domestic interruptions. His father, in response, praises the artists of the past who conquered such difficulties and worse: "Dass sie es in Not und Tod verstanden, aus diesen zersplitterten Spänen, die wir Existenz nennen, ein Ganzes zu zimmern und wohlgefügt zu hinterlassen, das war ihr rühmlichstes Meisterstück" (163). Kürnberger means to say that the exemplary life, not the creative work, is the more important product of the artist, a thought echoing the best of the Biedermeier in its insistence upon the "whole life." It is too bad that Kürnberger's remarkable musical perception in the first pages of *Giovanna* has no aftermath. Edgar's music, be it opera or quartet, is forgotten in the involvements leading to the establishment of Giovanna's identity.

Johanna Kinkel, the wife of the more famous Gottfried, reveals precious little respect for music or its practitioners in her shorter musical tales. In *Der Musikant, eine rheinische Bürgergeschichte* (1849) a young man overcomes the disgrace of having been a Spielmann. Tillchen falls in love with Franz, a violin player at his father's inn. Vitalized by her affection, Franz takes over the family business. Tillchen's brewmaster father, who cannot forget Franz's past, refuses him his daughter's hand, but the determined youth marries her nonetheless. Franz and the brewmaster are finally reconciled when the latter comes to realize that his son-in-law has been transformed: "Der junge Mann sah ganz verständig und ehrbar aus, hatte eine schöne, männliche Haltung, und war durchaus nicht im Bänkelsängerstil gekleidet ... [Der Vater] verglich ihn mit allen Umstehenden, und fand ... dass er sich seiner nicht zu schämen habe ..."[6] By becoming completely unartistic, the former musician erases the past. Another brief story, *Aus dem Tagebuch eines Komponisten* (1849), has an air of Kreislerian humor about it, but demonstrates even less regard for music than *Der Musikant*. A composer is plagued by noisy neighbors. One of them, a lieutenant, loves to practice a "tolles Musikdurcheinander" on the piano. The composer resuscitates some compositions by one Hucbaldus, a medieval Flemish monk, and has them played at dawn on a serpent and two bass trombones. The lieutenant gives up his apartment. Early church music was once an object of veneration for the composer in literature; now it is used in practical jokes.

In the longer *Musikalische Orthodoxie* (1849) Johanna Kinkel gives music a more dignified treatment. A young pianist, Ida Fernhofer, infatuated with the handsome widower, Count Selvar, is disillusioned when the Count one day brings an Italian soprano to his villa. Ida has already begun to suspect that the Count's musical taste is not impeccable: "Wie ein Donnerschlag traf es sie, als Selvar ihr vorschlug, Variationen von Herz über ein Thema von Rossini einzustudieren" (320). Fleeing to the city before the doubly sinister threat of Italian music and the Italian musician, Ida makes her way as a piano teacher. A concertmaster, Sohling, helps her to appreciate other composers than those of the German eighteenth century, her previous household gods. She is introduced to the best of Weber, Mendelssohn, Spohr, Chopin, and Spontini. Sohling has an advanced musical taste for a literary musician; he may not know the ultra-modern Wagner, but he is conversant with the leading lights of the generation preceding that composer.

Plainly the authoress possesses the necessary musical knowledge to continue her work on the same enlightened level; but the domestic bias of the time gets in the way. Sohling and Ida marry, although she does not abandon her pianistic career. Years later Selvar hears her play her husband's works in a concert. Selvar's regret at the prize he lost is aroused less by Ida's musicianship than by the rosy children's faces he sees when he visits the couple. Then the surprising Johanna, having given her tale the perfect Biedermeier close, adds an epilogue, spoken by Sohling, which makes us think we have sprung ahead to the sensual refinements of a later age: "Soll ich es [Selvar] nicht danken, dass er dich so lieben gelehrt? Denn die losgefesselte Glut deines wilden Herzens hat mich überwältigt und nimmer hätte mich die unbewusste erste Liebe einer unreifen Seele so beglückt" (370). Of course, sensuality is carefully placed in the service of the happy marriage.

Johanna Kinkel's novel, *Hans Ibeles in London: ein Familienbild aus dem Flüchtlingsleben* (1860), contains a similar melange of features pointing to Romanticism, to the authoress' own period, and to the future. Hans Ibeles is a German Kapellmeister and composer forced to emigrate to London in 1848. Like the Narziss of Emil Brachvogel and Mann's Adrian Leverkühn he is thus a musical figure associated with historical developments, but little space is devoted to his political misfortunes, since in England all of his energies are directed to the re-establishment of his career. Ibeles finds himself in a painful musical situation. He is compelled to give music lessons, yet ". . . die kleinliche Seite des Klavierlehreramtes war ihm gründlich verhasst. Er hatte wie alle tiefern Komponisten sehr reizbare Nerven, und sein musikalisches Gehör war so empfindlich, dass schrille Töne und unreine Harmonien ihm einen physischen Schmerz verursachten, der bis zu krankhaften Anfällen gesteigert wurde, wenn eine Ohrenmarter lange anhielt."[7] But with his Kreislerian nature he could endure even less readily the life of a "musical servant" that befalls the organizer of concerts for the English nobility. (Evidently the mid-century English attitude toward the composer had not changed since Ludwig Spohr's visit to England in 1819-20; compare the remarks of Spohr on the degrading treatment which he received in London.[8]) Ibeles says: "Als Führer des Orchesters empfand ich mich wie ein Priester, den Cultus des Schönen dem Volke vermittelnd. Als Lehrer kann ich ehrenhaft als Gleicher mit Gleichen verkehren . . ." (I, 363), but a "maître de plaisir" he will never be.

The strain of teaching estranges Ibeles from his wife, Dorothea. His two oldest sons, who, he had hoped, would be musicians, instead go into business. Dorothea thinks to please her husband by having the Ibeles daughters given music lessons, but her efforts are apparently in vain. Ibeles meets a beautiful "former slave," Miss Livia (actually an adventuress, Mrs. O'Nalley). One night, inspired by Livia's charms, he composes the passionate song, "Der Schatzgräber." His distant playing inspires a frightful dream in the sleeping Dorothea: "Wilde Musik klang von fern, und Orpheus, von den Mänaden zerrissen, sank blutend zu ihren Füssen. Er trug bekannte Züge, sie wollte die Arme ausbreiten, und sein Haupt auf ihren Schoss legen . . . Ein tödliches Grau sank herab, die Lebensfarben der goldenen Natur erblichen—das war das Bild des Landschafters Turner von der Sündflut. Sie rang mit übermenschlicher Kraft:

Hügel auf Hügel heran, immer den geliebten toten Leib in ihren Armen nach sich schleppend. Immer neue schlammigere Wogen rollten ihr entgegen. Endlich ward sie mit ihm in den Abgrund geschwemmt, und wie auf jenem berühmten Bilde die Kunst die letzte Mahnung an die Mütterlichkeit geschaffen, so fühlte sie sich als eben diese weibliche Gestalt, die schon versinkend mit sterbenden Armen das jüngste Kind aus den Fluten emporhält" (II, 251). The transformation of Orpheus into a child held high in the mother's arms offers an exaggerated symbol of the change in the musician-hero from Romanticism to Biedermeier; nowhere else is the protective element of the musician's new domestic milieu so drastically put. The "muddy waves" of sensuality are Johanna Kinkel's special equivalent of the madness threatening a Kreisler; some decades later they would swallow up a host of figures in the German musical novel and drama.

Succumbing to Livia's blandishments, Ibeles has written background music for her "melodrama," a declamation of oracular verses. Contrary to his vow never to appear before a noble company in England, Ibeles agrees to perform the work with Livia at a country estate. Dorothea has also been invited to the performance by an old friend; when Ibeles sees her he pursues her to her room and a reconciliation is effected. He has had the opportunity to compare his wife with the adventuress: "... die Poesie haftete nicht mehr an der Feuerblume, als er sie im Schatten der einfachen deutschen Rechtschaffenheit sah" (II, 325). Hans has arrived safely in the port of domesticity. The question comes to mind: would Hans Ibeles have been better off artistically, if not personally, if he had followed Livia? Her influence causes him to write music of a kind he has never undertaken before. Possibly he would have been destroyed, as Dorothea's dream predicted, but in the Romantic mind destruction would not have been too great a price to pay for the new artistic experience, and Hans, in his nervosity as in his concept of the musician as a priest, is a belated Romantic. Yet the genteel literary-musical tradition of the mid-century is too strong for Hans and his creator, and he returns to his motherly wife and accomplished daughters.

Still another tale treading shyly in the path of Romanticism is the *Enthusiasten* (1864) of Alfred Meissner; its hero, Baron Stein, is a harmless descendent of Rat Krespel and the Baron von B. Stein is inordinately proud of his elaborate music room and prouder still of its principal treasure, an Amati violin. A visiting virtuoso, Torrentini, informs his host that the entire instrument, except the back, is counterfeit. The Baron, with a trace of old Romantic madness, "geriet immer in den wildesten Affekt, so oft er an der Türe seines verödeten Musikzimmers vorbeistreifte."[9] One day he discovers the schoolmaster, Bleivogel, playing what seems to be a real Amati, the property of the local church. Wearisome negotiations between the Baron, Bleivogel, and two priests ensue; Pater Kressmann, who is willing to give the Baron the violin in return for some land, dies and is succeeded by Pater Risbeck, an eccentric determined to keep the instrument. Torrentini discovers that a rascally violin maker has built an "Amati" especially for the Baron by stealing the back of the church's instrument. The backs are exchanged and the Baron, who has been sharing the authentic violin with Bleivogel, has the schoolmaster return the now wholly false Amati to the church. In doing so Bleivogel smashes the instrument, and the Baron must make good the loss with his stolen treasure. The next day Risbeck gives Bleivogel the Amati for his own; Torrentini finds another real Amati for the Baron. The two enthusiasts live happily ever after.

The mad but somehow heroic excesses of a Krespel have been supplanted by petty thefts and tiresome deceptions. The object of the Baron and his accomplice is to possess a true Amati; to them the musical quality of the instrument means less than the name, for which the Baron is prepared to commit "jeden Akt der Rebellion . . . dem Standrecht trotzen, das Schaffot riskieren" (XV, 90). Nevertheless he has Bleivogel do his thieving for him. All the Romantic verve has gone out of Meissner's characters, although they may, like the Baron, move against the fairy tale background of the marvelous music room. Nor has the vitality of the Romantic personality been replaced by a substitute feature from the ideals of Biedermeier; an interest in the musical instrument as an inspiring piece of craftsmanship, a theme of Stifter's *Nachsommer,* is evidenced only in the fascination of the maker's label for Meissner's enthusiasts.

Adalbert Stifter was relatively uninterested in the music of his contemporaries. His brief friendships with the Schumanns and with Jenny Lind made no lasting impression upon him, and his rare bits of musical criticism do not evince a deep understanding of the art. It is small wonder then that music appears comparatively seldom in Stifter's writings; yet the master of Biedermeier prose had pronounced ideas on the art which he respected but did not love. In the first of Stifter's two important musical utterances, *Zwei Schwestern*, there is evidence that Stifter fears music and attempts to domesticate it; in the second, *Der Nachsommer*, it is regarded as a pedagogical means.

Zwei Schwestern (published as *Die Schwestern* in *Iris*, 1846, and revised for the sixth volume of the *Studien*, 1850) begins in the musical Vienna of the 1840's; from all the attractions offered there, Stifter chooses two young violinists, the Milanollo sisters, as his inspiration. Otto Falkhaus, the narrator, arrives in Vienna by coach; among his fellow passengers are two girls (they turn out to be the famous sisters) and an elderly man, who on account of his pale face and black clothing is jestingly called Paganini. The keynote of the novella is struck when "Paganini" answers: "Wer weiss, ob es nicht ein sehr grosses Unglück für mich wäre, wenn ich wirklich Paganini wäre."[10] The Romantic musician, tormented by his demon, has become an object of sympathy among the more sensitive of his observers. When Falkhaus and his Paganini-like friend attend a concert of the Milanollo sisters, the friend demonstrates his sympathy more overtly; he bursts into tears, saying "Ach, Du unglücklicher Vater" (IV, I, 89). The narrator himself is conscious of anxiety for the older sister, Theresa, who plays from the heart: "Er musste mit Befremden in das Antlitz eines noch so jungen Kindes schauen, das schon so empfand" (IV, I, 86). Stifter implies that the child is flirting with destruction by her intimate contact with so dangerous an art; but his narrator hastens to add that the innocence of Theresa's performance fills him "mit einer tiefen, schönen, sittlichen Gewalt" (IV, I, 86). Music must not of necessity destroy; it can also educate.

"Paganini's" outburst at the concert is not prompted by general sentiments alone; he is thinking, as we shall discover, of his own problems and his children's. While visiting the Lake Garda region some years later, Falkhaus rediscovers his "Paganini," whose real name is Rikar. At Rikar's prosperous farm Falkhaus learns the secret of his friend's tears. He had lost his fortune and was reminded of the impending unhappiness of his daughters, Maria and Camilla, by the sight of the Milanollo sisters. Yet Stifter lets us think that his sadness was directed in particular toward his younger child, Camilla. Camilla has been an excellent violinist since childhood, and her passion for music stems, quite Romantically, from a violin solo heard during Mass at the Milan cathedral. Her attitude toward music is still Romantic; Falkhaus first hears her playing at night, under the stars, and her music, despite her tender years, is the expression of "ein schreiendes Herz, welches seinen Jammer erkannt hat" (IV, I, 143). Camilla has paid for her association with the dangerous art; the happy child has become a delicate and overemotional girl, and Rikar predicts, like a latterday Krespel: "unser Kind wird an dieser Kunst sterben" (IV, I, 205).

However the Biedermeier, embodied in the older daughter, Maria, has already taken measures to check the Romantic cancer. During the Rikars' financial distress the mother demanded that Camilla support the family by violin concerts. Maria saved the nervous Camilla from the concert stage by founding a large garden around the isolated Rikar home, a plan which revived their fortunes. Furthermore, Maria was careful to surround Camilla in her music room with handsome objects of ebony, a music stand, a case for Camilla's scores, tables for her violins; the musician, beholding the beautiful things whose educational value Stifter so esteems, is made proof against the excesses of Romanticism. Eventually, by an act of renunciation, Maria gives her sister back her happiness. A neighbor, Alfred Mussar, asks for Maria's hand in marriage; Maria, knowing that Camilla loves Mussar, rejects his offer. She tells Falkhaus: "[Camilla] würde den Schmerz im Herzen halten, bis es bräche. Sie hat ohnedem dieses Herz durch das Spiel ihrer Geige . . . noch mehr gelockert, dass alles Uebel viel, viel tiefer eingreift" (IV, I, 232-233). Mussar marries Camilla instead, and when Falkhaus returns to Italy after some years' absence, he finds a Camilla admirably representative of the Biedermeier, "tüchtiger, tätiger, und an den Wirtschaftssorgen teilnahmsvoller" (IV, I, 246). After Camilla has received the guest in her new home "mit einer lieben Geschäftigkeit," she plays "etwas Heiteres und Kräftiges" on her violin (IV, I, 247). Romanticism has been vanquished, and Maria, we hope, will marry the narrator as her reward.

In *Der Nachsömmer* (1857) Romanticism is no longer treated as a problem. Instead, the novel's musical sections concern the homely zither, its performers, and more important, its construction. Heinrich Drendorf, the hero and narrator of the novel, first learns to know the zither during his wanderings through the Austrian mountains. Otherwise not musically inclined, he has nevertheless attempted to train his ear for the instrument's "Klänge und Unterschiede" (VI, 289). Later he hears the ladies of the "Rosenhaus," Mathilde and Nathalie, performing zither duets, and he resolves to play the instrument himself as one of the educational processes of his formative years, just as he collects stones, sketches bas-reliefs, or learns Spanish. Oddly enough he obtains his first zither from a huntsman, a type of Spielmann, who, as it were Romantically, does not have a particular region as his preserve but wanders through the forest at will. The huntsman is also the most accomplished and most famous zither player in the mountains. Unfortunately this figure appears but briefly in the course of the novel. Stifter does not reveal the cause of the huntsman's wanderlust or what connection it may have with his musicianship. The huntsman becomes Heinrich's teacher and introduces him to a master zither maker, from whom we discover the secret of Stifter's interest in the instrument. There is a loving description of the construction of Heinrich's zither: its finger board is of ravenblack wood decorated with mother-of-pearl and ivory, its bridges of pure silver, its boards from a fir tree specially chosen by the master, its feet ivory balls (VII, 3). But of its tone Heinrich says merely that he has never heard a sweeter one, and of the huntsman's performance: ". . . ich hatte weit und breit nichts gehört, was an die Handhabung der Zither durch diesen Jägersmann erinnerte" (VII, 3). Stifter has chosen the zither because he knows the instrument and because, with its complicated and ornate structure, it admits one of those loving descriptions of the object so common in *Der Nachsommer*. The zither, a single example of the many educational means employed in the novel, educates more by its plastic beauty than by its sound.

Stifter reveals other musical opinions in the discussion of the zither. Having chosen an instrument intended for amateur use, Heinrich teaches his sister to play it (again the domestic impulse of the musician in mid-nineteenth century literature). After instructing the girl in the elements, he hires a Viennese professional as their teacher; however he is careful to inform his sister that the Alpine huntsman plays far more beautifully than the master from the city, another example of the common distrust of the professional musician. Klothilde, visiting the mountains with her brother, is taken to hear the old zither maker tell of his fortunes. The mountaineers, who can recognize his best zithers, are too poor to buy them; the wealthy travelers, distracted by frills, cannot distinguish the virtues of a truly good instrument. The master zither maker, one of the many skilled workmen in *Nachsommer*, is the closest we come to a professional musician in Stifter's works, if we except the brief appearance of the Milanolio sisters; he is an artisan, a handworker. Trained both as a maker and performer, he still cannot create the same impression with his playing as the less highly skilled huntsman. Like the Viennese musician, he possesses too much "Fertigkeit." We can note an important change in attitude: in the eighteenth century the musician had been admired as an artisan who cultivated his craft to the full extent of his powers. In the Romantic period the musician was still regarded as a professional, but "genius" was not denied him. Now the element of "genius" has been reduced by the Biedermeier writer to a matter of "feeling," of a vague "beauty;" this quality is more a possession of the amateur than the professional musician. Stifter is the most enthusiastic eulogist of the craftsman in German literature, yet he does not wish the performing musician to be thoroughly skilled.

Der Nachsommer nevertheless throws a light into the future of the musical novel. Music is one of the lesser means by which the inhabitants and guests of the "Rosenhaus" are led to Stifter's ideal of "Einfachheit, Halt, und Bedeutung." The conception of music as a general pedagogical means is not original with Stifter; its most famous application is that in the "Pedagogical Province" of Goethe's *Wilhelm Meisters Wanderjahre*, where the boys are taught music, vocal and instrumental, as a part of the Province's educational program. Music is the first step toward "Bildung" in the Province, ". . . denn von ihr laufen gleichgebahnte Wege nach allen Seiten."[11] Stifter does not put the same emphasis on music as Goethe, since he is primarily concerned with achieving culture through well-ordered surroundings, yet the origin of his employment of music among his pedagogical means is unmistakable, despite the fact that he clothes music in the form of a beautiful object. We have in Stifter a curious phenomenon: an artist living in the most musical of cities during the most musical of centuries, who nevertheless receives his musical inspiration from the plastically minded Goethe. It is only in the twentieth century that a writer more musically inclined than either Goethe or Stifter has turned to the old form of the "Pedagogical Province" and given music a more important place in it: Hermann Hesse in his *Glasperlenspiel*.

Theodor Storm is not, strictly regarded, a representative of the Biedermeier in literature; rather he is the Biedermeier's descendant. In his novellas on music we find common thoughts from the Biedermeier world: the conception of music as an amateur art and a profound concern with pedagogical problems. In *Eine Halligfahrt* (1870) the quiet Biedermeier spirit in music is briefly challenged by a remnant of Romanticism. The hero of the tale, "der Vetter," spent his later years with his books and his violin on an island in the North Sea. Like so many of Storm's heroes, he had been involved in a shadowy love affair which ended unhappily. Musically his life was more successful, a fact revealed in the diaries which the narrator receives after the old man's death. His greatest joy was playing the classical masters before an audience at the home of Eveline, his beloved. One of these concerts is described at length. A group of children sing Schumann's settings of Eichendorff poems, and their voices "hover unsuspectingly over the abyss" of the songs. Meanwhile parents gossip comfortably and cavaliers pay their customary compliments. The violinist can see no objection to their actions: "Ich weiss nicht, ob der Kapellmeister Johannes Kreisler davongelaufen wäre; ich sass ganz still und horchte auf den süssen, taufrischen Lerchenschlag der Jugend."[12] The change in attitude since Hoffmann's day becomes evident in this passage: the listener may enjoy music wholeheartedly if he desires, but he should not be angry if others prefer to chatter instead. Music is no longer a sacred matter. The violinist himself begins to play, and at first remains calm. During his performance, however, a quality of the old Romantic musician creeps into him; feeling the sparks fly under his bow, he holds the listeners enchanted. The latter-day musician is not without warmth or emotion; perhaps he is even more completely "feeling" than the Romantic musician, since he has achieved a non-professional view of the art. Storm's position on music is more ambivalent than that of his immediate predecessors. He professes Grillparzer's love for the eighteenth century, and follows Stifter in his efforts to "tame" music, but we cannot overlook the fascination which the Romantic element in music evidently had for him.

Ein stiller Musikant (1874-75) is concerned with the musician as a symbol of quiet renunciation. The hero is not unlike Grillparzer's Spielmann, and, as in Grillparzer, there is an autobiographical element; Storm portrays himself and his son Karl, an unsuccessful musician. Ferdinand Tönnies, a friend of the Storms, has left an account of Karl's role in the composition of the novella.[13] A misfit at the Gymnasium, Karl was educated by the elder Storm and by tutors. In accordance with his father's wish the boy undertook musical studies and demonstrated the most refined taste; unfortunately he was easily embarrassed and seemed to complete an intellectual task only with a sensation of pain—a psychic condition similar to that of Grillparzer's musician. Storm's novella springs from the tension between stern father and sensitive son; it might be termed Storm's confession of his failure as a parent, and indicates once more the strongly social bias with which the mid-nineteenth century saw the artist's problem.

One day Christian, the hero of the story, and his father are playing a four-handed sonata of Clementi. In the rondo the boy fumbles and his father slaps him in the face. Although father and son later become reconciled, the child remembers the scene for the rest of his life. After attending the conservatory, Christian becomes director of a Liedertafel in a small town. An emergency forces him to supplement one of his programs with his own piano performance. His most enthusiastic supporters as he practices for the concert are Signora Katerina, an ancient opera singer, and Ännchen, the daughter of his landlord. The former is not merely a grotesque like the old soprano in Hoffmann's *Fermate*. With her practical musical knowledge she is of great aid to the young man. As for Ännchen, she cannot praise Christian's efforts enough. On the night of the concert an awful fear seizes Christian when he learns that a famous pianist is to be present in the audience. He believes that he is once more in his father's house: "... auch mein Vater stand plötzlich neben mir; und statt in die Tasten griff ich nach seiner Schattenhand" (II, 358). Thus Christian's father, like those of Hoffmann's music-hater and the Spielmann, has destroyed his son's confidence in himself. Running from the hall, Christian flees through the streets until he reaches a brook; leaning on a tree trunk he listens to the melody of the current and thinks of a song from Schubert's *Die schöne Müllerin*. The thought of death comes to him, but he is saved by the approach of Ännchen.

Christian has come very close to a Romantic end and in Romantic surroundings. The temptation is rejected, however, and the story continues in a quieter vein. Ännchen marries another and has a daughter who develops an excellent voice; Christian spends his last years in bringing Ännchen's child to the concert stage, a triumph he does not live to see. The young singer, as a gesture of thanks to the departed, includes his compositions in her concerts, honoring him as her teacher. To be sure, Christian does not surrender his life in the manner of the Spielmann; but, more the artist than his Viennese predecessor, he makes the artist's sacrifice—he devotes himself to the perfecting of someone else's art. There is a curious trace of the artist's idealistic selfishness in his deed; he has trained the girl to sing in the style of Mozart's day, which he learned from old Signora Katerina. Nevertheless, his immortality proves to be more that of the home than the concert hall. In the final paragraph we see Christian's pupil as a happy mother, lulling her children to sleep with his songs. The ending is like that of Tieck's *Musikalische Leiden und Freuden*, in which the soprano, trained in the eighteenth century style, retires to domestic bliss after a few performances.

The Biedermeier predominates in *Ein stiller Musikant*, but one of its Romantic features will receive new importance in the literature of the twentieth century. The motif of death coupled with music and nature has been borrowed by Thomas Mann and used by him notably in *Der Zauberberg*, where "Der Lindenbaum" from *Die Winterreise* leads Hans Castorp toward his (possible) death in battle. Music is likewise the prime indicator of the death-urge in little Hanno Buddenbrook (who during his mortal illness dreams that he runs into "den Schatten, die Kühle, den Frieden"[14]); in *Doktor Faustus* the composer, after his fall into childlike dependency, spends hours sitting beneath a giant linden tree on his family's farm, a symbol of Frau Leverkühn's triumph over her intellectually dead son.

Also, in *Ein stiller Musikant* Storm touches briefly on another theme which has some currency in the modern period, for example in *Doktor Faustus* and in Friedrich Huch's *Enzio*: the musician's relationship to a girl from a lower class, a relationship bringing with it conflict and sometimes disaster. The Romantic struggle to have the musician recognized as a member of respectable society has succeeded to such an extent that he is now quite aware of his middle-class dignity. The musician (in literature and in life) is not degraded by his choice of profession. It is no longer a rule that the young musician must learn his trade by orchestral playing or hack-work; he is educated in much the same fashion as any other student. The conservatory has become the equivalent, socially and educationally, of the university.

Storm's Christian is not overly conscious of a difference between himself and Ännchen; possibly he would have married her, had it not been for his failure. In *Es waren zwei Königskinder* (1884-85) the relationship of the musician to a girl of a lower class receives a more outspoken treatment. The story concerns Marx, a half-German, half-French student at the Stuttgart Conservatory. Proud and sensitive, a conscientious and brilliant student, he falls in love with Linele, a handworker's daughter: "... ein sonst tadelloses Mädchen; aber sie sprach nicht ganz richtig Deutsch, sie schwäbelte ein wenig, was zwar von den jungen Lippen lieblich klang; von Französisch gar war ihr Gewissen völlig frei" (III, 316). Despite his love, the ambitious Marx lets fall a remark concerning her lack of culture. Their relationship breaks off and the student takes to drink; one night he makes the mistake of insulting as stupid German mercenaries some soldiers stationed in the city. Enraged, they smear him with soot and have him taken to jail. Too proud to effect a reconciliation with Linele, who might have consoled him, Marx shoots himself. We cannot be sure whether the piece is a study of the sufferings of the proud half-Frenchman or the nervous and ambitious musician; certainly Franco-Prussian enmity has a role in the tale. Is Marx's feeling of superiority toward Linele a result of his Gallic pride or of his musical talent? If Marx is brought to a fall by pride, then Storm is offering still another argument for the victory of domesticity over art. Even the exceptional man should seek happiness in the arms of a simple girl, Storm would imply, and there are far worse helpmeets than a Swabian maiden. If Marx's arrogance stems from his genius, however, then Storm has begun to honor the Romantic gods once more, although in a negative fashion. Marx's very suicide makes us take him seriously; here at last is a musician with something of the passion of Berglinger and Kreisler. Shortly after the writing of *Es waren zwei Königskinder* the problematic musician again becomes a familiar figure on the literary stage, and Storm, in his last musical work, points the way from the serene "amateur" tradition of musical literature to the hectic days around the turn of the century, where the musician takes himself, and now and then his art, very seriously indeed.

II.

In the middle decades of the nineteenth century a second musical tradition existed in literature, running parallel with the serene current, but springing more immediately from the Romantic past. Concerned less with the actual musical advances of Romanticism than with its colorful aspects, it would seem to have Heine rather than Hoffmann as its inspiration. The demonic musician is retained, but usually in historical guise, or with his supernatural tinge explained by social causes, so that the reader, while pleasantly excited, need not be afraid. Much of this "neo-demonic" literature fills the same requirement as the diabolical virtuoso in the concert hall; the audience loves to know fear in anonymous safety. Yet some works in this style—especially where the demonic element is treated with restraint—reach a high level of literary creation.

The musician in Nikolaus Lenau's poetry is a Weltschmerzler, gloomy and diabolical. In fact the musician, apart from an occasional passage in the lyrics, appears in Lenau only as the devil himself (in the poet's short epic, *Faust*) and as the legendary gypsy violinist Mischka. Both these figures may seem to merit classification with the products of the Romanticists, the devil as violinist with Heine's Paganini, and Mischka with Brentano's Michaly; but a change has taken place in the attitude of literary men toward the demonic musician. Hoffmann, Brentano, and Heine deal with their musicians as contemporary figures; Kreisler is a "modern man" in every respect, Michaly a figure Brentano may have met during his sojourn in Bohemia, Heine, writing in the same decade as Lenau, describes real musicians whom he has known. Lenau, like Grillparzer, looks to the past for his musical idols: Beethoven is to him a figure out of an age of giants that has passed and will come no more. The true Romanticist can believe in the demonic musician as a contemporary, the epigone of Romanticism cannot. Therefore he must turn the highly gifted musician into a figure out of legend or history, while the Biedermeier artist devotes his attention to a more humble type.

Lenau conceived his *Faust* while residing in the Schwarzspanierhaus in Vienna, where Beethoven spent his last years; there, in 1833, the scene from *Faust* which most concerns us was composed: evidently the section, "Der Tanz," laid in a village inn, proved to be the easiest of composition for Lenau. (The inn, which Lenau liked to associate with music, turns up on several occasions in his lyrics; compare "In der Schenke," "Der Steiertanz," and "Die Werbung;" "music at the inn" also appears twice in *Mischka*). One evening Faust and Mephistopheles enter a village where a marriage celebration is taking place. Overcome by the beauty of a peasant maiden, Faust is too timid to approach her. Mephistopheles, disguised as a huntsman, borrows a fiddle and begins to play. Thereupon follows a description of the devil's fiddling that bears comparison with Heine's passage on Paganini. The difference between the two passages is this: while Paganini overcomes the imaginations of all his listeners as a part of his performance, Mephistopheles sets out deliberately to seduce only Faust and the girl through his playing. The demonic musician has become intentionally evil; music for Kreisler was primarily the instrument of good, Krespel's Svengali tendencies succumb to sublime music, and Heine's Paganini calls up images heavenly as well as diabolical. Mephistopheles uses music to ends appropriately satanic. His melodies rise and fall like waves around a bathing girl; suddenly she is overcome by a youth hidden in the reeds; a suitor persuades his beloved to submit to him; two rivals fight over a girl, and as the defeated one slinks away, the lovers embrace:

> Und feuriger, brausender, stürmischer immer,
> Wie Männergejauchze, Jungferngewimmer,
> Erschallen der Geige verführende Weisen.[15]

Everyone in the inn begins to dance; Faust and his brunette whirl out the door toward the forest. Mephistopheles' fiddling has accomplished its purpose.

Lenau's other violinist, Mischka, is a more sympathetic figure than Mephistopheles, but the effect of his performance is no less disastrous. Gypsy violinists are always favorites of Lenau, who, no doubt fancying that he himself resembled them, often exaggerated their artistic worth. Of the three gypsies in his famous lyric "Die drei Zigeuner," two are obviously musicians. One fiddles a fiery song; the other sleeps, his cembalo hung on a tree beside him. The fiddler might be Mischka himself. The first part of *Mischka* (completed 1835) is more a genre picture of Hungarian life than a story of Mischka's doings. Three hussars come to an inn where Mischka and his band are performing. Once Mischka too was a hussar, and he gives musical expression to his adventures through an ancient Hungarian battle song. The hussars, drunk with his music, burst out into the night in search of the Turks; the dancers imagine that the spirits of the heroic past parade before them. The passage is as effective in its way as the description of Mephistopheles' fiddling, and the same techniques are used. Lenau does not merely describe the images called forth by the music as Heine does; he draws upon his greater technical knowledge to intersperse passages where the music itself is depicted, or where the various instruments of the band represent certain emotions or natural phenomena. The hammering of the cembalo depicts the storm of battle, the violin the spring wind rustling over the dead, while the bass burrows in the depths: "Ob er dort dem wilden Hass / Grab an Grab im Boden grübe" (I, 392). In *Faust* certain violinistic effects were used (rising double steps to represent two voices rising in passion); in *Mischka* the tremolo suggests the trembling of the bridge leading into the land of spirits.

The second section (1842), less a tour-de-force, reveals more of Mischka's character. Mischka's only joy is his daughter, Mira. While Mischka is fiddling for a wedding, a young nobleman makes his way to the gypsy's hut and seduces the girl. Deserted, she wastes away and dies; the Count has decided to marry a woman of his own class. Mischka is engaged to play for these nuptials too; on the wedding eve he steals some hairs from the tail of the Count's horse. Having strung his bow with these, he appears in the dance hall. His music is full of the spirit of revenge, the bride begins to cry, despair spreads through the entire company. The young nobleman leaps upon his horse and rides away; in the dark his horse stumbles and its rider is killed. Mischka disappears forever; a shepherd boy says that he has seen him bury his violin in his daughter's grave. Mischka's act stems from a just cause to be sure; nevertheless he has employed music as a means of driving the Count to his death. Lenau mentions in passing that the gypsy also has put a curse on the horse's hooves; but the emphasis is laid upon the magical power of Mischka's playing, a power enhanced by the fact that his bow is strung with hair from the Count's steed. The musician in Lenau has become a completely demonic figure, dealing death to his listeners. He has however sacrificed breadth, losing all the facets of his character save the ability to rule others through music.

The implications of Lenau's two figures are greater than their literary value. The historical concept of the demonic musician now becomes widespread in German literature, and we have the appearance of Wagner's Tannhäuser, Brachvogel's Narziss Rameau and Friedemann Bach, and, above all, Mörike's Mozart. But there is another side to Lenau's figures: they are the predecessors of a demonic musician who, seemingly legendary, is nevertheless part of the contemporary scene, "der schwarze Geiger" in Gottfried Keller's *Romeo und Julia auf dem Dorfe* (1856). Keller was never noted for his musical interests, and he was far removed from the Weltschmerz of a Lenau, yet somehow the figure of the demonic musician has crept into his works. It would be convenient, of course, to classify the black fiddler, since he is the product of bad social conditions, as a Romantic Spielmann transformed to meet the exigencies of Poetic Realism; but he possesses a demonic quality—even a supernatural quality—otherwise unknown among the middle nineteenth century's pictures of the contemporary musician. Ibeles with his wild song and Christian with his thought of suicide pale beside him; he is like a figure out of Lenau, put into modern clothes.

"Der schwarze Geiger" is one of those eccentrics who appear so often in the pages of Keller's works, but he stands farther outside society than any of Keller's other "originals," and has a character unsoftened by any air of comedy. A number of factors serve to emphasize his grimness. The fiddler is a personfication of the guilt of the two fathers, Manz and Marti. Considered sociologically he might also be taken as the incarnation of the lawlessness from which the young lovers seek to escape. The fact that he is a wandering musician enhances his diabolical aura; he is more gifted, more independent, and more dangerous than Seldwyla's usual grotesques. Since there are few musicians in Keller's works, apart from the fiddler, it is impossible to determine by comparison whether Keller believes that the fiddler's musicianship gives him a power which the author's other outcasts do not possess. The earlier Keller had much in common with Romanticism and it is not impossible that he was influenced by a figure from Hoffmann, Tieck, or Brentano. Ermatinger in his biography has pointed out the influence of the Romanticists in many of Keller's stories;[16] and a section in Keller's diaries from 1843 consists of a long eulogy of Hoffmann (Ermatinger, II, 105ff.).

The fiddler, realistically enough, is set against a background of moral degeneration among the peasantry; he himself is the grandson of a ruined village musician, the original owner of the land lying between the fields of Manz and Marti, the litigious peasants. The two realize that the fiddler is the rightful heir of the disputed acre, but decide to cheat him out of it, rationalizing that he would drink up the purchase money within a month. The fiddler, a member of the "homeless ones," earns his living by playing at dances, patching pots, and helping the charcoal-burners and pitch-boilers. His appearance would suggest his quality of pariah: he wears a black felt cap and a black smock, his hair and beard are black, his hands and face are sooty[17]—even his fiddle, one suspects, is black. Only his cudgel-like nose would seem less threatening than preposterous. He knows very well that he has been cheated by the fathers of Sali and Vrenchen; but since he has no certificate of baptism the courts will have nothing to do with him; the word of the "homeless ones" who witnessed his birth will not be taken in court.

Keller motivates the actions of the fiddler in a realistic and reasonable manner. His attempts to persuade the children to join the wanderer's band may easily be explained as deriving from a desire for revenge. He himself admits that he is pleased to find the children of his enemies brought to a choice between separation and the vagrant life (VII, 178). However this satisfies his vengefulness; he has become so attached to the gypsy existence that he sincerely recommends it to Sali and Vrenchen. The aura of evil which surrounds him may actually be a reflection of the social decay with which he is associated, but Keller cannot dismiss the older Romantic tradition of the demonic musician. Certain features of the fiddler's physical appearance are uncanny; even his little cap, neither round nor square, seems constantly to be changing its shape. He has the habit of appearing and disappearing like a magical being. Sali and Vrenchen wish to avoid the strange fellow; nonetheless, as if under a spell, they follow him. It is he who suggests to the lovers —but vaguely aware of love—that they will go the way of all flesh, and he who performs the mock marriage ceremony: "Sie liessen es geschehen, ohne ein Wort zu sagen, und betrachteten es als einen Spass, während es sie doch kalt und heiss durchschauerte" (VII, 180). Finally the lovers join in the procession of the "homeless ones" as they move off down the mountain behind the fiddler, who plays as wildly as he can and springs about like a ghost. The demonic musician attempts to lead the young lovers into social destruction by the melodies of his violin. Elsewhere in the novella little is said of the fiddler's music; only once, when the lovers approach the "Paradiesgärtlein," is its power mentioned: Vrenchen forgets her suffering and desires nothing save to dance with Sali. During the weird bridal procession, while passing before their former homes, the lovers are seized by an abandoned mood and dance feverishly with the others in the steps of the fiddler: Keller skillfully combines the theme of moral degeneration with that of the fiddler's supernatural powers. Sali at last comes to his senses and forces Vrenchen to stand still while the band goes off into the distance.

What shall we call the fiddler? A master of suggestion, a frightening example of life among the "homeless ones," a demonic fiddler? Keller is intentionally ambiguous in order to excite all these thoughts. At any event, the fiddler has found not unlikely subjects on which to work. Sali and Vrenchen, for all their will to remain "respectable," reveal an unusual sensitivity to "evil music" and to the "evil musician's" promptings. But Keller, in the closing pages of the story, indicates that he is well aware of music's essential nobleness. When the lovers exchange rings, in the second mock ceremony just before boarding the boat, they indicate that they are joined in a purer union than that consecrated by the fiddler. They undergo a kind of transfiguration and the transfiguration is accompanied by music. As they float to their deaths, they experience cosmic music: "Die Stille der Welt sang und musizierte ihnen durch die Seelen" (VII, 182). The composition of *Tristan und Isolde* was completed three years after the publication of *Romeo und Julia*. Are we far removed from the world of the "Liebestod"?

Elsewhere in Keller music usually has a good if simple connotation. Heinrich Lee is saved from destruction by the sale of his flute, Salomon Landolt is an enthusiastic hornist, a German folksong momentarily reunites Regine and Erwin in *Das Sinngedicht*, while at the conclusion of the same collection the shoemaker's singing of Goethe's "Mit einem gemalten Bande" finally brings Lucie and Reinhart together. The Minnesinger Hadlaub, in the tale of the same name (1878), is less a musician than Hoffmann's Heinrich von Ofterdingen, Eichendorff's Florio, or Wagner's Tannhäuser; he is primarily a collector, and once he has won his noble bride (he is a townsman and a commoner) he settles down in Zürich to complete his precious collection. During his wanderings Hadlaub meets a more tragic and more Romantic figure: the Lower Austrian singer who possesses only his harp and a bag full of tattered songbooks. Hadlaub, a representative of the rising bourgeoisie, inherits the old man's songs but not his wanderlust.

Keller's semi-musical novella, *Das Tanzlegendchen* (1872), penetrates more deeply into the problems of the art than the works just mentioned. Its pious heroine, Musa, cannot resist the desire to dance, until one day King David appears to her as she is "dancing her prayers." He announces that the post of dancer being vacant in Heaven, Musa may occupy it if she will dance no more on earth. Henceforth Musa leads a saintly life, and when she dies, she is received into Heaven by myriads of dancing youths and maidens and invited to dine at the table of the nine Muses, who on this day alone may join the celestial ranks. Finally the Virgin arrives, whispering to Urania that she will not rest until the Muses can remain forever in Paradise. On their next annual journey to Heaven the Muses prepare a song, modeled after the customary angelic chorales, to show their good will. Their song sounds gloomy, almost rough; the heavenly throngs, seized with homesickness for the earth, begin to weep. At last the Holy Trinity itself silences the Muses and exiles them from Heaven forever. Keller has placed life according to natural law over against a life of resistance to earthly beauty as represented first by Musa and then by the blissful choirs. Keller's bias is of course well-known, yet he is fairer to the ascetic concept here than elsewhere. He realizes that art can exist within both spheres; we have on the one hand the joyous picture of the angel bands which accompany David and which receive Musa in Heaven, on the other the Muses, who are so beautiful that "die kleinen Musikbübchen" flatter them to obtain fruits from their hands. The two spheres are placed in an interesting musical juxtaposition, which hints at a problem to be treated more fully by Mann in *Doktor Faustus*: the split between music whose appeal is sensuous and music aimed only at the ascetic side of the listener. In the eighteenth century the great composer, while a servant of God, could and did write "sensuous" music without any thought of a conflict. Berglinger and Kreisler are in this respect relatively unified; neither is aware of a contradiction in serving God with a sensuous art. With the continuous accentuation of the sensuous element in music during Romanticism, and the neglect of the church forms, the chasm becomes wider still; the religious composer disappears from literature. What is striking in *Das Tanzlegendchen* is that even the non-musical Keller sees fit to crown his collection of "pagan" legends with a musical tale in which both principles are given almost equal rights.

A cause for Keller's lack of interest in music may be his acquaintance with Richard Wagner, certainly the archetype of the nineteenth century musician. Nothing could repel the hardhearted Keller more than the atmosphere in which Wagner held court at Wesendonck's Zürich villa. Wagner on the other hand, prompted perhaps by Keller's inability to pose, believed that the writer lacked talent; the composer says in his autobiography that the government would make the best use of such an honest fellow. This contrast of personality and of attitude toward art accounts for much of the paucity of literature concerning musicians during the flowering of Poetic Realism: the musician's art had remained Romantic, the musician had come to regard himself as a "chosen being," and society was ready to agree with him. Literature had however taken a quieter path; the mature Keller was most interested in the individual against the background of practical politics and everyday society.

It is impossible to imagine a non-Romantic Wagner. Hoffmann was the literary passion of Wagner's youth, and it is more than coincidence that the two operas of Wagner containing musical figures are to some extent inspired by tales of Hoffmann. The relationship between *Meister Martin der Küfner und seine Gesellen* and *Die Meistersinger* is to be sure more one of mood and atmosphere than of plot, although it is conceivable that Meister Martin influenced the creation of Hans Sachs, and the nobleman, Conrad, that of Walther von Stolzing. However the relationship between *Der Kampf der Sänger* and *Tannhäuser* is more interesting, since in both the works the demonic musician is presented in a pronounced form. Heinrich von Ofterdingen in Hoffmann's story is a reflection of certain facets of Kreisler's nature, put into historical form; the love of both Heinrich and Wolfram von Eschenbach for the Countess Mathilde is related to that of Kreisler for Julia, since the love-object in each case is a representation of music in the form of a woman. Heinrich's love turns to evil; he is in league with the magician Klingsohr and his messenger, Nasias, a fact which makes him seem close to Heine's Paganini or Lenau's musicians. Having learned a new type of music from Klingsohr, who is rumored to associate with uncanny powers, he is bested in the Contest of Song. Banished from the Wartburg, he is told to return within a year to do battle with a chosen master. Klingsohr may judge the contest. A figure resembling Heinrich is vanquished by Wolfram, the defender of Minnesong; "Heinrich" disappears in a cloud of smoke. Later Wolfram learns that it was not Heinrich but a vision conjured up by Klingsohr that he defeated, and through Wolfram's splendid song Heinrich himself has been freed from the powers of evil.

Wagner, in *Eine Mitteilung an meine Freunde*, denies any influence on his *Tannhäuser* either by Hoffmann's tale or Tieck's *Der getreue Eckart und der Tannenhäuser*, although he admits he is acquainted with both stories; he attributes his conception to a *Tannhäuser-Volksbuch* and the Middle High German poem of the *Sängerkrieg*.[18] This assertion is repeated in the *Leben* (XIII, 287-288). Wagner is not quite just toward Hoffmann, but he gives Tieck no more credit than he deserves. (Tieck's Tannenhäuser is not a musician and his pact with the devil does not take artistic form.) Hoffmann's Heinrich stands much closer to Wagner's Tannhäuser: both are artists, once devoted to the ideal, but now won over by sinister powers, Heinrich by Klingsohr, Tannhäuser by Venus. Wagner's second act is based on Hoffmann's tale: Heinrich's efforts to seduce Mathilde and Tannhäuser's praise of sensual delights in the presence of Elisabeth are similar; likewise the characters of Wolfram and the Landgrave are taken from Hoffmann's story. The song in praise of ideal love which Wolfram sings during the "Sängerkrieg" (II, 22) is specifically called for in Hoffmann, as is Tannhäuser's praise of sensual delights (II, 25). Wagner omits the battle of ideal and learned art between Eschenbach and Klingsohr, substituting a theme more attractive to him: the struggle between feminine purity (Elisabeth) and feminine sensuality (Frau Venus). In the same way Tannhäuser is not redeemed through the efforts of Wolfram; this task is accomplished by the saintly Elisabeth. Hoffmann's version does not have the religious connotations of the opera: Heinrich is saved for a life of service to art through the bravery of Wolfram, who wins Elisabeth.

Hoffmann thus formulates the problem less sensually than Wagner. Heinrich falls in with Klingsohr not because of an inclination toward debauchery on his part, but because he is tired of what Klingsohr calls in their interview on the mountainside "die gar schlechte schülermässige Singerei der sogenannten Meister" who have no conception "von der eigentlichen tiefern Kunst des Sängers" (X, 74). The theme of the opposition between feeling and intellectuality in art is taken up once more during the battles between Wolfram, Klingsohr, and Nasias. Mathilde is only the bait in Klingsohr's trap: intellectuality—the truly evil factor in art—masquerades as sensuality. This Hoffmannesque paradox should be carefully noted, for Thomas Mann employs the same theme in the interview between Leverkühn and the devil in *Doktor Faustus*. Wagner however concerns himself with the less subtle powers of Elisabeth and those of Frau Venus. At mid-century the figure of the easily tempted musician becomes more common in literature, being propagated in particular by Brachvogel's *Friedemann Bach*. Yet *Tannhäuser*, long the most popular of the Wagnerian operas, must have helped inspire the increasing popularity of the dissolute musician in literature.

Perhaps Joseph Viktor von Scheffel should not be mentioned

in close proximity to Wagner; there is nevertheless a certain resemblance between Walther von Stolzing and Scheffel's famous Jung Werner in *Der Trompeter von Säkkingen* (1854), however different the two figures may be in essence. Walther and Werner, descended from the guileless vagabond of Romanticism, have become ready to meet life on its own terms. More responsible individuals than the footloose Romantic hero, they are capable of becoming good citizens. The conflict between life and art is hinted at: the revolutionary musical ideas of Walther, the fact that Werner is believed to be a mere wandering musician, place hindrances in the way of both heroes, but having proved their ability, they win the young ladies of their hearts and settle down to a happy and prosperous life.

With *Die Meistersinger* Wagner intended to write a popular and comic opera, but the work's "popularity" is somewhat narrowed by the composer's determined interjection of his own problems into the battle between Stolzing and his critics. As for comedy, the opera hangs perilously between that genre and a more serious one. Walther, with his unorthodox music, might well be rejected by the Meistersingers, and there are unmistakably tragic features in the conception of Hans Sachs. But Jung Werner's tale could scarcely have a tragic conclusion. It is inconceivable that Scheffel, writing superficially and for a large audience, might have left Werner as the pope's Kapellmeister. When Werner is forced to leave the castle of Margareta's father, Scheffel hurries to bring the lovers together once more in Rome; the unhappy intervening years are added to give the poem some sort of climax. The age of Hoffmann, in which the question of the musician's religious conversion was still of import, is long since past. Oblivious of the musical problems of contemporary Germany, Werner does not on the other hand embody the concern with the human being characteristic of the Biedermeier writers. Without a dark side to his nature, and a performer on the hearty trumpet, he has no connection with Lenau's wandering violinists. His playing is sentimental like himself:

> . . . sein Blasen
> Zog melodisch durch die Nacht hin.
> Lauschend hört's der Rhein im Grunde,
> Lauschend Hecht und Lachsforelle,
> Lauschend auch die Wasserfrauen . . . [19]

The poem is nostalgic and Romanticizing, reminiscent of that Germany immortalized by the cheap lithograph and the light operetta.

In 1856, the year of the appearance of Mörike's *Mozart auf der Reise nach Prag*, Albert Emil Brachvogel completed his dramatic picture of the musician, *Narziss*, and two years later he published *Friedemann Bach*, the novellistic counterpart of the play: both Mörike and Brachvogel employ the life of the musician as a means of painting a Kulturbild, and in Brachvogel's play the musician becomes a symbol of his time. (The learned Wilhelm Riehl also published in 1856 his *Kulturgeschichtliche Novellen*, containing the best-known works among his several antiquarian tales on the musician.[20]) It is indicative of the attitude toward music in the literary Germany of the mid-century that so many historical pictures of the musician appeared within the space of three years. No comprehensive treatment of the musician had been produced in literature since Romanticism. Now that the creative musician is portrayed full length once more, the portrait is a historical one. Johanna Kinkel's *Hans Ibeles*, coming in 1860, achieved no literary fame comparable to the works of either Mörike, or Brachvogel, or Riehl: *Hans Ibeles* of course has a contemporary scene.

The son of a Breslau merchant, Brachvogel demonstrated such a distaste for formal study that he became an engraver's apprentice, then an actor, and finally a journalist and author. Largely self-taught, he was very proud of his knowledge, and long passages in his works are reminiscent of the text-book, a tendency likewise to be seen even in such a superior artist as Thomas Mann. *Narziss* and *Friedemann Bach* were by far the most popular of Brachvogel's many creations. *Narziss* became the rage of the German theater and held the boards until the nineties. *Friedemann Bach* was equally popular in the field of the novel, and possesses the dubious honor of being a forefather of the best-selling historical novel of the twentieth century.

Brachvogel chose the musician as a hero for his play and novel on sensational rather than aesthetic grounds. Of Narziss Rameau's musical talents we learn only that he is—or was—a musician; the musical element in the Bach novel is to be sure much stronger, yet Brachvogel has a larger store of anecdote, true and false, concerning the Bachs than he does knowledge of their music, which he doubtless had little opportunity to hear.

Brachvogel was perhaps led to his subjects by literary rather than by musical suggestions. He would have known Diderot's *Le Neveu de Rameau*; as for *Friedemann Bach,* Brachvogel may have been drawn to his subject by the reference in Forkel's classic *Über Johann Sebastian Bachs Leben, Kunst, und Kunstwerke,* a work which is mentioned in the novel. Forkel, in his catalogue of Bach's students, includes the composer's eldest son: "[Friedemann] kam in der Originalität aller seiner Gedanken seinem Vater am nächsten. Alle seine Melodien sind anders gewendet als die Melodien anderer Komponisten, und doch nicht nur äusserst natürlich, sondern zugleich ausserordentlich fein und zierlich. Fein vorgetragen, wie er selbst sie vortrug, müssen sie notwendig jeden Kenner entzücken. Nur schade, dass er mehr fantasierte, und bloss in der Fantasie nach musikalischen Delikatessen grübelte, als schrieb" (Forkel, p. 81). The musician's exotic nature, was nicely suited to attract a journalist who had already treated the half-mad Narziss Rameau. Eduard Mörike is interested in setting down the spirit of Mozart and of his time as he knows them through a study of the composer's music; Brachvogel is concerned with an exaggerated picture of the musician himself and a gaudy portrayal of the age in which he lived.

Brachvogel's Narziss is only allegedly a musician. He appears to be more a jester and an offensive sycophant than a creative artist. However he does have some traits which Brachvogel may think of as belonging to the artist (they appear again in *Friedemann Bach*). He is loved by two women, the pure Mademoiselle Quinault and Madame de Pompadour; he is also very nearly mad. Pompadour had been his wife when he was a poor musician; in the course of the drama Narziss discovers that the king's present mistress is actually the woman who, having deserted him, tried to bribe him to leave France. At the same time the discovery is revealed to the court through the machinations of the evil Duke Choiseul; Narziss scorns the renewed love of Pompadour and she dies of shame and chagrin. After beholding a vision of the coming revolution, Narziss also perishes. The efforts of Quinault to restore to Narziss his lost self-respect have been in vain.

Narziss is a more starkly outlined figure than Friedemann Bach in his boundless egoism (". . . ich habe mich doch so lieb, mein Gott!—so lieb!")[21] and his equally boundless self-contempt.

In this respect he reminds us a little of Kreisler, eternally wavering between ecstasy and despair; nonetheless the source of Kreisler's wretchedness is his burning genius, that of Narziss his betrayal by his wife. Narziss also resembles Kreisler in his constant revolt against the noble society around him, but Kreisler has a different reason for bitterness than Narziss: Kreisler's chief complaint is that the nobility does not honor music and accept the musician's genius; Narziss revolts against the organization of society which has turned him into a miserable parasite. Quinault and Julia are like one another too: young women from the middle class connected with a court, they both attempt to give aid to the artist (if that term may be applied to Narziss). In contrast to Julia, the distant ideal, Quinault becomes interested in Narziss long before he takes the slightest notice of her. Narziss, perhaps a little bored, finally admits that it is pleasant to have someone take a friendly interest in him. More he will not say.

Narziss possesses a superficial resemblance to the Romantic hero; but his most important feature is that he represents the use of the musician as the symbol of an age's downfall, or more accurately, of a nation's sickness. His apocalyptic vision does not prophesy the future age of equality; it depicts the destruction of the period which has produced him. Undoubtedly the play's climactic passage was effective on stage, with whatever distaste we may read it today: "Ja, die Sindflut—Es regnet Feuer vom Himmel und Galle und Tränen! Aus den Sümpfen des Elends und Verbrechens steigt das entmenschte Geschlecht und heult durch die Strassen nach Blut! Blut! Blut!" (381). Neither this passage nor the others in which Narziss attacks both the decadent nobility and himself deserve to be mentioned in connection with the controlled art of Thomas Mann. But Brachvogel is the first author in German literature to employ the device used as a basis for *Doktor Faustus*: the musician as the representative, at once product and accuser, of a diseased age.

(Apart from Johanna Kinkel, another successor to Brachvogel in the association of music and political life is Wilhelm Raabe. In *Das Horn von Wanza*, 1881, the aged Aunt Sophie Grünhage narrates the story of her musician father's embroilment in a difficult political situation. After the Wars of Liberation Aunt Sophie's father, who had played for King Jerome of Westphalia, lost his position; he was forced to flee to Halle, where he earned a meager living by teaching the students violin and flute: "... die Bezahlung war schlecht, und auch sonst hat die edle Kunst Musica meinem armen Vater nicht viel abgeworfen."[22])

Friedemann Bach shares a trait of character with several musicians in later German literature: women cannot resist him. The wife of the powerful Minister von Brühl attempts to seduce the young composer. Unfortunately for her plans, Friedemann falls desperately in love with her daughter Antonie. Cast into jail because of this love, he goes mad, and once more the theme of insanity appears, so common in the portrait of the musician. Storm's Marx is another musician driven to a kind of madness by unjust imprisonment; Berglinger, Rochlitz's Karl, Kreisler, "Ritter Gluck," the Baron von B., Krespel are all mad to a degree, but their madness is directly connected with their art. The madness of Bahr's "Armer Narr" and Thomas Mann's Leverkühn is given a double cause; physically it results from syphilitic infection, spiritually from too great a devotion to music. Brachvogel does not present any single ground for Friedemann's madness: it may be that the loss of Antonie has weakened his senses, or that the shame of imprisonment has caused his mind to snap. Brachvogel is not a careful writer; and after the imprisonment of Friedemann, his story becomes a hodgepodge of sensational events. Falling ever lower in the social scale, plagued by madness, Friedemann at last joins a gypsy band; he wanders to Berlin where he dies, attended only by his faithful gypsy mistress.

The above resumé will show what caused the popularity of the book; it is a catch-all of historical fact, scurrilous anecdote, frenetic imagination, and bare-faced sentimentality. Its opinions on music are much too enthusiastic to be taken seriously; the descriptions of musical performances read like a parody of Heine's fullblown style, and Friedemann's moments of inspiration make the religious passions of Berglinger seem colorless. When Antonie reveals her love to Friedemann, he ecstatically composes an oratorio on the last days of Christ: "Auf seinem schönen, jugendfrischen Antlitz, welches das volle, losgebundene Haar in schwarzen Locken umflattert, glänzt die strahlende Majestät der sich gebärenden Idee, die in prophetischer Glut und Klarheit aus dem Gedankenmeere seines Hirns emportauchte und sich mit der Siegesgewissheit auf dieser breiten, kühnen Stirne, ihrem Throne niederliess."[23] In Heine the figure of the contemporary musician had become equally important with the music he produced, a legitimate technique in the depiction of a virtuoso; in Brachvogel a composer from the relatively impersonal eighteenth century receives inspiration from above—and the reader is treated to a picture of the physical phenomena attendant upon the exalted state. *Friedemann Bach*'s importance lies primarily in the influence it must have exerted on the musical literature of succeeding decades, many of its themes, especially the sexual aberrations and moral decay of the musician, being extremely popular at the turn of the century. Otherwise it must be denied any artistic importance. Its connections with the musical figures of Romanticism are few, its connections with the ideals of Biedermeier none.

The greatest picture of the musician from the mid-century was produced by an author, Eduard Mörike, who had little contact with the musical currents of his day, never met a prominent musician, and seldom heard a full orchestra. Occasionally Mörike attended performances of major classical works, such as Mozart's *Don Juan* or Beethoven's First Symphony, but he was hardly an ardent concert-goer. A retiring nature and an extreme sensibility to music prevented him from attending public performances; he was often so excited by music that he felt an irrepressible desire to give his nervousness expression in violent motion. He much preferred to hear music in the home and, mostly through the piano arrangement, he came to know Haydn, Mozart, and Beethoven thoroughly. He took no part in the Wagnerian controversy; even Schubert's *Erlkönig* is said to have impressed him as being too complicated. The narrow boundaries of Mörike's musical world are quite congruent with the character of the solitary poet. In Mörike's opinion music, like poetry, must be cultivated alone, an attitude contrary to the principal musical current of the nineteenth century, a period of virtuosi and of the rise of the great orchestras. For this reason, perhaps, Mörike was most strongly moved by the memory of music, or by a sound recalling a melody, rather than by an actual performance. In his poem, "Ach, nur einmal noch im Leben," he says that the creaky gate of the Cleversulzbach vicarage plays an aria from Mozart's *Titus*, and in a letter from 1832 he describes the reactions which a thunderstorm aroused in him: "In unglaublicher Schnelle stand uns das Wetter überm

Kopf. Breite, gewaltige Blitze, wie ich sie nie bei Tag gesehen, fielen wie Rosenschauer in unsere weisse Stube und Schlag auf Schlag. Der alte Mozart muss in diesen Augenblicken mit dem Kapellmeisterstäbchen unsichtbar in meinem Rücken gestanden und mir die Schulter berührt haben, denn wie der Teufel fuhr die Ouvertüre zum Titus in meiner Seele los, so unaufhaltsam, so prächtig, so durchdringend mit jenem oft wiederholten ehernen Schrei der römischen Tuba, dass sich mir beide Fäuste vor Entzücken ballten."[24] Not only does the passage reveal Mörike's love of music as an art of the memory rather than an art of performance; it also betrays the secret of his attitude toward his idol, Mozart. Like Hoffmann he sees the demonic quality in the composer; Mozart is not the creator of Rococo filigree work but a deep and powerful personality. Characteristically Mörike mentions the *Titus*, a work from the composer's last and most Romantic period, that of the *Requiem* and the *Clarinet Concerto*. For Hoffmann, however, Mozart and even Gluck had been almost his own contemporaries. Mörike calls the composer "der alte Mozart" and sees in him a representative of an age long since ended. Likewise, he writes of Haydn: "Manchmal ist sein Humor altfränkisch, ein zierliches Zöpflein, / Das, wie der Zauberer spielt, schalkhaft im Rücken ihm tanzt."[25] We have watched the growth of the historical attitude toward music in earlier writers. German literary thought had lost touch with the development of German music, and even the most forward-looking of musicians turned to the past for his themes. Mörike's Mozart is the finest product of this historical attitude, and at the same time represents an unusual case of the philosophy of Biedermeier applied to the great creative artist.

Mörike himself cannot of course be called an artist of the Biedermeier alone. His earlier lyrics and his novel *Maler Nolten* are products of that Romanticism associated with the "nightside of nature," and with the probing of the subconscious; certain themes are struck in *Nolten* only to appear years later in *Mozart*, made softer and more subtle. Chief among these is the association of music and death. In the novel the dark figure which pursues Nolten, at last driving him to his death, is placed in a manifest relationship with music: the nemesis speaks to Nolten through music, despite the fact that Nolten is a painter. At the opening of the novel Nolten's sketches are described:

in one of them a woman, an organist, plays in the midst of a wild landscape, peopled by strange and sometimes gruesome figures. A youth with closed eyes and suffering features leans on the organ and holds a burning torch, a golden-brown moth rests in his hair. The skeleton figure of death treads on the bellows (II, 18). It is not difficult to guess that the youth is Nolten, and the organist Peregrina (or Elisabeth the gypsy girl), the sensual power which finally destroys the painter. The symbol takes an ironic form in that, shortly before her suicide, Agnes, Nolten's fiancée, sings the hymn of religious consolation, "Eine Liebe kenn' ich, die ist treu," accompanied on the organ by Henni, a blind boy, while his little sister takes the place of death at the bellows. On the night before Agnes's burial Nolten awakes believing that he hears the tone of the organ once more (II, 423). Springing from his bed, Nolten follows the music, only to fall dead in the chapel. The watchers by the body of Agnes plainly hear the weird music just before Nolten collapses. Henni, who has begun to regain his vision, claims that his first sight was of a woman at the organ; Nolten stood beside her. At the time of *Nolten*'s composition Mörike obviously possessed a darker and more Romantic conception of music than we should expect from an author who would someday write such a classic of the comfortable life as *Der alte Turmhahn*. The hero may be a painter, but Romantic music remains the means by which the world of spirits, in particular spirits of evil, communicates with him.

When compared with Nolten, or with Berglinger and Kreisler, Mörike's Mozart appears to be completely tamed. The plot of *Mozart auf der Reise nach Prag* hinges on a charming little incident which evidences Mozart's willingness to conform to the standards of conduct in Rococo society. During a midday pause on the journey to Prague Mozart wanders into a handsome park. Carelessly he picks an orange from a favorite tree of the Count to whom the estate belongs; the tree has been intended as a betrothal gift for Eugenie, the fiancée of the son of the house. The composer and his wife are invited to dinner; in order to make amends for his faux pas, Mozart plays the finale of *Don Juan*. The next morning the travelers leave, accompanied by the good wishes of their noble hosts. Superficially nothing has occurred: the betrothal party has been made all the more successful by Mozart's unexpected presence; the composer and his wife have had a pleasant interruption of their journey.

Remembering the deeds of violence which are the order of the day in Irenäus's park (*Kater Murr*), we are somewhat startled to learn of the excitement aroused by the plucking of an orange. Hoffmann's savage opinions are prompted both by the boundless idealism and the irony of Romanticism. Mörike intends to paint a pleasant picture of Rococo society, his thoughts colored by the Biedermeier atmosphere in which he himself lives. The Rococo-Biedermeier relationship between Mozart and his wife is done with special charm: the vivacious wife accepts the moods and humors of the composer with amused tolerance, although she cannot resist a half-teasing complaint now and then. Quite unlike Hoffmann's Julia, at once fascinated and repelled by the demonic Kreisler, Frau Mozart believes she knows every foible of the composer. She regales the company with a long account of her husband's habits, describing in detail his thoughtless purchases, his love of practical jokes. The fact that supposed friends take advantage of the composer and persuade him to improvise for hours on end arouses her to anger. However she hesitates to mention publicly a certain Signora Malerbi (once more the evil Italian musician) who has charmed her husband, nor does she dwell very long on her husband's love of company, his almost feverish desire to attend dances, his passion for masquerades. Mörike, while offering a relatively full account (in Constanze's narrative and elsewhere) of the husband's peccadilloes, mentions nothing of the historical Constanze's own inclination to useless expenditures or of her flirtations. Mörike's Constanze is a product of Biedermeier; while hardly so ideal as one of Stifter's women characters, she is nevertheless a perfect wife, whose foremost thought is the wellbeing of her husband and the preservation of her home. Unlike Julia, she totally lacks artistic ability. Both Mozart and Constanze are far more human in their proportions than either Kreisler or his beloved, who remain noble exaggerations. No trace of the Kreisler-Julia relationship exists between Mozart and his wife.

Care is taken to embellish the Rococo-Biedermeier conception of Mozart in other respects. Many of the details about him serve to render him harmless, a little eccentric but nonetheless lovable. The garden scene, the tales of his wife, his gracious and courtly bearing during the entertainment, and his composition of a duet for the betrothal party, all indicate that he knows well enough how to get along in the world; his moods may mislead him now and again, but he is no Kreisler who despises company and regards music as a sacred matter. It matters nothing to Mozart if his noble melodies are used for amusement. A compromise of mutual acceptance and tolerance has been reached between artist and society; the family of the Count receives Mozart's little foibles without a murmur, Mozart delights in the party's employment of his genius for its entertainment. We think of the words of the cousin in Storm's *Eine Halligfahrt* when he describes the musical evenings of his Biedermeier world. Kreisler would not be at home in this atmosphere. Mörike subtly emphasizes the association he has made between the philosophies of Rococo and Biedermeier by allowing Mozart to tell the story of his youthful experiences in Italy. While in Naples the composer and his father visited a palace overlooking the sea. There the young Mozart received those memories of Italy which caused him unconsciously to pick the orange. His description of a mock sea battle (in which oranges were used as ammunition) moves the fiancée, Eugenie, to say: "... wir haben hier eine gemalte Symphonie von Anfang bis zu Ende gehabt und ein vollkommenes Gleichnis überdies des Mozartischen Geistes selbst in seiner ganzen Heiterkeit!... ist nicht die ganze Anmut 'Figaros' darin?" (III, 242). Mozart's elegant tale of Rococo pageantry delights what is in reality a Biedermeier audience: Mörike has united the two periods in his work without slighting either eighteenth-century manners or nineteenth-century idealism. "Rococo" for Mörike does not mean the artificial world of shepherds and shepherdesses; he stresses in it rather the element of innocent joy which he finds exemplified by Mozart's music. He has transformed the gaiety inspired by a pageant, hardly a Biedermeier event, into that caused by the description of the pageant in refined society.

Thus far the portrait of Mozart is relatively innocuous. However Mozart in Mörike's mind was not merely a composer of works of gentility, as the passage cited concerning *Titus* will attest. It is true that the letter in question was written in 1832; but not all the Romantic elements vanish from Mörike's nature with the years. At the beginning of the novella, after but a few pages of narrative, the action pauses and Mörike inserts a section concerning Mozart's personality that reads as if it were borrowed from a biography of the musician. While this account of the extreme nervousness which plagued Mozart is couched in a somewhat moralizing style, it is nevertheless easy to see that Mörike is conscious of a connection between the composer's genius and the unhealthy impulse toward companionship which drives him from coffeehouse to coffeehouse. We are forced to the painful observation, Mörike says, that Mozart, aspiring to the loftiest goals of the imagination, nevertheless did not possess "ein stetiges und rein befriedigtes Gefühl seiner selbst" (III, 218). Mozart cannot be made to fit comfortably into the Biedermeier ideal.

In the "biographical" passage the author derives the unhappy features of the composer from his feverish desire for company; in *Nolten* the downfall of the artist is traced to his sensuality. During Constanze's narrative a contradiction has become evident. A certain pleasure in the sensuous can be noted in Mozart's account of his Italian adventures; now Constanze is forced to avoid mentioning the more serious of Mozart's foibles. Mörike half slyly, half shamefacedly describes in an aside the relationship between the composer and Malerbi: "Diese Römerin war durch Mozarts Verwendung bei der Oper angestellt worden, und ohne Zweifel hatten ihre koketten Künste nicht geringen Anteil an der Gunst des Meisters" (III, 256). Some even say that she had tricked him over a period of months and "kept him hot enough on her gridiron." Does Mozart's nervous gregariousness take sensual form in Malerbi's case?

At the end of the story, there is another hint that Mörike has allowed a little of the fault of Nolten and perhaps of himself to creep into what was intended to be a charmingly stylized portrait from musical history. Mörike says expressly that Mozart's performance of the finale from *Don Juan* has stirred Eugenie, the fiancée, most deeply of all. Eugenie rather than the good Frau Constanze represents the feminine and musical ideal; Eugenie senses the imminent death of Mozart, just as Julia in *Kater Murr* (and Countess Constanze in *Nolten*) know when danger threatens their artist-heroes. Eugenie lies sleepless during the night (like Julia and the Countess Constanze), and in the morning locks the piano keyboard which Mozart's hands have been the last to touch. Before she leaves the room her eyes fall upon the poem which represents her premonitions:

"Ein Tännlein grünet wo, / Wer weiss, im Walde." The pattern to be found in *Nolten* repeats itself in *Mozart*. Nolten is betrothed to the simple Agnes, representative of all the domestic virtues; his sensual nature leads him to an affair with the Countess, who understands his talent far better than does his fiancée, and he is at the same time pursued by the dark form of Elisabeth, the gypsy. Mozart is married to the domestic Constanze, and understood by Eugenie; the figure of Elisabeth could be identified with that of the Italian Malerbi. With the sudden emergence of Eugenie, Mörike's own creation and not a historical figure, the resemblance between the two heroes becomes strikingly apparent. The feminine figure, who is a musician and who speaks to Nolten through music, lures the painter to his death; Mozart, worn out by a nervous impulse which Mörike allows to be interpreted as taking sensual form or perhaps being even of sensual origin, predicts his own death in music, the meaning of which is only understood by a woman not his wife.

Mozart, born of a fusion between Rococo and Biedermeier, has Romanticism lurking at his core. The Romantic element becomes most overt in Mörike's portrait of Mozart as a musician. Like Hoffmann, Mörike chooses the *Don Juan* to express the musical "night-side" of the composer: his performance of the finale causes Eugenie to think of his impending death. Mörike describes this music in terms which are certainly not those of Biedermeier; were it not for the questions of the company assembled in the drawing room, we should think we were in Hoffmann's theater again. In the description of the graveyard scene, where the statue of the Commendatore addresses the Don, this Romanticism reaches its height. The great trombone passage and the subsequent chorale receive verbal expression in the famous: "Wie von entlegenen Sternenkreisen fallen die Töne aus silbernen Posaunen, eiskalt, Mark und Seele durchschneidend, herunter durch die blaue Nacht" (III, 270). Even the most sober person is forced to cross the boundary of the human imagination, beyond which one perceives the transcendental. Such sentiments are scarcely those of the Biedermeier artist; the musical description resembles those of Hoffmann and the closing section of Heine's Paganini-essay. Mörike may seem closer to Hoffmann than Heine, for Mörike's composer-performer does not appear in the images he calls forth; he does not depend on the dramatic effects of the virtuoso. Yet Mörike has not remained untouched by the growing interest in the musician himself, considered apart from his works. Hoffmann's *Don Juan* is primarily a description of the opera, an interpretation of its dramatic values; Mörike's words on *Don Juan* concern the music as an expression of Mozart's own death-touched personality, not as a part of a well-nigh perfect music drama. Hoffmann, the arch-Romantic, says little of Mozart himself; Mörike devotes an entire novella to him. Hoffmann never interpreted the personality of a real composer; that was a liberty he took only with his own creations. Now the musical tale, on its historical detour, finds it easy to approach the demonic personality set at a safe distance in the past—and difficult, except in the purposeful ambiguities of a Keller or the domestic circumlocutions of a Kinkel, to deal with the demonic musician of the present.

In 1861 Ferdinand Kürnberger published a tale, *Der Dichter des Don Juan*, which forms an amusing pendant to Mörike's novella. Lorenzo da Ponte, Mozart's sometime librettist, is living penniless in Amsterdam with his wife, Nancy; they tell one another stories to forget their hunger. (After a number of vicissitudes da Ponte wins a position as poet to London's Italian opera.) One of da Ponte's tales concerns the writing of *Don Juan*. Through da Ponte Kürnberger discloses more freely than Mörike how Romantic the concept of the composer has remained: "Nachts werde ich für Mozart schreiben und mir denken, ich lese die Hölle von Dante . . ."[26] Indeed, the demonic tradition is so strong that Kürnberger transfers the supernatural quality from composer to librettist; da Ponte confesses "dass ich den Don Juan betreffend zuerst von dem Gesichtspunkte des Dämonischen ausging" (II, 50). Kürnberger points like a minor and franker Mörike toward the revolution about to be effected in German literary thought on music.

At the time of Mörike's death there entered on the German intellectual scene a thinker opposed both to quietude and historicity. Friedrich Nietzsche instead was interested in the great and disturbing personality. As a young man he found his ideal in Wagner. The initial result of the relationship, *Die Geburt der Tragödie* (1872), provides a theoretical justification of music as the basis of tragedy. Tragedy is born of music, the Dionysian art; tragedy, the mediator between music and the listeners, represents a myth, which "schützt uns vor der Musik, wie er ihr andrerseits erst die höchste Freiheit gibt."[27] In return for this freedom—that of appearing in the most Dionysian, the most orgiastic manner, but disguised and given form by the myth—music grants the tragic myth such a penetrating metaphysical significance as word and picture can never afford. The listener hears "der innerste Abgrund der Dinge" (I, 147) speak to him. As Nietzsche says in the last chapter of the essay, tragedy and music should be inseparable. Wagner has reunited these two sister elements in a single work of art, the musical drama, and thus has broken the grasp which the "opera" (according to Nietzsche a Socratic or Apollonic form of art) had maintained over the musical stage for centuries. Music has at last been recognized theoretically as the "demonic" and the tragic, rather than the mathematical and the serene art; and Wagner is for Nietzsche the rediscoverer of this truth, lost since the Greeks. According to Nietzsche's pamphlet, *Richard Wagner in Bayreuth*, tragedy and Wagner have appeared together: ". . . so endlich erwächst der grösste Zauberer und Beglücker unter den Sterblichen, der dithyrambische Dramatiker" (I, 545). Not only music as Dionysian art, but the musician as Dionysian creator have been given justification and in a form destined to excite the most fervid interest.

Nietzsche's opinions on the "dark powers" inherent in music have been uttered before in German literature; their presence in Mozart, for example, had long ago been noticed by Hoffmann. Nietzsche calls the composer Wagner an explorer of the utmost depths of suffering: ". . . so steigt sein Weltblick in die Tiefe . . . dort sieht er das Leiden im Wesen der Dinge . . ." (I, 552-553). Yet this quality, later to be fully developed by Mann in *Doktor Faustus*, can already be noted in Kreisler, with his sudden glimpses into the darkness. It is the nervous sensitivity which, reduced to a lower grade, characterizes (and distresses) a host of other literary composers. Nietzsche has however spread the doctrine of music and musician as Dionysian, as demonic elements throughout all levels of German intellectual life. That he was tremendously aided by Wagner's music cannot be denied, but the credit for the actual formula remains his own. The profusion of novels and dramas about the musician which began to appear in the century's last decades can be traced in part to the popularity of Nietzsche and Wagner in musical circles. In Sudermann's *Das Hohe Lied* the heroine knows, besides the work of her father, only the compositions of Wagner, and her sole other contact with current intellectual life is through a music critic, who thinks to seduce her by giving her Nietzsche to read. The young musician in Friedrich Huch's *Enzio* has but two intellectual interests apart from his own compositions, the correct interpretation of Nietzsche and the correct performance of Wagner.

Nietzsche and Wagner reawakened interest in music as a matter of intellectual speculation in Germany. Following the relative harmony of thought which existed between music and literature during Romanticism, the two arts grew apart during the period from the deaths of Beethoven and Schubert to the founding of the theater at Bayreuth. Music remained a Romantic or post-Romantic art. Literary men on the other hand were devoted to ideals directly opposed to those of the best musical art of the day. Where music had remained Romantic, producing geniuses like Berlioz, Chopin, and Wagner, literature on music had turned to renunciation and domesticity or to historical pseudo-demonism. The Nietzsche-Wagner partnership brought music and literature together again.

A few words might be added concerning the later break between Wagner and Nietzsche, since it predicts certain developments which musical thought was to take after the composer's death. The Nietzsche who received the libretto of *Parsival* in 1878 was completely dedicated to Hellenistic, to "southern," to "joyous" art, while Wagner had "cast himself helpless and broken" at the foot of the cross (III, 6). Even after Wagner's death in 1883 Nietzsche did not cease to do battle against him; the philosopher launched a final attack in *Der Fall Wagner* and *Nietzsche contra Wagner*. *Der Fall Wagner* opens with the famous eulogy of Bizet's *Carmen*: Nietzsche has heard the opera twenty times. He cannot bear the sound of Wagner's brutal, artificial, yet "innocent" orchestra any longer; Bizet's orchestration is the only one he can still endure: "Diese Musik ist böse, raffiniert, fatalistisch; sie bleibt dabei populär . . ." (VIII, 7). Yet still more important is Bizet's depiction of love, translated back into nature as hatred unto death between the sexes. In contrast to this completely "natural" music stands the chaste Wagner of *Parsival*, the composer of music without a future.

With Nietzsche's conversion to the ideals of "southern"

vocal music (and by implication to the works of Donizetti, Bellini, and Verdi) we see the legitimation of the Mediterranean musician on the German musical scene. "Southern" music must henceforth be accepted as a worthy sensuous counterbalance to the idealism of German music. This point of view is fruitful for literature: Heinrich Mann re-evaluates the Italian performer, and Werfel glorifies Verdi. For the development of music itself Nietzsche's argument was a dead end; the age of great "natural" music was past. It would still experience a late Italian blossoming in Puccini, but it had never flourished in Germany, while *Carmen* remained an isolated phenomenon on the French operatic stage. Such is not the case with Wagner's return to religion, however decadent, however "death-inclined" it may have been: Bruckner and Mahler, Reger and Pfitzner all compose important music connected in one way or another with Christianity. Yet the literary musician, going through his most sinful age, manages substantially to avoid religion until Adrian Leverkühn begins the study of theology.

Chapter III

THE POST-WAGNERIAN AGE

In the years after the death of Wagner the musician became an extremely popular subject for literary treatment in Germany. The German public could look back upon a musical tradition generally accepted as the greatest in Europe, and many neighboring nations were developing their own music in the German manner. While other German and Austrian composers, Brahms, Bruckner, Mahler, Strauss, and Wolf for example, did not yet have the international following of a Wagner, they nevertheless served as evidence that their nations stood at the forefront in creative music. Italy had once been the home of virtuosi, but Germany had established a standard of excellence for the performer hitherto unheard of. The average German had come to realize that his country held the musical leadership of the world, just as it had held the intellectual leadership during the age of Goethe. The conception of the musician as a chosen being, formalized by Nietzsche and embodied by Wagner, had received general acceptance, penetrating not only into other cultures but also into the broad masses of the German reading public. This public expected the musician to be a "genius," abnormal, unhappy, but nevertheless consecrated, a person to whom all privileges were to be granted. German authors met the occasion in accordance with the public's expectations.

Scarcely a musical figure in the literature of the time remains untormented by a problem better treated by the psychoanalyst than by the aesthetician. A tendency in this direction could already be noticed in Brachvogel, and even Mörike intimates such an interest. Yet Mörike's concern with eroticism harks back to Romanticism; in that period the musician's sensuality had largely been sublimated toward ideal ends. In the musical literature of the period 1883-1918 there exists however little interest in the musical values which may arise from the sexual aberration. Music as such disappears in favor of a discussion of a conductor's unhappy marriage or a composer's overpassionate nature, so that the work might concern the unusual individual in general instead of the musician in particular. The sexual theme admits of endless variations: the temptations of the woman artist, the mentor or virtuoso who uses his personality to seduce others, or the itinerant musician, for whom the possession of the good citizen's sister symbolizes his entrance into society.

Only in isolated works is the future of the musical art discussed; authors seem to regard the late Romantic splendor of German music as something bound to endure. Nor is there concern with music as a pedagogical means; music is rather associated with irresponsibility. Yet the age makes its valuable contributions: it accepts nineteenth century music as a model, and in this way the tendency of previous decades to regard music as an art of the eighteenth century is counteracted. It refurbishes the figure of the professional and contemporary musician. And it shows a healthy objectivity in its occasional criticism of its own favorite son, the genius-composer, and in more frequent parodies of his brother, the virtuoso.

A melodramatic short novel of Ossip Schubin (Lola Kirschner) from 1884, *Die Geschichte eines Genies,* gives some inkling of the various fates awaiting the composer. It places the worldly-wise composer Alphonse de Sterny over against the shy half-gypsy "genius," Gesa van Zuylen. Abandoned by his mother, Gesa is reared by a music copyist. De Sterny makes the young violinist, a brilliant performer of gypsy music, his protégé. After several concert tours the now mature Gesa returns to Brussels and the home of the copyist. Falling in love with the copyist's daughter, he undertakes an American tour in order to raise money for their marriage. In Gesa's absence de Sterny seduces his fiancée; she commits suicide on his return and he, broken-hearted, becomes a drunkard. Later he learns that de Sterny has stolen his compositions and used them as his own; one of them, *Satan* (a favorite compositional theme at this time: see *Der Kraft-Mayr* below), is played by the orchestra in which Gesa ekes out a living. Now nothing can stop Gesa's decline; he ends his life in Paris as the "raté de Montmartre."

Schubin treats de Sterny in a way that would have been unusual a few years earlier. The musician de Sterny is a dangerous man, of a type seldom met since Romanticism, an evil mentor and a composer wrapped into one; musicians of his ilk are destined to become more frequent in the post-Wagnerian period. Developing his sensual side, Schubin lets him say ". . . im Schlamm fühlen wir uns manchmal wohl . . .;"[1] yet instead of making him wholly diabolical, she gives him some good-natured domestic traits. Fond of his creature comforts, he likes to sit by the fire with a bottle of wine. Gesa is essentially a Romantic figure too, yet the fate which befalls him is not madness or musical destruction. As much defeated by his own weakness as by the machinations of de Sterny he is the first of a series of young composers who fail to rise above the struggle of existence. Schubin's novel juxtaposes two chief musical types of the age, the cynical—but not supernatural—possessor of the masterful personality and the tormented youth.

Ernst von Wolzogen's *Der Kraft-Mayr* (1897) has four composer-figures: the earnest but terrible-tempered Florian Mayr from Bayreuth, the megalomaniac Antonin Prczewalsky, the demonic Peter Gais, and finally the Olympian Franz Liszt himself. Florian, called the "Kraft-Mayr" because of his Bavarian temperament and physical strength, is a piano teacher in Berlin. Having punished his clumsy pupil, Thekla Burmester, he is dismissed by her foster parents, and Prczewalsky takes his place. Thekla secretly loves her violent Florian, but is compelled to endure the attentions of the Pole, who has cast his eye on the Burmester fortune. Just how modest a musician Prczewalsky is can be detected in his conversation: "Die Gräfin Proskowsky hat für mich Gift genommen, und der Fürst Smirczicky hat sich mit mir schiessen wollen. Aber ich hatte keine Zeit, ich hatte . . . ein Konzert in Warschau, wo ich meine Symphonie Opus 7 dirigierte. Die Fürstin Smirczicky liess mir dabei einen Lorbeerkranz reichen."[2] Even a beating from Florian does nothing to improve Prczewalsky, one of the funniest (and most brutal) satirical portraits in the novel.

Wolzogen does not confine his criticism of the genius-composer to non-Germans. Before leaving Berlin for Weimar, where he becomes the student of Liszt, Florian hears the "music drama," *Satan,* of one Peter Gais. Wolzogen turns the whole battery of his satire upon the performance: ". . . der dämonische Peter Gais war eben dabei, die Hölle loszulassen. Der Bechsteinsche Konzertflügel, grössten Formats . . . zitterte unter den wuchtigen Tatzen seines genialen Bändigers" (I, 54). During the performance Gais himself sings: "Nach einer längeren Weile ging ihm freilich die Stimme ganz aus, und da begann er zu pfeifen mit vollem, tremolierendem Ton. Das war jedenfalls angenehmer anzuhören als sein dämonischer Gesang . . ." (I, 56-57). Schrempf, Gais's librettist, excuses the master's faults with "Herr Gais hat doch nun einmal den Dämon . . ." (I, 68). The words "dämonisch" and "Dämon" are the special targets of Wolzogen's mockery. The composer can no longer create around himself an aura of the supernatural, unless he wishes to be made fun of.

However, if the composer has lost his claim to contact with another world, he still has many privileges not granted the ordinary mortal. In the company around Liszt the innocent Florian meets a Hungarian pianist, Ilonka Badacs, whom the master calls "mein Täubchen, mein höllisches" (I, 138). Ilonka seduces Florian, and he, plagued by his conscience, confesses to Liszt. The latter absolves him with the words that might be a motto for most musicians of the time: "Ein Künstler kann nicht existieren ohne die Ekstase: der Rausch der Sinne befruchtet die Phantasie, und es ist ganz gewiss, dass ein Mensch ohne Sinnlichkeit kein Künstler sein kann" (II, 39). Liszt in his own person offers an example of this concept of the artist; however Florian is too sternly devoted to musicianship (and too much in love with Thekla) to become a sensualist.

The remainder of the novel is concerned with Florian's unswerving service to music. He loses the favor of Liszt through the intrigues of Prczewalsky. (The Pole has received a second thrashing from Florian for daring to present a tone-poem, *Finis Poloniae,* to Liszt.) Ilonka partially succeeds in reuniting the master and his pupil, and Florian expends all his energies in preparing a performance of Liszts *Christus* in Berlin. Just before the concert a letter from Liszt denies Florian the right of presentation, and the young musician collapses. After a long illness he begins his musical career once again, having proved himself by his iron devotion to Liszt's creation a true musician, "der heutzutage eigentlich schon ein überlebensgrosser Kerl sein muss, wenn er den Namen verdienen will" (II, 32). These are the words of Florian's perceptive friend, the Baron von Ried, who detects in the usual musician of the day a strain of moral and intellectual rot. The novel ends when Liszt, recognizing his error, obtains a professorship for Florian at the Munich Conservatory; at last "der Kraft-Mayr" can marry his Thekla.

While the work of a satirist, Wolzogen's book is by no means negative; he is hopeful for the future of German music if its fate is left in the hands of men like Florian Mayr. Nevertheless, the reader feels uneasy after putting down *Der Kraft-Mayr*. The composer should be a more sensitive type than Florian, who is prone to solve even musical problems with his fists. Florian, "der reine Tor," has fewer descendants in the musical novel and drama than Gais, Prczewalsky, and Liszt. Gais in particular has many fellows in literature. (And it must be admitted that Wolzogen, unsympathetic to Gais as he is, lets the tolerant Liszt excuse the demonic composer: "[Gais] erschiene . . . ihm dem Grössenwahn verfallen, dem traurigen Schicksal starker Künstlernaturen, denen es an Erfolg gefehlt hat. Einige wenige unbedingte Anbeter, die einen solchen Verkannten in seiner Selbstüberhebung bestärkten, wirkten oft noch schlimmer auf ihn ein als völlige Vereinsamung," II, 58.) Gais, the composer of *Satan*, and Leverkühn, the composer of *Dr. Fausti Weheklag*, are not completely disparate figures. In literature immediately subsequent to *Der Kraft-Mayr* the supernatural talents of the demonic musician may be replaced by problems of a sexual nature; but the supernatural tradition is not dead, as Thomas Mann will eventually bear witness.

The psychological problems of the composer are given thorough treatment in a number of works. Emil Strauss in his novel, *Freund Hein* (1902), describes the youth of a musically talented individual who, kept from the art by that familiar figure, the stern father, at last kills himself. Heiner, who has felt that he should be sent to a conservatory without further ado, has been forced to repeat year after year of work at the Gymnasium. Frequently the novel becomes an attack on the examinational system of German secondary schools rather than a portrayal of a young artist. The father's opposition to a musical career stems from his own youth; the son of a violin virtuoso, he was also seized by a "musical passion" and almost allowed music to cause his failure in the law examinations. Strauss is careful to point out that the father's musical interests remained a "passion" which could be laid aside, but that in Heiner "die Musik der eigentliche Lebenstrieb war und überdies ein schöpferischer Trieb, für welchen Ausspannung und Ruhe, Abwechslung und Gegengewicht Gesundheitsbedingungen sind . . ."[3] The distinction made between the "passion" of the mere performer and the "life-impulse" of the creative musician is of particular importance for this period. In the preceding era the performer had been of nearly equal rank with the creative musician; the composer Bellini and the violinist Paganini are treated in much the same fashion by Heine, for example. Now however, the performer—whether exhibitionistic virtuoso or devoted artist—is regarded as a musician of a lower order than the composer. The gifted dilettante, such as the cousin in Storm's *Eine Halligfahrt*, is no longer possible. Music, and in particular the composition of music, has become a matter of supreme importance once more, a return, however superficial, to the ideals of Romanticism.

Heiner's sufferings may be termed Kreislerian, for they too result from a consciousness of the contrast between art and life. The youth visits a professor in whose subject he is particularly weak, hoping to obtain encouragement; when he learns that the teacher is a bad amateur musician, he feels he has debased himself by desiring to confide in such a person. His relationship with a young girl, a childhood playmate who later appears to him as musical inspiration, is again reminiscent of Kreisler's love for Julia; in both cases the beloved figure is shadowy and the love remains platonic. However, Strauss betrays the psychoanalytical interests of his time in his descriptions of Heiner's dreams, where he probes into the connection between the adolescent eroticism of Heiner and the youth's musical impulses. A girl, vaguely resembling the friend, comes to Heiner in a Grecian dress, and he believes that he is taken up into the Dionysian background with temples and dancing youths and maidens against which the vision moves: "da fühlte er auf einmal sich selbst dort stehen, mit dem Thyrsos klingend den Takt schlagen und sich im Odem der ausströmenden Musik wonnig erbeben" (299). Yet his realization that the friend is a real and quite respectable young lady has much to do with his suicide. This consciousness of the split between the ideal and reality is expressed in a scene from Heiner's last days: the girl passes down a forest road in a carriage while Heiner lies hidden beneath the trees; despite the fact that he might reach out and touch her, he creeps back into the woods where he later shoots himself.

By the friendship between Heiner and Karl Notwang, Strauss indicates in still another way the boy's consciousness of his lack of fitness for ordinary life. Strauss's treatment of the friendship theme is again more strongly sexual than similar phenomena in Romanticism. Notwang is a handsome youth whose one aim in life is to be independent; the master of every situation, he nevertheless has a warm affection for the dreamy Heiner. Heiner is likewise attracted to Notwang, but his attraction contains strong elements of hate. After they have sworn eternal friendship, Heiner beholds in his imagination the white teeth, "the blooming eyes, the silver-shining eyes" of the friend, "und ein Zorn und Abscheu gegen dieses Bild zuckte in ihm auf; aber es wich nicht, es lachte strahlend weiter . . ." (229). The dislike for Notwang also becomes an element in Heiner's death. The older youth attempts to help him revolt against his father, but Heiner resists the effort; his opposition stems not only from his love for his father, but also from his desire to escape the domination of Notwang, who could assume the father's role.

The passages concerning Heiner the musician are far less satisfactory than those concerning the hero's psychological problems. The descriptions of Heiner's compositions are of the most imprecise kind, although the "trio for piano, violin, and cello" shows Hoffmann's influence in the attribution of specific emotions and moods to the various instruments, the violin indicating "impatient desire, defiance, and blind passion," the piano representing the thunder and lightning which frighten arrogance, the cello the pain, "der sich an sich selbst ersättigt hatte" (188). Strauss also tries the stratagem, later used with varying subtlety by Jakob Wassermann and Thomas Mann, of introducing details from the lives of actual composers in order to enhance the veracity of the hero's musical character. Of such a nature is the incident, based upon a well-known Mozart legend, in Heiner's childhood where, persuaded to hold the trumpeter's music at a band concert, he is overcome by sickness at the first chord. The introduction of the vignette fails its purpose. The author does not take the trouble to devise new anecdotes about the musician's life; he employs those familiar to the reader possessing even the most superficial acquaintance with music.

In contrast to the musical sections the school incidents are original in nature; and Strauss demonstrates considerable inventiveness when he describes the traps which Heiner's subconscious lays for his intellect. While the boy is studying mathematics, he notices that instead of solving his equations he has read the letters as notes and in this way has sung an entire page to himself (243). Strauss interprets this mental trick simply as an expression of the boy's unhappiness in school. He does not indicate that Heiner has stumbled upon a relationship between music and mathematics (and a mechanical mode of composition), themes to be exploited by Mann in *Doktor Faustus* and integrated into the *ludus* of Hesse's *Glasperlenspiel*. Strauss is a modern in his attitude toward social and psychological developments; musically he has remained in the Wagnerian era, during which music was approached as an emotional rather than a coldly structural art, and so he ignores an opportunity for weaving extremely progressive musical thought into his novel. Considered musically *Freund Hein* must be classified among the treatments of the musician as a demonic figure, but the musician is overshadowed in importance by the attack on the social convention which crushes him. The book is in essence not a musical novel, but a study of the pedagogical and social problems plaguing the gifted child.

Like Heiner, the hero of Friedrich Huch's *Enzio* (1911) is a Romantic in his musical outlook, is dominated, he believes, by his father (although the domination is one of weakness rather than strength), has a friend more capable of life than himself, and finally commits suicide on the threshold of his career. Neither Heiner nor Enzio has to be a musician in order to carry out his creator's purpose: they could as easily be painters or poets. Thus music, in Huch as in Strauss, comes out second best, but where Strauss, belaboring the flaws of the Gymnasium, often approaches the level of Anklageliteratur, Huch, having stronger psychological interests, subtly depicts the destruction of the artist through an uncontrollable sexual desire.

There are three important musicians, all composers, in *Enzio*: the hero himself, his father, opera director in a small city and writer of comic operettas, and Enzio's friend Richard. The principal musical episode in *Enzio* concerns a performance of Wagner, who obviously has remained the ideal composer for Huch. Enzio is an outspoken Wagner enthusiast; Mozart's *Don Juan* seems antiquated to him, but upon hearing the *Ring* he writes to Richard: "Ich hatte keine Ahnung, dass es so etwas gibt! Dass eine Musik so weit in ihren Ausdrucksmöglichkeiten gehen kann..."[4] His father is a Wagnerite of a more practical stamp. Overlooking the soprano's shortcomings and the fact that his orchestra is too small, the director regards the production of *Tristan* on his little stage as one of the great musical events of his life. Enzio however mocks his father's sincere efforts by calling the orchestra "ein kleiner Haushalt, wo einer oft gleich für zwei arbeiten muss . . ." (311). Richard, not so ardent a Wagnerite as Enzio or the Kapellmeister, is nevertheless a complete Romantic in his devotion to Beethoven, who he says has exerted the greatest influence upon his own work (219). Huch's musicians continue to regard the Romantic spirit in music as a living force, capable of forming their own compositions. Enzio and his father, products of the same milieu, are not at all different in their artistic ideologies. The son is merely less inclined than the father to compromise with practical conditions. The musical clash between the two has its origin in the jealousy and fear which reign in the Kapellmeister's home.

Enzio dislikes his father musically and personally. The latter, a charming but sensual man, has for many years had a liaison with Fräulein Battoni, the sometime Isolde. His wife, Caecilie, devotes her love to Enzio, who responds all too easily to his mother. As Enzio matures, he becomes momentarily involved with Fräulein Battoni, but rejects her upon learning his father's secret. Henceforth mother and son form an indissoluble league against the Kapellmeister. As matters begin to go downhill for Enzio—he hastens from one exhausting love affair to another, and his compositional powers are on the wane—he places the blame for his decline ever more frequently at the feet of his father. He blurts to his friend Richard in their last conversation together: "Ich bin der Sohn meines Vaters und sein Schicksal sehe ich vor mir," and "Das Leben meines Vaters steht wie ein Orgelpunkt über meinem eigenen Leben" (502). Enzio turns against Richard in his final days, and this loss of his best friend is prompted by envy on Enzio's part, behind which there lies the old fear of becoming like his father. Richard, not bearing Enzio's "curse," will become a successful composer, while Enzio's musical career has been ended by the paralyzing idea that his father's fate awaits him.

After Richard's departure, Enzio's thoughts of his father shift from the musical field to that of personal relationships. Thinking of his coming marriage to the virtuous Irene, Enzio realizes that his bride would share the fate of his mother in her unhappy marriage; he would be unfaithful to his mother in the person of his wife. Enzio has not been quite just in attributing his downfall to his father. The real mainspring of Enzio's being has been Caecilie, and his fear of becoming like his father only disguises his basic anxiety: that he will disappoint his mother as she has so often been disappointed before by his rival. Rival is what the Kapellmeister is to Enzio; the boy is unconsciously the victim of an incestuous passion for his mother, who to all appearances returns his love. Like Frau Leverkühn, for whom Adrian has a concealed but decisive affection, Caecilie gives her son a mixed assortment of boons and burdens. Caecilie has herself awakened the sensual nature of her son, allowing him an unnatural intimacy even in childhood. While Enzio is at the conservatory, Caecilie's influence is continued by the simple Bienele; the mother promotes the affair, and even after Enzio's suicide takes Bienele and her child (of whose approaching birth Enzio has not known) into her home. Enzio, trying to flee his mother's (and Bienele's) love by resorting to mistresses like the nymphomaniac South American girl, Teresita, succeeds only in bringing about his physical collapse; he is forced to return to his mother's care. It is through the same possessiveness of his mother and her representative that Enzio is preserved for a time from destruction—but it is his mother who has encouraged his sensuality, and, more important still, has led to the fatally imitative rivalry with his father. The boy's compositions can be interpreted as his attempts to beat his father at his own game, and thus to show his mother that he is his foe's superior. Enzio, stimulated by Caecilie to be sensual like his father and yet better than he, and to be musical like his father and again better than he, finds himself at the end in a condition of physical, moral, and artistic exhaustion from which there is no escape but suicide. Irene's repugnance at Enzio's debauchery has played the smallest role in his death, and his regret at the loss of his musical gift has not whispered the final command in his ear: he has betrayed his mother, has become like his father, and is therefore, he judges, unfit to live. Enzio, sane until the end, never realizes the sinister role his mother has played in his life; Leverkühn, mad, tries to take revenge.

In *Freund Hein* and *Enzio* the musician comes to a premature end; in Hermann Bahr's one-act play, *Der arme Narr* (1906), the musician's life is cut short by madness. Bahr's play is a not very penetrating treatment of the contrast between the practical brother who has devoted his life to business and the aristic brother contemptuous of all bourgeois standards of conduct but true to his art. Bahr's attitude is summed up in the motto from Nietzsche printed on the dedication page: "Dass der am schönsten lebt, der das Dasein nicht achtet." In the course of the action the industrious Vinzenz, dying of an incurable disease, is shown the futility of his existence, while Hugo, the mad brother, demonstrates the value of an artistic life, meanwhile convincing Sophie, Vinzenz's daughter, that she too should forget the respectable standards of her father and live as she desires. "Frage nicht. Lebe. Lebe. Lebe. So lobst du Gott den Herrn."[5] What Bahr says through Hugo has been given more sincere expression by other authors. The play however does possess some interest, its hero being the first musician in German literature whose madness is definitely attributed to a physiological cause. Bahr makes it clear that Hugo's mental decay is the result of his youthful indiscretions. Hugo is partially modeled on Hugo Wolf, who had died three years before the publication of the play. The play is as much an apology for Wolf's life as it is a bearer of Bahr's own ideas; and as the playwright allows Hugo to declare that he regrets nothing, so he praises the character of Wolf. The manner in which Bahr gives a loftier significance to his hero's malady looks ahead to Mann's *Doktor Faustus,* where the hero is likewise overcome by insanity resulting from venereal disease. The final scene of the play, where Hugo defends his life before the assembled company of more prosaic individuals, resembles the episode near the end of Mann's novel in which Leverkühn both defends and accuses himself. Both Bahr and Mann are completely Romantic in their conception of the musician as the chosen individual mediating between man and powers greater than himself. Hugo speaks of descending to the ocean bottom, to the "Gottesgrund:" "Da hab ich für die Menschen dann das Leuchten heraufgeholt" (86). Leverkühn (who also makes an imaginary submarine journey) takes the more pessimistic view of things and calls himself one who has loaded the sins of the century onto his shoulders by inviting the devil to be his guest; but in doing so he also designates himself as the exceptional individual. The privileges of the exceptional personality are expanded to the utmost in Bahr's play. Even the burned-out genius is now to be honored; any social stigma attached to his disease is to be forgotten in a period when the artist, to speak with Wolzogen's Liszt, requires ecstasy at any cost.

A freakish psychological treatment of the musician is to be found in the little work, *Kapellmeister Kreisler* (1906), of Richard Schaukal, like Bahr an Austrian. *Kapellmeister Kreisler*, an "imaginary portrait" consisting of thirteen "vigils" supposedly written by Hoffmann's musical hero, is not original, but it provides an instructive contrast to the genuine Kreisler stories. The erotic element in Kreisler, idealized by Hoffmann, is presented in a much crasser light. The brutal incident between Caecilie and George in *Die neuesten Schicksale des Hundes Berganza* is plundered by Schaukal for its more unpleasant details. The element of adultery is also introduced by giving Kreisler a wife, a character taken from Hoffmann's own life. The figure of Hedwiga from *Kater Murr* adds another feature to Kreisler's adulterous visions, and a liaison is mentioned as leading to Hedwiga's suicide; Kreisler and his wife must flee, but during their escape the wife is killed, an event arousing no grief in the musician. Undoubtedly Schaukal intends these lurid happenings of the final vigil as a kind of wish-dream, although it must be granted that he avoids the clinical quality of some of his contemporaries (such as Schnitzler) by his effort to imitate Hoffmann's more exalted atmosphere.

In his portrait of Kreisler's psyche Schaukal stresses a detail not to be found in the Kreisler-writings and which does not seem to have played a major role in Hoffmann's own life: the composer's love for his little daughter, Caecilie. The Hoffmann couple had only one child, named Caecilie in honor of music's patron saint. It is certainly tempting to play with the possibility that the girl might have been a source of joy to her unhappy father, had she lived, a temptation to which even so solid a biographer as Walther Harich almost succumbs, but Schaukal's interpretation of the figure seems a gross exaggeration. Hoffmann's Julia-cult is changed into a child-cult. Kreisler has transformed his little daughter into a saint: "Ich bete zu meiner kleinen Heiligen"[6] and it is his child whom he sees "in jedem Weibe, das mir etwas bedeuten will, das wie ein Auge sich auftut nach dem Paradiese . . ." (79). Just why Schaukal emphasizes this feature is difficult to say; Hoffmann was less interested in the figure of the child than many Romantic writers, and although the child was important to Romanticism as a symbol of purity, it is strange to see it substituted for Hoffmann's ethereal embodiment of music, the Julia-figure. An explanation might be that the woman-artist has come to possess quite a different meaning for the authors of the present period. In earlier literature there appear a number of female musicians who are the very essence of purity; but rarely is a woman-musician in the literature of the post-Wagnerian period free from a sexual taint. The ideal, when it is still called for, is now best represented by the very young child. The child ideal will appear in Wassermann's *Das Gänsemännchen*, Schickele's *Symphonie für Jazz*, and, most brilliantly, in Mann's little Nepomuk Scheidewein, the joy and inspiration of Leverkühn's last years.

The problem of the composer and his relationship to his wife, is the subject of Arthur Schnitzler's play *Zwischenspiel*, written in 1904. The hero of the play, Amadeus (after Mozart) lives in what he believes is a happy marriage with his wife Caecilie. Therefore he does not worry about a possible liaison between Caecilie and Prince Sigismund, while she has no fears about his relationship to his pupil, the Countess Friederike. Amadeus seems domesticated, perhaps even more so than Mörike's Mozart. In addition, he has the highest regard for his wife as an artist, a fact of which he often reminds her. When he composes an opera, the soprano role is written for her alone. Unfortunately he carries his Kreislerian regard for the woman as embodiment of music so far that he allows a division to arise between his treatment of his wife as an artist and as a woman. He makes a short concert tour with Friederike, a woman whom, as he tells himself, he cannot truly love because he despises her as an artist, persuading himself that he is thus not unfaithful to his wife, since she still remains the beloved ideal. His wife however is by no means a placid Constanze Mozart, but a modern woman; she also wishes to have certain rights as a woman and as an artist other than those which Amadeus is willing to grant her, and so the marriage is finally broken up. Amadeus has been led to cause the failure of his marriage by two factors: his all too prosaic acceptance of Caecilie as his faithful wife and his extreme idealization of her as an artist, both faults which are to be expected in the nature of the genius. Schnitzler, unlike other authors of the period, does not grant the genius unlimited privileges; a marriage satisfactory to both parties, not the production of a work of art, should be the matter of prime importance. However Schnitzler is enough influenced by the contemporary conception of the genius to grant that Amadeus could not have acted otherwise. A true genius, he is childlike, incapable of the dissimulation that would be required to make his marriage a success: he cannot act the part of the eternally interested lover when he needs peace and quiet in which to create his works. As his friend Albert says at the beginning of the play: "Verstellung liegt deiner Natur fern. Wenn du einmal in die Lage kämst, einem Wesen gegenüber, das dir nahesteht, Komödie zu spielen, so gingst du daran zugrunde."[7]

Jakob Wassermann in *Das Gänsemännchen* (1915) considers the musician in marriage and then proceeds to more artistic themes. It is typical of the period that while the section of the novel dealing with the *mariage à trois* of the composer Daniel Nothafft is successful, that which concerns Daniel's musical development is not. Nothafft is probably the most plagued musician in German literature; yet his tribulations are social and psychological, not musical. Unlike most literary composer-heroes, his chief handicap has been a grinding poverty, depicted with all the grubby detail at Wassermann's command. While the problem was a real one in the lives of many historical composers, it is not commonly treated in the novels concerning the composer, although it appears in some of the works concerning the Spielmann and his descendants. Poverty has in general been avoided: some writers, such as Hoffmann, Mörike, and Thomas Mann, are more concerned with questions of music and the musical genius, others devote themselves to a psychological consideration of the musician. Only Brachvogel, in his *Friedemann Bach*, has heretofore said much about the destitute composer, and that destitution is so romanticized that the reader does not realize its grimness, an effect which Brachvogel has intended: the description of poverty is dull when extended throughout the course of the artist-novel. Wassermann disregards this fact; there is scarcely a page of his novel which does not catalogue Nothafft's distressing circumstances. As a result we learn a great deal about Nothafft's struggle for existence, and relatively little about his efforts to compose.

The tale of Nothafft's financial woes turns upon a melodramatic device: he has been cheated of his inheritance by a rascally uncle. As a result he never receives a formal musical education; borrowing a page from the life of Brahms, Wassermann puts his hero to work as a pianist in a bordello, whence he passes to employment as a teacher and as conductor for a wretched opera troupe. When he finally obtains his inheritance, he has become so involved with a number of women that the money is of little help. Like Mann's Leverkühn he meets a prostitute, the Zingarella; after her suicide Daniel keeps her death mask with him as a source of inspiration. Of Daniel's numerous other affairs the most interesting is the "marriage" with two sisters (patterned on that of the poet Bürger) which culminates in tragedy. A later marital experience with a young girl completes Daniel's disillusionment: she betrays him with another man and disappears. Daniel realizes that as an artist he has arrogated every privilege to himself without assuming responsibility for his acts. The Goose-Man, a figure which surmounts a Nürnberg fountain, has come to serve as a patron saint for Daniel. When the composer is in despair over his betrayal by his wife, the Goose-Man appears with the command: "Wende deinen Blick ab vom Phantom und werde erst Mensch, dann kannst du Schöpfer sein. Bist du Mensch, wahrhaft Mensch, dann bedarf es vielleicht gar nicht des Werkes, dann strahlt vielleicht die Kraft und die Herrlichkeit von dir selber aus."[8] Daniel returns to his boyhood home, and lives in saint-like retirement, surrounded by his pupils, who revere him because of his humanity and his selfless devotion to the art. The majority of Daniel's works have been burned up in a fire, the composer has however come to realize that not the work but the man is important. His students and his son receive all his attentive love.

Nothafft began to write music without the slightest training; Wassermann leads us to presume that he, like Wagner, teaches himself by studying the scores of the classics. His compositions, all for chorus and orchestra, perhaps betray a Brahmsian nature; his chief production is the composition of Goethe's "Harzreise im Winter," a poem likewise set to music by Brahms in his *Alto Rhapsody*. We know nothing of how Nothafft stands in relationship to the musical problems of his day (the composer presumably comes into his maturity in the nineties). Wassermann maintains strict silence on the operas Nothafft conducts and the methods he uses, preferring to describe his troupe's financial troubles. The novel contains in effect fewer passages about music than any other of the longer works with a musician as hero; its conversations on art consist of generalities about the nature of genius, its rights and its duties. The musical purpose of the book is to demonstrate the bankruptcy of the old Romantic conception of the genius, or, more accurately, the bankruptcy of an exaggerated version of that conception. The loving care with which Wassermann investigates Nothafft's destitution is not a result of his desire to describe a very typical condition in the life of the actual composer; Wassermann intends rather to provide a cause for Daniel's moral blindness. Nothafft has been so poorly treated by life that he reacts by demanding too much from it. Nor is the series of women who fall into Daniel's hands adduced in an effort to point out psychological complexities in the composer: through these women he may express his rights as an artist. As the problem of Nothafft's blindness is stated in the least subtle terms, so its solution deals in extremities. The novel's closing pages indicate not only an irrevocable abandonment of the worship of the abnormal personality, but of the creator in any form. The burning of Nothafft's compositions symbolizes the rejection of art for life; when a student asks him: "Und das Werk, Meister?," he merely smiles (605). Instead of preaching a more modest attitude for the composer akin to that of a Bach, Wassermann baldly denies him. Wassermann's solution, as we shall see, achieved a not inconsiderable progeny.

The unlimited rights of the artist have been extended to the woman musician. In Romanticism woman had been an ideal figure, in Biedermeier and Poetic Realism a housewife, real or potential. And in Romanticism, only the Italian women musicians had any trace of evil about them; however Wilhelm Hauff, otherwise so unoriginal, understood the unhappy position of the woman singer: his Giuseppa is treated as if she were a piece of property, a fair prey for all. The rare "bad women" of Biedermeier, Mundt's Fanchon, and Gutzkow's Lodoiska, are painted sympathetically, but Johanna Kinkel is less forgiving in her portraits of Italian singers and Anglo-Irish adventuresses. In the late nineteenth century the problem of the woman musician begins to receive more common and more varied scrutiny: if she follows her profession and yet allows herself to be controlled by others, she is regarded as immoral; if she insists on her rights, either as a woman or as an artist, she may wreck her life. The majority of the works about women musicians may be considered a part of the feminist movement of the time. A musical milieu is chosen because the woman artist has more arguments for emancipation at her disposal than the non-artist. Thus a confusion arises in almost all portrayals of the woman artist: an argument is seemingly offered for the right of woman to live as an artist, but suddenly this argument changes into one for woman's rights as a human being.

The first of the stories in this group was written in 1874, yet it is like a work of the nineties in almost every respect. Only the conclusion of Ferdinand von Saar's *Die Geigerin* indicates a more conservative standpoint: in the final analysis Saar has little regard for woman's artistic rights. His tale concerns three musical sisters, Anna, Mimi, and Ludovica. Anna's fate is that of the woman musician in the Biedermeier; she marries and has children. Mimi takes the primrose path and becomes a cabaret singer, as well as the mistress of a succession of wealthy men. Ludovica suffers the most unhappy fate: she falls desperately in love with Alexis, a financial speculator, who uses her to obtain money from the narrator, a scholar. The scholar, in love with her, accedes to her wishes, and even after he learns that Alexis has deserted Ludovica for Mimi, he attempts to persuade his rival to return to the more respectable sister. Later, mortally ill and deserted by Mimi, Alexis dies in Ludovica's arms. Ludovica then marries a degenerate baron whom she supports by giving music lessons; when he orders her to prostitute herself to gain more money, she commits suicide. In this harrowing story Saar asks: "Wie es kam, dass [Ludovica] in törichter Umkehrung der Verhältnisse für diejenigen zu sorgen bemüht war, welche für sie zu sorgen die Verpflichtung hatten [?]"[9] The tendency to "Hörigkeit," later to become so much a matter of concern to Wedekind and Bahr, is already present in the character of Ludovica. Mimi, on the contrary, represents the more independent type of woman we shall get to know in transfigured form in Hofmannsthal's *Der Abenteurer und die Sängerin*: like Vittoria, Mimi has left woman's usual and respected place to venture into what may be called "the world of art" (in Mimi's case it might more accurately be called the world of no moral scruples). There she has placed herself on an equal footing with men, has used them, and has apparently triumphed over them.

Ludovica's relationship to art casts a light upon the whole problem of the woman in music. Her musicianship is none too firm. When she is about to throw herself away in her devotion to Alexis, the scholar reminds her that she has her art to console her. She replies that once music was the only joy in her life: "Aber jetzt hass' ich [die Saiten] und nur manchmal überkommt es mich, darin zu wüten, dass sie zerspringen wie mein Herz!" (VII, 192). For most of the women in the literature of the period, music is an emotional matter from the beginning, and when a stronger emotion appears, music is forgotten without a qualm. From this cause, too, arises the fateful confusion between artistic and human values in works on the woman musician; reacting with her emotions alone, she cannot separate art from life. Only the heroine of Heinrich Mann's *Die Branzilla* is able to make an absolute separation of the two and she does so at the cost of becoming a monster.

In some of the works on the woman musician music is given almost no treatment, while all emphasis is laid on the social problem. Such is the case with Sudermann's popular but undistinguished *Heimat*.[10] The old father-daughter conflict of the bourgeois tragedy is given a new form: the daughter is an artist. She has left her unhappy home to seek fame as a singer; a social rather than a musical impulse has made her devote her life to the art. Magda's family at first accepts her upon her return to her home city during a concert tour, but when it is learned that she has had an affair with the man who now wishes to marry her, a tragic outcome ensues. Sudermann is obviously on the side of his heroine. He does not condemn her for her moral downfall; he damns those who have forced her to the steps she has taken: her officer father, her stepmother, and her seducer. The dramatist removes the problem entirely to a social plane: Magda's desire to become an artist has social motives, her love of the artistic life is a social one, and her downfall social. She has not given much to music, and she pursues a musical career only for the material well-being it offers her; when she decides to remain at home, she regrets the loss of her freedom and of whatever comforts she possessed in her career as a singer. Sudermann's play, written in 1893, strikes the tone for future and more subtle works concerning the woman artist. Music plays a negligible role; the social and moral question is more important.

As might be expected, Schnitzler, in his short novel, *Frau Berta Garlan* (1901), takes a relatively anti-artistic attitude. His thesis is that the really good woman should not attempt to live the life of an artist (that is, to live immorally), however convinced she may be that she is acting in a noble fashion. She can only cheapen herself by such a decision. His heroine, a widow, supports herself and her son by giving piano lessons in the provincial town to which her husband had brought her from Vienna. Learning that a former conservatory sweetheart, now a famous violin virtuoso, is in the capital, she goes there and gives herself to him. Emil, the virtuoso, consents to see her now and then when he is free from his other engagements, but Frau Berta comes to realize that "sie nicht von denen war, die mit leichtem Sinn beschenkt, die Freuden des Lebens ohne Zagen trinken dürfen."[11] Berta is no artist—Emil says that she has a pretty talent for salon music. She tries to convince herself that she loves Emil as a musician, and can imagine no greater joy than that he play for her, but Schnitzler mercilessly exposes her self-delusion; unsatisfied by her brief marriage, aroused by the attentions of other men, her adventure with Emil has been "die letzten Schauer einer verlangenden Weiblichkeit" (II, 180). At the conservatory she had rejected Emil; now he becomes the principal object of her desires. Any artistic pretenses she may have had are removed. The novel is not a study of art at all, nor even of the rights of woman as an artist; it is a description of the transient moral collapse of a virtuous if pedestrian woman.

In the two plays from 1906, Bahr's *Die Andere* and Wedekind's *Musik*, the outcome is not so positive as in *Frau Berta Garlan*. Schnitzler's Berta comes to her senses and devotes herself to the rearing of her child, but Bahr's heroine dies of disease, and Wedekind's goes mad. In *Die Andere*, the heroine, a sensitive violinist, is seduced by a coarse impresario, Amschl, who finally deserts her when he sees she is about to die. *Die Andere* has inherited much of the apparatus of Saar's *Die Geigerin*. Both heroines, violinists, are in love with worthless individuals, and both are hopelessly loved by good and devoted men, in Saar's novella a scholar writing a *Geschichte der Menschheit vom Standpunkte der Ethik*, in Bahr's play a brilliant professor of history. Saar and Bahr give their works a certain Viennese melancholy; viewing the tragedies of their heroines as inevitable, they are not so morally indignant as Wedekind.

Bahr is however more depressing than his forerunner, since Saar's Alexis at least is charming, while Bahr's Amschl is the epitome of vulgarity. The relationship between Alexis and Ludovica has the semblance of a love affair. Amschl is in contrast an ugly representative of the Svengali-type, whose power over Lida, the violinist, is hypnotic; as soon as he appears, she falls into a state of cringing obedience. The element of fear inherent in the relationship between the two is suggested in a scene which occurs just before they set out upon a concert tour, and but a few hours after Lida has decided (in vain) to marry the history professor. Amschl scratches his finger on a rose stem; taking the stem from its vase, he lets it whistle sharply up and down through the air; then, threateningly, he says to the paralyzed Lida; "Hauen sollt' man dich, Lämmchen! Einfach . . . 'mal stramm verhauen. Das schlimme Kind."[12] Amschl's domination of Lida is the most interesting feature of what otherwise is a dull and confused play. Lida is on the threshold of a neurosis (she cannot stand excessively bright light or loud noise), and a possible connection exists between this hypersensitive condition and the heroine's final illness; but Bahr does not make the connection clear, just as he merely implies that there may be a link between Lida's hypersensitivity and her musicianship. An attempt is made to give the play a greater significance by the addition of a political background: the professor, Hess, is offered a vital government post which he rejects because of his broken heart, and as Lida dies a revolution breaks out. The play's value remains in its brief but trenchant treatment of the problem of "Hörigkeit."

Wedekind's *Musik* confines itself to a single theme, the degradation of the trustful singer by her teacher. The bond between Klara Hühnerwadel and Josef Reissner differs slightly from that between Lida and Amschl. Klara is a respectable but ambitious young woman whose desire it is to become a Wagnerian singer; she seems willing to go to any lengths to achieve this ambition. Unfortunately she falls into the hands of Reissner, whose exploitation of her musical enthusiasm ends in a visit to an abortionist. An opportunity comes for her to accept an excellent position in Switzerland, but she is forced by the discovery of the scandal to flee to Antwerp. At her teacher's request, she returns to Berlin and to a jail sentence for abortion: he has convinced her that only in Germany is there a possibility of an artistic career. After Klara's release Reissner fathers her second child, upon whose birth she insists. The child dies and Klara goes mad. Does Klara continue to follow her teacher's wishes out of sexual attraction or devotion to music? Throughout the first four acts the play seems to be a horrifying set of variations on the Griselda-theme. However in the last act the emphasis is shifted. At its climax Klara cries: "Musik! Musik!—Was habe ich um deinetwillen auf Gottes Welt schon ausgestanden."[13] Wedekind intends the spectator to think that Klara has lived in the conviction that she has been serving music, although she has in truth been the victim of a perverted passion for Reissner. The closing line would indicate such an ironical meaning for the play. A friend, who has followed the whole sordid story, remarks upon seeing the beginning madness of Klara: "Die kann ein Lied singen!" (V, 104). At any event Klara has the saving illusion which neither Ludovica nor Lida possesses; she at least thinks she is serving the art of music.

In *Die Andere* and *Musik* there is a tacit disapproval of granting too much freedom to women, but both playwrights destroy the effect of their criticism of the artistic life by making the women artists prey to implausible monsters. In this respect Schnitzler has proved himself cleverer by depicting his Emil as a by no means predatory fellow; Amschl and Reissner can hardly be considered as valid objections to the artistic life. Thus far no argument has been presented for the woman as artist, but rather for the rights of woman as a human being. Sudermann turns his play into a question of morals; Bahr and Schnitzler consider psychological phenomena. Wedekind apparently argues for the rights of woman as an artist, but Klara too is the victim of a psychological flaw.

None of these tortured women musicians can claim intellectual achievements in music; creatures of emotion, their emotionalism forms their attitude toward the art. In the novels of Max Dauthendey, *Josa Gerth* (1892) and *Raubmenschen* (1911), there are women musicians of a more clever type; but here the emotions—and Dauthendey's frenetic action—get in the way of the woman's mental work. Josa Gerth is a high-strung young woman whose first "love affairs" are with feminine musicians, Fräulein von Auer, a concert pianist, and Josa's piano teacher, Martha Starke. Josa Gerth is inordinately sensitive to music, experiencing her strongest feelings for her two idols when she hears them play. Fräulein von Auer's music, in the description of which a Kreislerian instability can be detected, stimulates Josa dangerously: "Sie stachelte die Töne, peitschte,—Flucht, Verfolgung—unbändige Lust, plötzlich—Schwäche, zitternde Ermattung, süsstaumelnd—ein Bäumen, Aufraffen—klaffende Tiefe, verzweifelter Sprung—Leere, Einsamkeit, kreisende Stille."[14] Martha Starke lulls Josa with her playing: "In Josa wurde es wunschlos, so ruhig . . . Von den Tönen umschmiegt schloss sie die Augen, und ihre Gedanken huschten wie Sonnenstrahlen durch rosenrote Einsamkeiten" (III, 453). The synaesthetic effects recall another feature of the music played by Kreisler to his club. Josa is a Romantic, more sensitive to music than her sister musicians of the fin-de-siècle, who are, ironically, professional musicians where Josa is not. Josa, like Antonie Krespel and that convalescent Romantic, Camilla Rikar, is not strong enough to survive a constant contact with music; the sound of bells brings her near to collapse: "Jeder Laut ein Bild. . . . Die Phantasie tanzte, wirbelte in tollen Sprüngen, von den Tonstimmen angefeuert. Allmählich begannen ihre Glieder zu schmerzen. Müde Sehnsucht zerrte an ihren Nerven" (III, 448-449).

Josa, ever the Romantic, becomes an enthusiast for religion and marries the theologian Theodor. The marriage is not a success, Josa's synaesthetic visions on the morning after the wedding notwithstanding (". . . ein Feuerwirbel löste sich goldtriefend, stieg gellend höher, immer goldschmetternder . . ." III, 512); and the bride, reacting against her husband, writes a book on free thought. After the marriage *Josa Gerth* says little about music; its second part concerns Josa's platonic love affair with a botanist (with whom she has synaesthetic conversations: "Sie . . . verglichen jede Farbe mit einem schrillen oder sanften Ton," III, 497), her desertion of Theodor, their reunion and final separation. Dauthendey's portrait of the Romantic woman musician against the late nineteenth century background remains one of those tantalizing and unfulfilled promises in the literature on the musician, like Rochlitz's *Aus dem Leben eines Tonkünstlers* or Kürnberger's *Giovanna*.

As far as music is concerned, *Josa Gerth* draws upon the past. *Raubmenschen*, building upon the thought of Goethe's *Wilhelm Meisters Wanderjahre*, predicts a future development of the musical novel—not that Goethean serenity has much influence in Dauthendey's hectic world. Rennewart meets an astronomer and his musician wife, Hanna, on board ship to Mexico. Once arrived in the tropics, Rennewart conquers a local beauty, who however is murdered by her fiancé. The astronomer also dies, and Rennewart and his widow, quick to fall in love, return to Europe together. In Paris Hanna is killed during a hotel fire. This outline of the bloodstained plot will reveal no intrinsic connection with music; yet Hanna possesses some most interesting ideas on the subject. Tired of the musical refinements of modern Europe, she hopes to find an artistic Garden of Eden in Mexico. In her studies of Aztec culture she discovers that music had a primary role in the structure of the Indians' state: "Die Kathedrale sei der Tempel der Sonne gewesen, links davon die Tanzakademie, rechts die Musikakademie, und an der vierten Seite der Königspalast. Und es sei damals Sitte gewesen, dass jeder Bürger sein Examen im Spielen irgendeines Instruments ablegte, um die Bürgerrechte zu erlangen" (III, 683-684). Music is a means of attaining social maturity, a means of education. Hesse in *Das Glasperlenspiel* will construct a state much like that of Hanna's Aztecs, although in his case it will be based upon a study of Oriental culture.

Hanna's reverence for the Mexican past contrasts painfully with her contempt for the Mexican present. When the Aztecs' descendants, having lost their noble art, sing about "tomales calientes," the disillusioned Hanna exchanges her admiration of Indian culture for a tradition even older but closer to the European soul. Before leaving for Mexico, Hanna was given a copy of the Apollo-hymn, recently discovered during excavations at Delphi. She does not play the hymn in the New World, but on the way back to Europe, after the ship has almost sunk in a storm, she performs it on the salon piano as an act of thanksgiving: "Diese einfache, wunderbare Harmonie, dieser wandelnde Takt griechischer Tänzerinnen, die um Apollos Altar wandeln, indessen das Altarfeuer senkrecht ins Himmelsblau nach Vereinigung mit der blauen Weltseele strebt, mit der Weltseele des Dichtergottes Apollo" (III, 928). Does European music need a return to the sincerity and simplicity (and to the religious-political function) which it had in the ancient world?

Hanna is capable of pondering questions which are beyond the capacity of her sister (and brother) musicians from the decades before 1914. She might easily be a contemporary of Werfel's Verdi, Mann's Leverkühn, or Hesse's Josef Knecht, all of whom are the products of a belief that European musical thought has grown topheavy and decadent, that "a return to the beginnings" must be made. However Dauthendey does not call for primitivism of the type Leverkühn occasionally proposes. He desires a return to an earlier culture, not to the absolute source of the art, to, as Mann's humanistic Zeitblom would say, "the howl." Dauthendey's musicologist is pregnant with the most fascinating musical thought. It is a pity for musical literature that she dies without attempting to carry out her reforms.

In other works from the period the woman as artist receives a more satisfactory treatment, but the confusion between artistic and human questions seems to remain unavoidable. Hugo von Hofmannsthal demonstrates this fact in his drama, *Der Abenteurer und die Sängerin* (1899), a picture of life in eighteenth-century Venice. Its principal characters are Vittoria, a singer, and Baron Weidenstamm, an adventurer who many years before has been her lover. Now the singer is married to a respectable nobleman, Cesarino, and passes off her and Weidenstamm's son as her brother. In one of those gorgeous speeches with which the play is replete, Vittoria tells how her voice too was born of her affair with the baron:

> In deiner Liebe, nur aus ihr genährt,
> unfähig, anderswo nur einen Tag
> sich zu erathmen, einzig nur bekleidet
> mit Farb', aus diesem Element gesogen,
> wuchs dieses Wunder, dies Kind der Luft,
> Sklavin und Herrin der Musik, Geschwister
> der weissen Götter die im Boden schlafen,
> das Ding, das ich so: meine Stimme nenne,
> wie Einer traumhaft sagt: mein guter Geist![15]

Reverence for the source of her voice at first prevents Vittoria from giving herself to the Baron once more; when she learns that the Baron, a common roué, has confused her with another love, she realizes the sordidness of her former relationship. Thoughts of her duty to Cesarino are awakened; thus she is led back to her husband first of all through her music, secondly through the realization that her adventure with Weidenstamm, however worthwhile its results may have been, was hopelessly immoral: "Auf dem Rand des Bettes sassen wir wie bleiche Mörder!" (191). The result is the same as in *Frau Berta Garlan*, but the problem is actually an artistic one (Vittoria loves the creator of her voice, not a sensual image), and the solution is achieved partially through artistic means. Again the question remains: is it Vittoria's indignation as an artist or as a woman that leads her to reject Weidenstamm? In all probability Hofmannsthal intends us to think it is both.

The main theme of the play is however that Weidenstamm emerges from all his adventures with empty hands, while Vittoria has received not only a handsome son but a beautiful voice, through which she has made her career and won her husband. Even the old and illustrious composer has not had Vittoria's good fortune; so aged that he no longer recognizes his own music, he sits babbling in a corner as Vittoria sings arias from his operas. The husband, Cesarino, also lives in a certain emptiness; he does not realize that his wife has never loved him and that she has been inspired to remain faithful to him out of wounded pride, feminine or artistic. In the final scene he appears as a sorry figure, despite his noble qualities; the Baron has departed, having convinced Cesarino that he was the lover of Vittoria's mother, not of the singer herself. Cesarino listens enchanted as his wife sings the aria from *Ariadne* which she has not essayed for years; ironically not he but the fickle adventurer Weidenstamm has made Vittoria perform her greatest number. Vittoria stands alone, surrounded by hollow figures; even the Baron cannot appreciate what he has inspired. Hofmannsthal has transformed many musical values of previous literature: the performer, not the creative musician, is important, the woman is not the inspiration but gives that rather thankless role to the man. Also, Vittoria is hardly to be called Weidenstamm's victim in view of the situation as it exists at the end of the play; she vanquishes those who seek to exploit her. As an artist she has triumphed over the composer and over the creator of her voice, as a woman she has triumphed over her former lover. She has done so at the expense of losing her last illusions concerning her single great passion, but she has become a greater artist and a nobler woman for all that.

Heinrich Mann in his short novella, *Die Branzilla*, has a heroine who sacrifices everything to art: it is questionable if she possesses any of the traits of the human being. The Branzilla is not destroyed by her devotion; she destroys others by means of it. In this respect she might seem to be an exaggerated version of Vittoria, who survives triumphant among the defeated men in her life; but she does not achieve the human victory of Hofmannsthal's heroine, her life being from start to finish artistic. Mann's story is a brutal one, told without the psychological refinements common in the works of the Viennese. The Branzilla allows her young patron, who reveres her, to be executed by the Austrian police so that she may save her career, she poisons a rival soprano, she falls in love with a tenor because he can sing almost as well as she, and punishes herself because she sees something earthly in her love. Her suspicions of her own weakness do not prove to be true; when he loses his voice she drives him to suicide. The tale ends as she forces her daughter to take up a musical career; she intends that her name shall be known to the public even after her death. Mann's singer is an isolated feminine representative of unswerving devotion to art; and her devotion does not take the relatively harmless form of Berglinger's or Kreisler's. Mann implies at the end of the tale that he thinks the woman mad: her daughter threatens repeatedly to have her confined in an insane asylum.

Yet Mann, writing an apology for the virtuoso, as it were, attempts to discover what prompts the Branzilla to commit her dreadful acts. She is an Italian and a devout Catholic, and to her, as to so many other musicians in literature, music is a divine service. She is as much dedicated to it—and through it to the service of God—as any nun to the service of the Church. After she lets her young admirer be executed, she tells herself that she has done well, for the nobleman was a stranger to her religion. He has loved her, not her art, and so has attempted to keep her from her salvation. "Denn ich lebte fern von den Freuden der Welt, hatte keinen Teil an den flüchtigen Lüsten der Menschen und arbeitete in der Zucht des Herrn für die Ewigkeit. Ich bin seine Nonne; nun will er mich in seine Gnade aufnehmen, ich soll seinen Glanz sehen."[16] During her love affair with the tenor, she turns once more to God in asking refuge from her earthly passion, and when the tenor loses his voice she views this misfortune as a just punishment "dafür, dass er sich selbst und die Kunst verliess und unheilig lebte" (X, 273). In Mann's opinion the virtuoso performer is as much a servant of the divine as the composer, and his service may demand even greater sacrifices (if the killing of others may be called a sacrifice) than that of the creative musician, who lives a less competitive life.

The Branzilla's devotion to music has been destructive to others; in Thomas Mann's *Tristan* a woman's love for music contributes to her own destruction. Frau Klöterjahn is the sickly wife of an industrialist. During her sojourn at a tuberculosis sanatorium in the Alps, she carries on a flirtation with an author, Detlev Spinell. The climax of their relationship is the piano performance by Frau Klöterjahn of excerpts from *Tristan und Isolde*. The doctors have forbidden her to play but she cannot resist the temptation. Soon thereafter her condition worsens and she dies. (Could Hoffmann's *Rat Krespel* have provided Mann with a part of his plot?) As elsewhere in Thomas Mann, Romantic music and death are equated. The longing for beauty is likewise a longing for destruction; and Frau Klöterjahn's brief fling at the artistic life has brought her death, in contrast to Berta Garlan, who is improved by her experience. Mann offers a choice between the realm of art, beauty, and death, and the gross but living world of Herr Klöterjahn and his little son. The choice is apparently made more difficult by portraying the "musical seducer" not as the young composer of *Rat Krespel*, but as the stunted grotesque, Spinell. It is he who persuades the sick woman to play once more: "Wenn Sie fürchten, sich zu schaden, gnädige Frau, so lassen Sie die Schönheit tot und stumm, die unter Ihren Fingern laut werden möchte."[17] But Mann views Spinell with sympathy, just as he has a basic sympathy for the decay inherent in Romantic music, although he parodies the cowardice of the little man and finally lets him run away in the face of the howling and healthy Klöterjahn child. Mann does not put his final blessing on either the world of Spinell or that of Klöterjahn, yet we are left feeling that he has decided in favor of the spokesman of art.

In Max Halbe's *Die Tat des Dietrich Stobäus* (1911) still another woman musician apparently dies for her art, but the boundary between the artistic and the human spheres is difficult to distinguish. Of all the erring sisters from the period, Karola Bergmann is the most lighthearted and, in a healthy way, the most sensual. Dietrich Stobäus undertakes an affair with the ballet dancer Karola; discovering her voice, he has her trained as a singer. For all her volatility Karola can turn even a shallow role into something much better: "Karolas süsse, innige Stimme hatte den gewöhnlichsten Liedchen, den seichtesten Couplets so etwas wie einen Schimmer von Ewigkeit, einen Unterton letzter menschlicher Dinge, von Glück, Liebe, Vergänglichkeit oder dergleichen verliehen."[18] Halbe, almost alone among portrayers of the woman musician, does not connect moral character and the quality of the music produced. Vittoria has her apotheosis while regretting the sins of her past, and the Branzilla, criminal as she may be, still possesses a code of conduct which Karola does not. Mundt's Fanchon and Saar's Mimi, morally weak, can excel only in frivolous music. Male musicians, on the contrary, often can produce noble music after their "fall;" witness Florian Mayr or Bahr's Hugo. Karola, musically speaking, is granted the same freedom of conduct as her male companions.

Nevertheless, literary musicians, male or female, sooner or later receive some kind of punishment for their transgressions. Only Wolzogen's Liszt seems to go scot-free; the Enzios, the Nothaffts, and the Hugos receive their just deserts, although not necessarily in a musical form. Karola suffers a fate as unhappy as any of the rest. Stobäus proposes marriage to Karola; refused, he pushes her from a cliff into the sea. (Or perhaps she falls: one of the novel's extra-musical problems concerns the actuality of Stobäus's "deed.") What is the motivation behind Karola's refusal? Does she think that she can better serve her art if she remains independent, or is she more attracted by the freedom of the artist's life, the public's acclamations? From what we know of Karola, we should guess that she refuses for the more selfish cause. Yet the pleasure with which she uses her voice should not be forgotten, nor has she ignored the words of the old singer Pellerini: "Die Kunst ist eine eifersüchtige Geliebte ... und niemand kann zweien Herren dienen, mein Kind" (189). And Stobäus himself does not know whether it is the woman or the artist he loves: "Wird es nicht immer das Weib sein, das in der Sängerin über die Menge triumphiert, und ist es nicht umgekehrt vielleicht doch die Sängerin, die ich unbewusst wieder im Weibe liebe, dies Theaterblut, dies Zigeunertum, was mich so sehr an ihr anzieht, mich nicht loskommen lässt?" (448-449). Perhaps the artist cannot be separated from the woman. Men, Halbe infers, are in part to blame for the indissoluble union, since in the woman artist they see the woman's desirability heightened. A taint of the lawlessness once imputed to all "entertainers" has clung to the woman musician. She will never be free of sexual connotations. Halbe, like the Mann brothers and Hofmannsthal, seems to speak in favor of woman's artistic rights; none of them takes—or is able to take—an unqualified stand.

The same confusion does not exist with respect to the virtuoso type; here opinions are sharply outlined. A small group, consisting of the Mann brothers and a few other writers, regards the virtuoso with understanding but recognizes the evil inherent in his conception of music; another and larger group parodies him. Heinrich Mann, as we have seen, discerns the quasi-religious motives behind the action of the Branzilla, but does not go so far as to condone them. However he, like his brother Thomas in *Das Wunderkind* (1903), realizes that there is a certain dignity in the virtuoso, a being at once selfish and selfless. The attitude of both the Manns toward the performer is spoken by a critic in Thomas Mann's novella, who says of Bibi Saccellaphylaccas, the child prodigy: "Er hat in sich des Künstlers Hoheit und seine Würdelosigkeit, seine Charlatanerie und seinen heiligen Funken, seine Verachtung und seinen heimlichen Rausch" (*Erzählungen*, 692). Thomas's artist, in contrast to the vital Branzilla, has that death-inclination we have already remarked in *Tristan*; he appears to be a naive child, yet an air of tiredness can be noticed about him. Much of Mann's sketch is concerned with the reactions of the various spectators to the boy's performance. Although captivated, it is doubtful that many of them have been exceedingly touched by the music which he plays. Mann does not let this music be of any artistic importance; the program, consisting of the boy's own compositions, serves merely to enhance the effect of his personality. When the virtuoso performs, it does not matter what music he plays, so long as he is at the keyboard. The virtuoso, completely lacking in critical sense, is the victim of a passion for music itself. The artist is devoured by his perhaps valueless music.

The two virtuosi who appear in Mann, Bibi and Rudi Schwerdtfeger in *Doktor Faustus,* are both children, Rudi not in years perhaps, but certainly in attitude: they make the child's efforts to win general favor without distinguishing between individuals. More than Rudi who, living in a later age, is confronted by composition fraught with technical difficulties, Bibi regards music as a kind of toy: "Es ist dieses prickelnde Glück, dieser heimliche Wonneschauer, der ihn jedesmal überrieselt, wenn er wieder an einem offenen Klavier sitzt—er wird das niemals verlieren" (686). Bibi takes special joy in those passages where a modulation is pleasing to his own ears; at these points his first thought is not for the public but for himself and his music. Even though he notices that the spectators have not given particular attention to his beloved passages, he is so pleased with the sound that he rewards the audience by casting his eyes toward the ceiling. Mann's virtuoso is composed of childlike pleasure in playing together with an equally childlike desire to win the favor of the audience. He cannot view music with the objectivity necessary to the creative artist, in whom the critical faculty is always active; he remains subjective, and music is the single possible joy in his life.

The singer, Heinrich Muoth, in Hermann Hesse's *Gertrud* (1910),[19] cannot bear to think that anyone withstands his personality: this element in his character is developed at the expense of his interest in music. Hesse's singer is in essence a melancholiac who must have the consoling and constant affection of a friend or a woman, of the entire audience or even of music itself (the composition especially favorable to his voice). Bibi's childlike joy in music is present in Muoth only from time to time. Indeed Muoth's most interesting feature is that he is the occasional virtuoso. He is intended to demonstrate the futility of the inconstant Weltschmerzler in art. Like a typical virtuoso he wins the friendship of the composer-narrator and the love of Gertrud, largely because he feels that neither of them has any regard for him. The composer's friendship he further exploits by obtaining from him a number of songs and a rewarding operatic role; in the meantime he marries Gertrud, whom the composer loves. For no apparent reason he tosses friendship, love, music, and fame aside and becomes a drunkard; at last he kills himself. As the Branzilla would say, he has received a just punishment, not having served music well. He has caused unhappiness only through his unbalanced character, not through any desire to devote himself more fully to music. Strictly regarded he has less claim to the reader's sympathy than the murderous Italian soprano. Hesse of course wishes that Muoth be placed in unfavorable contrast with the narrator, who, a cripple and having renounced happiness in its usual forms, decides in the end to lead an almost saintly life. Hesse's single portrait of the virtuoso is not a satisfactory or a complete one; Muoth remains a foil to the narrator and a frightening example.

The virtuoso is reduced to a Spielmann in other works: Ernst Zahn's short story, *Der Geiger* (1905), considers the fate of the virtuoso-nature in a Swiss mountain village, Carl Sternheim's *Bürger Schippel* (1913) renews the old theme of the efforts of the musician to obtain admittance to society and couples with it a discussion of the virtuoso in a debased form. Zahn's story concerns the fortunes of an untrained violinist, who possesses the spark of genius. With naive obstinacy the Troger-Jakob refuses to attend a conservatory, saying that he is happier as he is. He falls in love with a summer visitor, but cannot win her with his violin playing, and so loses the respect of the villagers; at last he disappears into the mountains. (The same plot, with a Jugoslavian setting and a more erotic twist, turns up in Joseph Friedrich Perkonig's novella, *Der Guslaspieler*, 1944.)[20] The story is a study of the virtuoso in little. The Troger-Jakob's traits are essentially those of Mann's Bibi; he attempts in his childlike way to win the affection of villagers and tourists alike; at the same time, satisfied with his playing, he does not attempt to learn the music of others. He is vain (and childlike) enough to be hurt when a professional musician says: "Von Kunst kann natürlich nicht die Rede sein, aber— nun—was man nicht alles schön findet in dieser schönen Gegend!"[21] Zahn's story provides an example of the completely defeated virtuoso, who can no longer make a claim upon anyone's attention and so ceases to exist.

In Sternheim's *Bürger Schippel* the doughty hero's hypnotic voice enchants his employers, otherwise class-conscious musical amateurs who despise Schippel because of his illegitimate birth. Schippel is not content with the passing artistic spell he is able to cast over his social betters; he desires permanent acceptance. Sternheim's drama early ceases to concern itself with the problems of the artist and becomes a satire on the foibles of the middle class. The members of a male quartet wish Schippel to be their tenor soloist so that they may win a contest, but refuse to accept him socially. When the sister of one of the members is seduced by a local prince, she is offered to Schippel as a wife in an effort to make him sing: he refuses her upon learning that she has been the prince's mistress, and is challenged to a duel by another member of the quartet, who faints at the dueling place (Schippel is about to do the same). The musician wins the duel and so is accepted by the bourgeoisie. The somewhat obvious satire might have gained power had Schippel acted out of a feeling of pride in his musicianship; such is not the case. Schippel's voice is scarcely mentioned after the first act of the play; he behaves as he does because of the injustices inflicted upon him throughout his life; his greatest desire is not to be understood as a musician, but rather to get the upper hand over his tormentors. As the brother of the seduced girl says to him: "[Sie] spielen so ein bisschen lieber Gott vor sich selbst," and Schippel answers: "Man hat's endlich nötig."[22] At the end of the play Schippel, accepted as a citizen, no longer desires to destroy the middle class; Sternheim says that the decaying bourgeoisie can remove its enemies by accepting them—an amusing social thesis, but hardly related to the contemporary problem of the musician.

It has become increasingly futile to treat the musician as a social outsider; not only is he accepted by society, he is admired as a Wagnerian "exceptional man." Such admiration is not confined to the actual creative genius; it is extended to give almost all musicians an aura of fascination. From this fascination derives the vast growth in the number of concert performers during the eighties and nineties of the last century; the advertisement pages in any of the great German musical journals from the period are astonishing by the number of singers and instrumentalists who offer their services to the public. The age of the incomparable virtuoso, such as Paganini or Liszt, has passed; these masters have been replaced by a host of lesser figures who cater to the public's insatiable desire for the "great artist." It is not strange, then, that a number of parodies of the second-rate virtuoso should appear in reaction against the rage; while of no great literary value, they are among the most comical literary productions of the period. Their salutary effect may be noted in the fact that in the period following the First World War the virtuoso disappears as a serious figure in German literature.

Wolzogen's Prczewalsky—both composer and virtuoso—has already been described, greedy, lecherous, bloated with conceit. Another virtuoso of Prczewalsky's type is Camillo Arsakoff in Adolf Stern's lengthy novel, *Ohne Ideale* (1882). A mixture of Slav and Italian, Camillo condemns German music: ". . . es ist notwendig," he tells his advisor, the Countess Platoff, "dass ich einige Zeit in Deutchland verweile und mich dort in musikalisches Ansehen setze. Das alberne Vorurteil vom musikalischen Prestige der Deutschen herrscht einmal."[23] With such views Camillo easily becomes a villain of the first water. Countess Platoff persuades Bernhard, Duke of Forstenburg, who is visiting at the same Italian resort as Camillo, that the pianist is his illegitimate son. Returning to Germany with the ducal household, Camillo sets out to seduce Bernhard's daughter, Stephanie, by playing Chopin to her. A birthday concert is arranged for the Princess, at which a "symphony-cantata" by Arsakoff is performed; the Kapellmeister, a German, expresses his opinion of this "russisch-italienischen Salat von Esprit und Sentiment und unerträglichen Raffinement" (III, 262) in no uncertain terms, and so we learn something of the nature of Arsakoff's compositions. But Arsakoff is not entirely superficial; in a conversation with Paul Lohmer, Arsakoff's equivalent in the non-musical action of the novel, the musician confesses that his art fulfills a physical need: ". . . selbst der Genuss würde mich schal dünken, wenn ich ihn nicht mit meiner Kunst würzen dürfte" (IV, 14).

Arsakoff conquers the willing Stephanie, but her father learns of the liaison and, still under the impression that the musician is his son, compels him to marry the graceless child of a Jewish banker. Stephanie tries to persuade Arsakoff to flee with her, and commits suicide when he refuses. (So shocked is Camillo by the thought of leaving his well-feathered nest that "er war wirklich einer Ohnmacht nahe und hielt sich mit Mühe aufrecht, IV, 108.) When last we see Camillo he has been richly punished for his misdeeds; depressed by his bride's company, threatened with exposure by Countess Platoff if he enters royal society again, he sees emptiness before him: "Ein Frostschauer schien ihm durchs Mark zu dringen, und in seinem wachen Traum wandelten sich die hässlich scharfen Züge der russischen Gräfin zum Bilde des eigenen freudlosen und reuevollen Alters" (IV, 284). Stern, with his odd mixture of sympathy and heavy-handed sarcasm, prepares the ground from which later and more skillfully parodied virtuosi grow.

The grimmest of the parodies is Frank Wedekind's *Der Kammersänger*, a play in three scenes written in 1897. In his introduction Wedekind calls the play "der Zusammenstoss zwischen einer brutalen Intelligenz und verschiedenen blinden

Leidenschaften" (*Gesammelte Werke*, III, 197), a not precisely accurate description stemming from Wedekind's rancour against those German theater directors who devitalized the figure of Gerardo into a depiction of a vain nincompoop. Wedekind says that "brutale Intelligenz" has been transformed into "eine übernatürliche Dummheit" (III, 198). In interpreting his play Wedekind has however gone too far in the other direction. Gerardo is not an intentionally cruel man; he attempts to avoid harming others, especially when his career might be injured in the process. His secret is that he is completely self-centered; as he tells the old composer, Dühring, who seeks to interest him in his opera, he has worked his way up from paper-hanger's assistant to "K. K. Kammersänger" by demanding that he be paid for every task. In the scene with Dühring, Gerardo most nearly reveals his true feelings, or lack of feelings, about art, but even here he does not confess his real conception of his position. Certainly he is not sincere with the giddy Miss Coeurne when he tells her that he regards art as a chaste goddess, to be served unselfishly; with his last visitor, his former mistress, Frau Helene Marowa, he speaks of a shadowy concept of duty. In no case does Gerardo confess the entire truth, and there is little reason why he should: all three of his visitors are as egoistic as he, desiring to take more from him than he from them. Dühring wishes the singer to endorse his impossible opera; Miss Coeurne intends to have her first sexual experience with her idol; Frau Helene, having tired of husband and children, believes she will find a new and more exciting life with the singer. Gerardo does not despise his visitors; he merely has other things on his mind: his practice hours are interrupted, he must catch a train to Brussels for a performance of *Tristan*.

That Gerardo has not told the complete truth to Dühring is demonstrated in the monologue which follows the composer's departure: the singer realizes that his earnings will be small consolation to him in later years, and obviously he has no overwhelming devotion to art. His often repeated expression of a desire to practice simply reveals his terror of a breakdown on the stage. The Kammersänger thus borders on the tragic: underneath what Wedekind calls the "brutal intelligence" there is an elemental fear; Gerardo is in a position where all too much is expected of him. While he is able to extricate himself with dignity from the situation with the childish Miss Coeurne, he must confess a good part of his actual insignificance to Professor Dühring, and confronted by the half-mad Helene he fails completely. Helene commits suicide—and he misses the train to Brussels, in his eyes the greater tragedy. Nor is he to be too severely criticized for his reaction; while his "brutal intelligence," coupled with a magnificent voice, has made him a famous singer, spiritually he has remained the paper-hanger's assistant, unable to appreciate his influence over others. Wedekind's battle between "brutal intelligence" and "blind passions" is at first comical; when we realize how empty the "brutal intelligence" is and what tragedy results from the illusions which it calls forth, we see that the play has a very dark side. It remains a most penetrating study of the virtuoso conceived as a hollow symbol, a supposed "genius" who cannot fulfill the promises he seems to make.

Hermann Bahr's comedy, *Das Konzert* (1909), considers the virtuoso with friendly scorn. Its hero, Gustav Heink, married to an understanding wife but attractive to large numbers of other women, is periodically involved in more or less serious extra-marital affairs, which he undertakes principally because he believes he must. During one of the latter relationships he is discovered by his wife, who pretends to take up a liaison with the newest conquest's husband. Gustav is momentarily frightened, but falls back into his old habits in the last scene. Bahr's virtuoso is a close kinsman of Wedekind's Gerardo; like the Kammersänger he hesitates to undertake the affairs which are thrust upon him, largely because he desires more time for rest, practice, and homely, even somewhat philistine joys. Gustav must salve his pride and aid his position by continuing to live the life of the "great artist." He is not in essence a musician but simply a very vain man; when his wife suggests that he might retire from the concert stage he cries out that a critic has called him "the still handsome Gustav Heink:" "Weil sie meinem Talent nichts anhaben können, die Herren hinter mir, in ihrer Ungeduld, die durchaus den Platz für sich haben will, rechnen sie mir jetzt meine Jahre vor, vielleicht geht's so, dem Publikum ist ja keine Verleumdung zu dumm."[24] Doubts appear in Heink's mind as they have in Gerardo's, but without the same tragic overtones, since Heink is worried in the main about growing old, while Gerardo asks a more pregnant question concerning the purpose of life. Heink can see a purpose: he would like to become a good husband and good citizen, if it were not for his pride; Gerardo, free of Heink's rosy illusions, realizes that his life has been and will be empty.

Tragic elements are not to be found in Gustav's relationship to others. The affair with the young wife, Delfine, which might have had serious consequences both for her and her scholar husband, is cut short by the clever efforts of Gustav's ever understanding Marie. The liaison begun in the final scene causes harm to no one, since Eva, the "victim," has really desired just this moment for years. Gustav himself consents to the affair with mechanical gestures; he can pretend for a little longer that he is a dashing youth rather than a prosaic and middle-aged man. Marie accepts Heink as he is; she does not believe his vows of eternal faithfulness ("Gustl, man soll nichts verschwören," 149), and would undoubtedly be astonished if he kept them. She realizes that he loves her and that his other affairs arise from his profession and his temperament. As she tells Delfine, he is but an overgrown child, and one can control him only if one possesses patience and strong nerves. The question arises, of course, if Gustav is worthy of the care which Marie grants him; in the answer lies the single tragic element of the play.

Carl Sternheim's story, *Schuhlin* (1915), stands on the borderline between the treatments of the virtuoso type and those of the evil mentor. Schuhlin is a pianist and composer who at first earns his living as a salon virtuoso; believing that the composer receives more acclaim than the performer, he writes a cycle of Hölderlin songs. For a time he wins the admiration of a select coterie, but eventually even his most ardent worshipers grow tired of hearing the same meaningless music over and over again, and turn against Schuhlin, who retires to the forests. There he is sought out by Klara, an adoring but dull-witted young woman, and later by Neander, who becomes his single student. After Schuhlin consents to marry Klara, a rivalry arises between the wife and the student, each attempting to outdo the other in service to the master; finally the student stabs Klara and commits suicide. Schuhlin proceeds (in the last sentence) to seek supporters "die die Mittel zu jenem Leben sichern sollen, das er als ihm gemäss und seiner Bedeutung zukommend, ein für allemal erkannt hatte."[25]

Like another virtuoso, Zahn's Troger-Jakob, Schuhlin goes to the wilderness to sulk when he is deserted; he does not persuade Klara or Neander to follow him; they sacrifice themselves to him voluntarily. At first he does not make a conscious effort to exploit them, as a Reissner or an Amschl would have done. However he does bear a resemblance to the evil mentor type in that he learns to play off one disciple against the other. More a charlatan than any of his fellow virtuosi, he seems to possess only the slightest musical ability, yet he never is assailed by doubts. The self-confidence of Wedekind's "Kammersänger" can be shaken, and with tragic results; Schuhlin remains comic in his monumental faith in himself. That his two followers are so absurd prevents their deaths from dampening the comedy; they die with all their illusions about the master intact.

In Schuhlin the virtuoso becomes a talentless sybarite, the evil mentor an impractical egoist. Kapellmeister Czepanek in Sudermann's *Das Hohe Lied* (1908)[26] seems to share Schuhlin's position as the weakly evil mentor. Czepanek does not appear in Sudermann's novel, but his influence is quite apparent. He has been the leader of the local singing club, a moderately talented but by no means remarkable musician, who squandered whatever ability he possessed. His leisure hours were wasted in drinking and the pursuit of the town's girls; during just such a chase he was forced to marry the mother of Lilly Czepanek, the novel's heroine, under pain of losing his position. However he did compose one work, an oratorio, *Das Hohe Lied*, which he believed to excel the music of Wagner. Sudermann never commits himself on the real quality of the composition. Lilly after having long carried the manuscript with her as a symbol of the ideal (which she has kept from pollution at the hands of degenerate officers and lustful business men), decides to commit suicide; she casts the composition into the water, and then realizes that she wishes to exist at any cost. Sudermann's Lilly has lived under the influence of her father, despite the fact that he disappeared while she was still young: the father's influence, apparently beneficent since it represents the ideal, has turned out to be harmful after all; it has caused Lili to refuse a spiritual compromise with life, although she has certainly not been loath to make the physical compromise. Having thus freed herself of her father's control Lilly marries her former love, the faithful philistine Dehnicke, and sets out with him for Italy, the object of her dreams. We can achieve our goal not by clinging to the ideal, but by surrendering it. The novel's solution of course causes us to entertain serious doubts as to the musical value of *Das Hohe Lied*; Kapellmeister Czepanek's real aim in life was perhaps not the pursuit of the artistic ideal, but rather of the young ladies who made up his Gesangverein.

The more cynical attitude toward the evil mentor is painfully obvious in Wedekind and Bahr. Reissner and Amschl are hypocritical creatures; neither Wedekind nor Bahr attempts to give them the Luciferian dimensions apparent in such a character as Rat Krespel. When Klara is taken to prison Reissner becomes the picture of righteousness. What is more horrible, his pose is accepted as genuine by both the prison officials and by Klara's mother; this duplicity on Reissner's part helps drive Klara into utter insanity. Amschl's character appears to have more of the demonic about it; the hypnotic powers which he exerts over Lida seem to relate him to Krespel and Abraham. Yet these mentors love Antonie and Chiara, in however overmasterful a fashion. Amschl regards Lida as a financial investment, and the sexual fascination which he so knowingly exerts upon her is the means of forcing her to undertake exhausting concert tours. Krespel goes mad after Antonie's death, Abraham borders on insanity after Chiara's disappearance; Amschl, called to the flat where Lida is dying, can merely evince a desire to escape from an embarrassing situation. Lida's importance for him has terminated together with her earning ability.

In Heinrich Mann's *Die kleine Stadt* (1909) the musician, whatever his talents, stands at the service of—indeed, is used by—his audience, which has become in this respect a kind of monster mentor. A shabby opera troupe visits a little Italian city, where the singers become the center of a struggle between the clergy and its opera-loving enemies. The churchgoers are led by the bigoted priest, Don Taddeo, his opponents by the lawyer Belotti. The troupe's two leading women are Flora Garlinda, the prima donna, and Italia Molesin. Garlinda is a baser Branzilla; ugly, ambitious in the extreme, she loves only a dream of success. Italia's talents are more sexual than musical; to her music is an excuse for an immoral life. Of the male artists, one, the lyric tenor Nello Gennari, uses his voice to win the love of Alba, daughter to a stalwart of the anti-operatic faction; another, the baritone Gaddi, is the strong foundation upon which the troupe is built. A good family man and a good friend, he does his best to save Nello from himself. What feeling Gaddi has for the art stems from a sense of solidarity with his ensemble. Perhaps the truest musician is the aged tenor, the Cavaliere Giordano, who has lost both his voice and his sexual powers (a connection is implied), yet who remains a loving servant of his art. In contrast, the town's resident musical director, Dorlenghi, is skillful at getting the best from his rebellious charges, but suffers from the same gnawing ambition as Garlinda, a fact for which she at once hates and admires him.

The intrigues arising from the proposed performances of Viviani's *Arme Tonietta* are so involved as to defy description. The performance takes place at last, and Mann devotes a hundred pages to delineating the great event. It matters little that the singers are often mediocre or worse; the audience has the main role. It jeers or is enraptured, laughs or cries; the singers are at its mercy. According to Dorlenghi, this musical triumph of the people was the composer's intention in writing *Tonietta*: "Ich habe also ein Volk gesehen! Das Volk, für das der Maestro Viviani seine Oper geschrieben hat . . . Es erfindet für uns, dies Volk, es fühlt und tönt in uns. In der Musik der 'Armen Tonietta' hat es seinen eigenen Tonfall wiedererkannt, seine Gesten, sein Tempo" (*Gesammelte Romane und Novellen*, VIII, 270-271). The concept is a new one in literature on the musician; heretofore the musician, not the audience, has been the controlling factor. Mann intends his novel as an interpretation of the Italian scene, and we must not take his allotment of total power to the audience as being equally applicable to Germany; in *Die kleine Stadt* Mann has transformed the familiar concept of music as an educational means to music as a means of expressing the people's will. It is little wonder that the Italian individualist Settembrini in Thomas Mann's *Zauberberg* entertains strong doubts about the benefits to be derived from the art.

However, the opera does serve the welfare of the little city. Belotti wishes to show his singers a historic bucket in the church's belfry, to which Don Taddeo refuses him the key. Belotti loses the ensuing lawsuit and many of his fickle supporters; but the charms of Italia bring peace to the city. Don Taddeo is aroused by the singer during confessional, and, tormented by his conscience, sets fire to the inn where she lives; then he saves her from the flames. Once more the theatrical party is in the ascendancy, and the priest makes a final peace with Belotti. The singers depart, leaving a member of their band behind them. Nello has sung his heart out in an effort to win Alba. He arranges to elope with her, but she, repentant, murders him at their trysting place; then she kills herself. The virtuoso has been sacrificed to love.

There are many anomalies in *Die kleine Stadt*: the all-powerful audience, the self-sacrificing virtuoso, the profound sympathy for the world of Italian music. More a cultural panorama of the Italian people than a musical novel, it nevertheless demonstrates an original mind at work on musical problems. *Die Kleine Stadt*—by its understanding of the "southern" spirit a descendant of Nietzsche's *Carmen* critique—stands as a link between Heine's Bellini-portrait and Werfel's *Verdi*: in each case the musician is the servant of the mass, and in each case woman has a dominant role in the musical world. Mann's prima donna has a strength of purpose unknown even to the ambitious town conductor, Italia is able to heal the wounds of the municipality, and Nello gives up his life for Alba's sake. Not men but women shape the destiny of Mann's city and its inhabitants. In *Verdi* woman may not be quite so active a force; there her strength lies in her ability at suffering, but it is strength nonetheless.

The musical literature of the period from Wagner's death to the First World War is for the most part one of bankrupt standards and ideals; while a number of problems are posed, few solutions are indicated. Among the composers, Heiner and Enzio commit suicide, Bahr's Hugo goes mad, Schnitzler's Amadeus sees his marriage wrecked. The women musicians seldom have a happier end, while the virtuosi seem doomed to impotent despair. Of the creative musicians (if we exclude the rough and ready "Kraft-Mayr") only Wassermann's Daniel Nothafft can be said to have reached any sort of satisfactory compromise with life, and this by the renunciation of his claims on art: he ceases to compose and becomes an exemplary figure. This is however not a solution for the artist but for the man alone.

Two other, less optimistic solutions are essayed in early works of Thomas Mann and Hermann Hesse. The musician may— unlike Heiner and Enzio—go victoriously to destruction, surrendering gladly to the death-urge inherent in Romantic music; or he may renounce all claims on life to devote himself to his art, and even there make the smallest demands. Hanno Buddenbrook stands as Thomas Mann's definitive picture of the musician before *Doktor Faustus*. That Hanno dies while still a child does not detract from his importance; the child is also Mann's representative of the virtuoso type. As *Tristan* indicates, Mann believes that the element of death and decay inherent in all art is nowhere so clearly expressed as in the music of the Romantic-harmonic tradition, which reaches its culmination in Wagner. The musician for the Mann of *Buddenbrooks* and the novellas is primarily a Romantic one, and his fate is correspondingly that of the Romantic: giving himself up to the charms of music he is destroyed by it. Hanno dislikes the orderly work of the schoolroom, and even at the piano is not as diligent as he might be when required to practice his exercises. His enthusiasm lies rather in the field of improvisation, "des Akkordsuchens;" the music of *Die Meistersinger* or *Tristan* alone can interest him apart from the creations of his own imagination. Music assumes a much more deadly role in the life of Hanno than it did in the lives of other musical youths of similar dreamy tendencies, the "Musikfeind," the Spielmann, or even Hanno's literary contemporary, Heiner. For these other musicians music plays a salutary part; only when they are deprived of it does harm (in one form or another) come to them. Hanno, here surprisingly like Rochlitz's Karl and like Mann's own Frau Klöterjahn, cannot exist without music, but he cannot live with it either: the emotional strain which it places upon him contributes much to the collapse of his oversensitive nature. The theme of the emotional demands upon the musician by his art is continued by Mann in *Doktor Faustus*; his Leverkühn is by no means free of Romanticism and can with justice be named Hanno's brother-german. But Leverkühn struggles to escape Romantic music, Hanno willingly dies for it.

Mann, in his treatment of music as purely Romantic, betrays a ruling tendency of the period: for him music has remained in the Wagnerian age, and the technical and intellectual developments made in the art since the death of Wagner mean nothing to the author of *Tristan, Das Wunderkind* and *Buddenbrooks*. (Even in *Faustus*, where he is abreast of the latest musical thought, his Romantic preferences shine through.) A like attitude is to be found in Hesse's *Peter Camenzind*, published in 1904, three years after *Buddenbrooks*. In Zürich Camenzind, the clumsy poet-hero of the novel, meets Richard, a handsome and wealthy student of music; Richard's intellectual horizon is determined by Nietzsche, his musical horizon by Wagner. Hesse however does not emphasize Richard's musical predilections; he is primarily interested in the friendship between the sophisticated musician and the naive poet, offering an unusual variation on the theme of the contrast between the musical unequal to life and the friend able to survive the struggle (incidentally, a contrast also present between Hanno Buddenbrook and his friend Kai). The musician Richard is not tormented by the problems of life; Hesse concentrates on the problematic nature of his real hero, Camenzind. Camenzind is awkward, unsure of himself, slow, Richard is polished, poised, and intellectually nimble. But strangely, the Sunday child Richard, like Huch's all too passionate Enzio, meets an early death by drowning.

In *Peter Camenzind* the friendship has its suspect side, an element already noted in *Freund Hein* and to recur in Hauptmann's *Die Hochzeit auf Buchenhorst* and in *Doktor Faustus*. (The homosexual aspect is less pronounced in *Gertrud*, where Muoth simply wants compositions from the composer, or in *Enzio*, whose hero's lusts are unambiguously heterosexual.) When Richard dies, Camenzind falls into a prolonged condition of melancholy. Even at the beginning of the friendship Camenzind feels an attraction to Richard quite separate from the spell which his music casts. As Richard plays (says Camenzind), "betrachtete ich mit heimlicher Lust den schlanken Nacken und Rücken des Spielers und seine weissen Musikerhände..."[27] At times Richard seems to be conscious of his role. While the youths are swimming he pretends to be the Loreley, and Camenzind is the unhappy boatman. Yet the "Loreley," not the "Schiffer im kleinen Schiffe," goes down to destruction. Does Richard die simply because he is one of those youths too beautiful to live? Or is he, the Wagner enthusiast, another Hanno Buddenbrook beneath his self-sufficient exterior, gnawed at by the poisons of Romantic music, toward which the later Hesse was to demonstrate considerable unfriendliness? Hesse does not say.

In *Gertrud* the loosely "poetic" quality of young Hesse's plot-construction finds a counterpart in the description of the narrator-hero's musical life. Like Wassermann's Daniel Nothafft, Hesse's determinedly unintellectual composer Kuhn does not seem to possess any kind of aesthetic theory. A song cycle and a chamber trio receive full, but subjective and non-technical descriptions; the opera written for Muoth is unidentified as to plot or style. As for the musical influences in the composer's life, these too remain in the limbo of disregard; however Hesse causes a Mozart enthusiast, Teiser, an orchestral violinist, to become the friend and critic of the narrator. Little is made of the Mozartian impact upon Kuhn's production; but Mozart's compositions have plainly had the greatest effect in shaping the happy, childlike personalities of Teiser and his sister. This detail, small though it may be, is not unimportant: it indicates the completely undemonic (and un-Romantic) attitude of Hesse toward Mozart, and the author's interest in the pedagogical powers of the art, which he develops to the full in *Das Glasperlenspiel*.

Vagueness in respect to the composer's musical life and accentuation of his personal problems make *Gertrud* resemble *Das Gänsemännchen*. The composers of Wassermann and Hesse eventually turn their backs upon the world, and devote themselves to a life of secluded renunciation. In Wassermann's novel this solution comes as such a surprise that it loses all effect; Wassermann gives us the feeling that he adds a "constructive" ending after having reveled in a garish depiction of Nothafft's financial and marital difficulties. Hesse's use of the renunciation theme harmonizes better with the plot of his novel. Early in life the narrator has been forced to limit his desires; a sledding accident has permanently crippled him. Both the great love affairs of his life have been distinctly unsuccessful (in contrast to those of a Nothafft or an Enzio); one girl drops out of his life after the accident, the other, Gertrud, marries the singer Muoth. As a performer of music the hero has likewise been unfortunate; his lameness has given him a diffidence quite incompatible with the occupation of the virtuoso. Intellectually too he is not outstanding; he realizes very well that he is not a brilliant thinker. As a creative musician he is able to make greater claims; yet precisely his talent affords him the most unhappiness. He cannot understand why others should receive recognition and love while he is more gifted than they. However he is taught, especially by the example of Heinrich Muoth, that no one, not even the artist, should make the slightest claims upon life or art: "Das Schicksal war nicht gut, das

Leben war launisch und grausam, es gab in der Natur keine Güte und Vernunft" (298). Eventually he gives up the hopes he cherished of possessing Gertrud after the suicide of her husband; he also slowly abandons composition, except for an occasional song or sonata, which he regards as belonging to himself and Gertrud (a slight echo of the Julia-theme). He has not become the "great example" for a group of admiring students, in the manner of Nothafft; instead he attempts to devote himself to a life of understanding, love, and consolation of others. The artist must make way for the human being; the personality of the "genius" has no rightful claims to make. The idea contains noble elements, but nevertheless a novel like *Gertrud* avoids the central questions concerning the musician, just as most of the other works from this period have done: what is to be the fate of the musician as artist in the modern world?

Chapter IV

THE AGE OF MUSICOLOGY

I.

The decades following the defeat of the Central Powers in 1918 saw an unabated popularity of creative literature on the musician. As an abnormal personality the musician exerted a dwindling but still potent fascination; in its twilight the figure committed deeds of violence or debauchery unknown even to the purple pre-war years. As a more edifying continuation of an earlier tradition there also appeared novels in which the musician learned to renounce—his art, his happiness, or his life. Finally, the growth of music as a learned matter fostered the *Verdi* of Werfel, the *Doktor Faustus* of Mann, and *Das Glasperlenspiel* of Hesse. The influence of musicology on literature, a development without an earlier parallel, deserves separate and detailed treatment. We must first make our way through the welter of works dealing with themes carried over from the past.

The actual musical interests of many writers from the twenties are evanescent. Heroes and heroines are made musicians in order to increase their aura of the exotic, or to excuse their misdeeds. And, nearing literary exhaustion, the musician of abnormal disposition frequently offers only enough material for the novelistic episode, the anecdote, the short tale. We meet truncated representatives of types we have known before: the unhappy youthful composer, the virtuoso, the woman musician, the Spielmann. Jakob Wassermann, in *Laudin und die Seinen* (1925),[1] shows a young composer driven to suicide by his affair with an actress. No Friedrich Huch, Wassermann does not present the erring musician in full view, but uses his death as a mainspring for the legal complications of which the book mainly consists. Gerhart Hauptmann offers a similar sketch of the young composer in *Die Hochzeit auf Buchenhorst* (1932), where the hero reveals vaguely homosexual proclivities, a subject which Hauptmann handles with a delicacy rare in the present period. The composer, Dietrich Kühnelle, the intimate friend of another musician, Hasper, convinces himself that he should marry the sister of the narrator's fiancée; losing his nerve at the last minute, he flees to America as a sailor—surely an unusual fate for the composer. Musically, Hauptmann's tale might have been written decades before, and, indeed, its setting in time is the *fin-de-siècle*. Kühnelle, playing a nineteenth century "war horse," a Liszt rhapsody, is described in the language of an Ossip Schubin: "Am Anfang musizierte und meditierte ein Erzengel. Aber aus dem Unterirdischen kroch und schlich ein Dämon herauf, der sich plötzlich mit tückischem Klauenhieb des himmlischen Instrumentes bemächtigte."[2] And Kühnelle's mind works as nebulously as that of any composer from the turn of the century: "[Er] hatte damals nicht die geringste Beziehung zu Philosophie und Religion. Kunst war das Ein und Alles für ihn. Ich kenne ausser ihm keinen Menschen, der einen so hohen, allumfassenden Begriff von Kunst besass. In diesem Begriff waren ihm Gott, Welt, Menschheit zusammengeschmolzen" (30). Has Hauptmann intended by the most subtle stylistic and intellectual means to conjure up the past? Then he has achieved a masterpiece of empathy into the musical spirit of his youth. Or have his musical opinions and predilections simply remained those of the post-Wagnerian era? Then he would demonstrate a musical conservatism not unknown to major German authors.

The virtuoso, reeling from the blows dealt him by Wedekind and others, is no longer the public's shining idol; the fears of the Kammersänger have become reality. Wilhelm Schäfer, in *Der Cellospieler* (*Anekdoten*, 1928), tells of a cello virtuoso who, deaf and aged, decides to drown himself after his wife's death. Saved and taken to an old people's home, he makes a pitiful attempt to play again. One day he goes for a walk beside the Rhine; melodies begin to form within him, and he realizes with difficulty "dass es Musik aus eigener Schöpfung war, dass er sie aufschreiben konnte, dass er, der immer nur ein Diener fremder Kunst gewesen war, nun im Alter noch begnadet würde, selber ein Meister herrlicher Musik zu sein."[3] Hurrying homeward, he stumbles over a chain, falls into the water, and is drowned. The virtuoso, a servant, is intended by destiny never to become a composer, a master. The reference to the virtuoso as "Diener" registers precisely the extent of the figure's transformation; but the point is made a little belatedly, a little sentimentally, and in a minor literary genre.

Albrecht Schaeffer in the story *Fidelio* (1918, collected in *Prisma*, 1925), says equally interesting things about the virtuoso in almost as miniature a form. The bass Peter Nehr kills a singer with whom he has had an affair. His prison sentence is a light one, since he pleads that he lost consciousness before committing the murder. Freed, he seeks money from his benefactor, then leaves for South America; his faithful wife is on the same boat. Nehr has a fault not to be found, at least in overt expression, among the earlier virtuosi: he suffers hideously from stage fright. (Storm's Christian, who has the classic literary case of the ailment, is not a virtuoso.) Nehr suspects that his stage fright (and the attendant release from it during performance) are indispensable parts of his make-up, "dass hier der Kern seines Lebens und Wesens lag, und dass er absterben würde, so er ihn herausnahm, ganz leer werden; und dass auch die Angst notwendig dazu gehörte und nicht wäre zu entbehren gewesen."[4] Before the "blackout" in which he killed his mistress he experienced stage fright; the fear of failure, which lay hidden beneath the actions of Wedekind's Kammersänger, has become all-consuming in Nehr, even, when combined with jealousy, making him into a criminal. Nehr is cured of his complex in a somewhat miraculous fashion; he sings for his benefactor's daughter, and "flügelschlagend um seine arme Stirn kreiste die Taube der Erlösung" (90).

Schaeffer's sensitivity in dissecting the anxieties of Nehr is a worthy counterpart of that skill with which the pre-war writers probed the musician's emotions. Schaeffer also takes up a thread from the past when he has his musician become a criminal, a tendency long discernible in both the virtuoso and the mentor. The brutality of Nehr's crime is ameliorated by the singer's psychological flaw, which he thinks he must cherish in order to practice his art. (In the same way we excuse Mann's Branzilla because of the musical motivation of her actions.) Other criminal musicians contemporary to Nehr are also excused by their authors; however the musical pardon granted them rests on much flimsier grounds.

The now forgotten Martin Borrmann offers a thief and a murderer who are among the most distasteful figures in musical literature. In *Der Zwerg und das Grammophon* (1925) a dwarf, Hugo, falls in love with one Fräulein Robinson singing "Du mein Schönbrunn." He buys a phonograph and the prerequisite record, but they fail to satisfy him; he steals the machine on which he first heard the recording, thus hoping to reproduce the enchanting sound exactly. (Fräulein Robinson's live voice, "sachlich, zu dick und zu wirklich,"[5] has disappointed him.) Arrested for the theft, Hugo goes mad when through his cell window he hears a hurdy-gurdy playing "Du mein Schönbrunn." Hugo's sufferings are no more moving than those of the organist Zebedäus in Borrmann's novel, *Venus mit dem Orgelspieler* (1922). The organist begins an affair with Dolly, an acrobatic dancer, but is forced into the background by the younger Lanatsch. Zebedäus, having lost his pupils and his post, becomes a clown in Dolly's act. Dolly further humiliates him by making him pump the organ while Lanatsch plays profane melodies. His patience at an end, Zebedäus breaks Dolly's back during a performance. Committed to an asylum, the organist escapes, and sails out to sea in a small boat, led on by a vision of the dancer. Zebedäus has the characteristics of the Romantic composer: he has written a great oratorio, he draws inspiration from religion, he has found a human incorporation of his musical aspirations in Dolly. Yet it is a long way indeed from Berglinger and Julia to Zebedäus's crazy mixture of faith, idealism, and lust: "Das Werk schrie unter ihm, die Orgel stürzte bergauf. Er spielte den Chor, in dem von den Tränen des Herrn berichtet wird. Sein Oratorium baute sich fernblickend hoch. Er sah auf Dolly ... In allen Tönen bäumte er sich nach ihr."[6] The author attempts to make us regard Zebedäus as a musical martyr, a Professor Unrat with genius, but he destroys his own case by the emphasis he puts on Zebedäus's erotomania.

In Alfred Neumann's *Rugge* (1920) the titular hero, a regimental musician, is at first glance a Romantic Spielmann, just as Zebedäus seems to be a Romantic composer. A fellow soldier complains: "Die Mannschaften seien überzeugt, dass der Spielmann Rugge des Teufels ist ... Er führe schlimme Reden, trommle Müdigkeit in die Beine, geige zur Nacht das Blut in Sturm ..."[7] Music, here as elsewhere in the twenties, has become a peg on which the author can hang a variety of adventures. Those of Rugge are unusually grisly; employed as a spy, he becomes a favorite of a perverted nobleman. Rugge is a terrifying example of the pass to which the musician can come in the hands of an author whose intentions are not musical. Music vanishes, depravity and derring-do have won the day.

The woman musician has fared no better. In Ludwig Winder's *Die jüdische Orgel* (1922)[8] a rabbinical student sacrifices everything to train a young singer for the opera; becoming a prostitute instead, she opens a nightclub together with her quondam Maecenas. In Borrmann's *Don Juan der halben Dinge* (1925)[9] a concert singer, Alice, tries to seduce the "Don Juan" by singing Mozart to him. In *Karriere* (1931)[10] Robert Neumann's Erna conducts the reader through the cabarets of the Balkans and the Weimar Republic; her forte is the song, "Rote Rosen habe ich gepflückt." Neumann's novel is at least an interesting account of the musical demimonde, and should some day possess cultural-historical value. Why did the writers of the twenties and thirties not deal at greater length and more realistically with the itinerant musician? Perhaps a modern equivalent of Springinsfeld would have arisen, a role hardly filled by the garish phantasms of a Borrmann or an Alfred Neumann.

This disappearance of music in a cloud of wild eroticism is the last stage in a development which began in the post-Wagnerian era, or even before. Happily, works also grew out of the same period in which the musician ceases to demand that his personal "rights of genius" be recognized. The blossoming of the theme of renunciation in the years after the war is not without resemblance to the Biedermeier's desire to push the Romantic genius into the background; but now the sacrificing musician assumes a greater variety of forms, and sometimes stands in closer contact with the music of his period.

Der Spiegel (1919) of Emil Strauss and *Der Geigenmacher* (1926) of Hermann Stehr deal with non-creative musicians who renounce. Both works are laid in the past, *Der Spiegel* in the late Rococo, *Der Geigenmacher* in an imaginary world. Like Stifter, whose style he imitates, Strauss is interested in the musician as pedagogue. His Josef is a typical Stifterian figure, perhaps more restless than most of the Austrian's creations. Josef tries farming, then enters a monastery and is sent by his superiors to study music in Vienna. Again discontented, he is about to leave the brotherhood when the emperor dissolves the monastic orders. Marrying the strong-willed Charlotte, who like him had once taken religious vows, Josef earns his living as a professional musician. An inheritance renders Charlotte financially independent, and husband and wife are gradually weaned away from one another. Josef dies of typhus, after having saved a traveler ill with the disease and neglected because of the fear of infection. Charlotte realizes that her pride has wrecked the marriage; she draws inspiration from her memories: "Josefs Bild ... beglückte sie so, dass sie an keinem Tage ihres schweren Lebens mehr die Heiterkeit des Herzens und Blickes verlor."[11]

The tale is meant to prove that character, not talent, is important. Josef's changes of occupation are not the struggles of the musical genius to attain his proper milieu. They are rather the efforts of a sincere man to find that position in which he may do the most good with the talents accorded him. Josef's musical career is as disillusioning as his experience in other capacities; for it does not grant him the spiritual peace he desires, and his concert tours keep him from his wife and children. The constant separation has encouraged Charlotte's obstinacy; in his absence Josef also changes sufficiently to warrant Charlotte's charge that he is "unberechenbar." The situation is not unlike that of Stifter's *Waldgänger*, where repeated separations cause two loving but stubborn people to grow apart.

Therefore Josef in his personal life is not quite the completely good man he strives to be. Only his final act of sacrifice transfigures him into an inspiration for his wife and children, thus letting him become the teacher in his most ideal form. Josef has always had something of the pedagogue about him: "Ich will gute Musik machen, die beste, die ich verstehe; aber das ist meine Natur, das macht mir keine Mühe ... Ich möchte aber auch etwas Schweres tun, wozu ich alle Willenskräfte zusammennehmen muss ..." (198). Hesse's Josef Knecht in *Das Glasperlenspiel* thinks the same thought; Knecht's life as *ludi magister* is all too easy for him, he likewise wishes to undertake something more difficult, and becomes the private tutor of a gifted but difficult child. Strauss's Josef is also forgetful of his own gifts, and decides to give up his concert tours in order to develop his son's talent, but perishes on his last journey, leaving behind only his example, not his technical ability. Josef Knecht is drowned just as he begins his new career as a tutor; the problem child is transformed by his example. Strauss's novel offers the most convincing argument before *Das Glasperlenspiel* for the musician as self-sacrificing pedagogue.

Stehr's *Der Geigenmacher*[12] concerns a master violin maker who cannot build a perfect instrument until he has learned to love and to renounce a peasant girl, Schönlein. Not properly a creative artist, the violin maker is still subject to a weakness of the recent composer, being the victim of excessive passion. Schönlein has promised herself to him if he will wait until she has completed certain tasks, a fairy tale motif. The violin maker approaches her too soon, and she disappears. He tries to atone for his error, but never finds his beloved again. Tormented by remorse but having learned renunciation, he fashions a violin in the shape of Schönlein's body. Upon hearing the sound of his masterpiece, he loses his peace of soul once more; the violins he builds thereafter cannot compare with the single product of his brief renunciation. The violin maker has lost the gift so painfully acquired.

Stehr's use of the style and motifs of the Märchen is tedious and detracts from the value of the message presented. The removal of the problem of the all too passionate artist (that is, the artist whose claims on life are too great) into the impossible world of the "Schönlein-Geige" does not add to the effectiveness of the story; the musician is too closely connected with such actual factors as current musical problems and the contemporary intellectual milieu to be separated so completely from reality. Much the same tendency can be seen in the nineteenth-century inclination to treat the musician as a historical figure; Stehr goes a step further and makes him a creature of myth.

In the musical episodes of Hesse's controversial *Der Steppenwolf* (1927) the narrator, the non-musician Haller, is given a lesson in humanity by two semi-mythical musicians, the magically talented saxophonist, Pablo, and the immortal Mozart himself. (The action takes place in the twentieth century.) At first it would seem that Pablo and Mozart represent opposed principles, the hectic fever of jazz and the noble serenity of classicism. Hesse declares that they are in essence related: Mozart, offering Haller a cigarette, is immediately transformed into Pablo. Both figures, so different in appearance, teach Haller to accept life as the "Urkampf zwischen Idee und Erscheinung, zwischen Ewigkeit und Zeit, zwischen Göttlichem und Menschlichem."[13] Even though Pablo plays "degenerate" music, smokes opium, debauches Haller's beloved Hermine, and expresses perverted desires toward Haller himself, he is still Haller's best friend in earthly affairs as Mozart is his best friend in the realm of the intellect. Mozart demonstrates to Haller that the music of Händel retains its nobility despite its cruel distortion by the radio: "Sie sollen die verfluchte Radiomusik des Lebens anhören lernen, sollen den Geist hinter ihr verehren, sollen über den Klimbim in ihr lachen lernen" (311). (And the music of cold "classical laughter" to which Mozart introduces his pupil is actually related to jazz in its gaiety and sparseness of means. In *Der Steppenwolf* Hesse prepares the disdain with which the "Glasperlenspieler" will treat the tragic lushness of Romanticism.) The solution presented in *Der Steppenwolf* is akin to that of *Gertrud*. The artist must learn not to demand that life be made ideal to correspond with his desires: Haller must accept the good and evil in Pablo, just as the narrator of *Gertrud* should have accepted the contradictions of Muoth.

The novels of Strauss and Stehr are innocent of new musical ideas; Hesse's *Steppenwolf*, although it introduces jazz, does not examine the influence of the Negro-American form on European music. Three other novels written during the twenties place the composer into contact with a totalitarian state, or with the twelve tone scale and musical primitivism, or with the world of jazz. Max Brod's *Das grosse Wagnis* (1918) puts the composer into an imaginary future, Otto Stoessl's *Sonnenmelodie* (1923) lets him essay a conflict with the contemporary world, while René Schickele, in *Symphonie für Jazz* (1929) makes the musician too much a part of certain currents in that world.

The composer-narrator, E. St., of *Das grosse Wagnis* has taken that not infrequent decision of his calling to withdraw from public life. War breaks out and he is drafted; ill and fatigued, he is spirited away by a friend to the underground city of Liberia, whose name is belied by its dictatorial government. There his musical ability earns him special favors; he also has the good fortune to meet an earlier beloved, Ruth. Ruth convinces the narrator that in his withdrawal from the world he has not attempted "das grosse Wagnis"—the effort to become a truly free and good man. (She has devised a complicated game called "das grosse Wagnis," intended to teach children freedom of the spirit; can Hesse, in writing *Das Glasperlenspiel*, have thought of her invention?) Liberia is shaken by a series of revolutions, the "mountain of Liberia" is blown up, and Ruth disappears. The narrator, no longer the selfish artist, wanders through the "war-world" as a prophet and teacher, thinking of Ruth and her "Wagnis," preaching the gospel of love, and pondering the education of youth. Arrested, he is shot as a deserter.

Der Spiegel and *Das grosse Wagnis* appeared at the same time, and for all their differences they concern the same theme: the teacher who, leaving his art to teach by his example, perishes in his pedagogical venture. Indeed, Brod's passion for pedagogy leads him to polemics against Romantic music and its estrangement from reality: "Das Resultat aller Konstruktionen heisst: Dekonstruktion ... deshalb musste Krieg und Militäreinberufung hereinbrechen, um den in Mönchseinsamkeit Weltabgeschiedenen heimzusuchen und zurück in die Welt zu ziehen."[14] But Brod is less serene than Strauss in his notion of how unselfish goodness is to be transmitted by the former musician. Strauss, like Hesse to come, has his hero work by the still example; E.St. is a noisier prophet of quiet love.

The serenity lacking in Brod's picture of renunciation is no more an integral part of Stoessl's *Sonnenmelodie*. Its hero, Johann Körrer, is burdened with the poverty we saw besetting Wassermann's Nothafft; musically Körrer is more important than his predecessor. Born in Wiener Neustadt, the son of a drunken zither virtuoso, Körrer picks up harmony at his father's side. Social injustice keeps him from a musical career; becoming a schoolteacher, he nourishes his musical ambitions by playing cello in an amateur quartet and attending the opera. He is repulsed by the sensual connotations, the literalness, and the overpowering "sense of instrument" to be detected in the Wagnerian orchestra: "War dies noch Musik? ... Die Töne sprachen nicht mehr ihre eigene unverwirrte Sprache, sondern alle möglichen Laute, aus ihnen summte das Holz, ächzte das Metall, pfiffen die Zungen, redeten Bäuche, stöhnten Lungen, damit das Meer, der Himmel, ein Becher verzauberten Weins, ein begehrlicher Weibeskörper, ein siecher Mannesleib, eine Hirtenflöte, das Säuseln eines nächtlichen Gartens nachgeahmt, nein wiederholt würden."[15] (Adrian Leverkühn has the same distaste for the instrument and uses tonepainting chiefly for ironic purposes.) Körrer, abandoning his cello, makes his debut as a composer. His concert for the Wiener Neustadt public is a fiasco; even his supporters are not prepared to receive his special variety of music. His compositions, based on the twelve tone scale, try to abandon both harmony and polyphony. The instrumental works consist of a succession of solo voices, playing without expression or accent: ". . . die Vielheit der Stimmen, die einander folgten, antworteten, und ergänzten, [war] schwerer zu fassen . . . als bei der gewohnten Musik, wo sie miteinander und gleichzeitig auftraten, immer dasselbe mannigfach wiederholten und abwandelten, bis es . . . sich ins Bewusstsein bohrte und hämmerte. Hier tauchte jede Folge der Töne . . . mit ihrer sachlichen Klarheit, mit ihrem eigenen Rhythmus, nur in gewisser Entfernung von ihren eigenen Akkorden begleitet, wie Bogen auf ihren Pfeilern stehend, auf . . ." (384-385). Körrer's songs, to Hölderlin texts, are "keine inbrünstigen Rufe bedrängter Leiblichkeit" but rather of "menschheitlicher Bedeutung" (379). Stoessl's descriptions of Körrer's compositions, written long before Thomas Mann portrayed the music of Leverkühn, prove that the latter author was not a pioneer in giving the tonal system of Schönberg literary form.

Some of the listeners judge that Körrer is mad, and during the war years he does briefly become the inmate of an asylum. After his release he discovers that the reputation of his compositional system has spread, but he continues to live in abject poverty. His intransigent condemnation of music other than his own ("Die Welt hat das Gehör verdorben. Sie wird am Getöse sterben. Sie will es so," 433) does not win wealthy patrons. As Körrer becomes more and more estranged from reality, he adopts a musical primitivism unlike the intellectuality of his Hölderlin songs; he dreams of an ageless melody from the sun, "einfache, unbetonte Melodie" (439), which he connects, in confused prose, with the music of the spheres. He continues his battle against musical instruments (an early symptom of his urge to primitivism), complaining that there are no longer "zwölf abgemessene, schwebende, klare Töne . . . sondern soviel Töne, als man Instrumente nebeneinander schart" (466). The novel ends when a loan company takes Körrer's piano away; his wife finds him playing the "sun melody" on glasses of water, the nearest approximation of pure music he can achieve. Just before his bankruptcy Körrer, like Goethe and Dauthendey before him, has busied himself with thoughts of a pedagogical province, a fantastic "Egypt" where king and priests have as their first task the preservation of "die Melodik der gleichschwebenden Temperatur, die atonale Musik . . . als einzige wahrhafte, mögliche, von der Willkür der Triebe und Leidenschaften freie, reine Musik" (490). Stoessl has attempted that combination which neither Mann nor Hesse in their pictures of modern musical culture directly essays, a synthesis of the atonal system with the pedagogical province. The fascinating if very uneven *Sonnenmelodie* leads from the musical treatments of renunciation to the musicological novel. Stoessl's Körrer has renounced that which we commonly know as music for a purer ideal, finally seen in pedagogical terms. His last audience, as he plays on the glasses, is his little son.

Hesse has implied a connection between the "classical laughter" of Mozart and modern popular music. René Schickele's *Symphonie für Jazz* denies that jazz may be a possible saviour of decadent European music. Schickele states instead that jazz is more emotion-laden, and hence more dangerous for the art as well as for its practitioners, than any previous musical phenomenon. John van Maray, the half-Dutch, half-Lothringian hero of Schickele's novel, is symptomatic for the evil arising from an intimate association with jazz. His attitude toward the new music is at first an ironic one—jazz is the proper vehicle to express his vast contempt for the world in general—but soon the master becomes the servant. "Erst trieb er nur Spass mit der Jazzmusik . . . behandelte sie als Gegenstand seines musikalischen Ingrimms . . . Er hoffte, schliesslich werde dem Publikum der Skandal klar werden, den er meinte. Das Publikum merkte nichts dergleichen, und John begann sich mit dem tönenden Umsinn . . . zu befreunden."[16]

In his personal life John becomes a perfect representative of his art. He has misadventures with psychoanalysts; his marriage to the beautiful Johanna goes to pieces. Johanna herself is infected by the bad habits of John's circle; after her separation from him she becomes involved with a publicist, a wealthy musical amateur, and an effeminate dance-band drummer. John meanwhile continues to work at jazz compositions, in particular a jazz symphony, in which the melodies, ostensibly beautiful, come "von den Orgien der vierten Morgenstunde in der gruselig bunten Unterführung des Bahnhofs. Sie hatten gerade Zeit gehabt, sich zu waschen und umzukleiden" (234). His decidedly impure inspiration is the vocalist Ursel Bruhn ("mein Nacht-Ursch"), for whom he composes song after song. Ursel introduces John to a bohemian group in which music is abused: a man in lilac pajamas sings venerable hymns while a girl dances with "wollüstigen Windungen und Streckungen des Körpers," and a Bach chorale is performed in the same fashion (199-200). John leaves Ursel in disgust, and Johanna, learning that John is in desperate need of a child on whom to lavish his love, decides to renew their union. She follows her husband to St. Moritz, where he has gone with little Angelica, his illegitimate daughter from a former liaison. Angelica dies after a skiing accident; before her death she commands her father to love Johanna once more. Realizing what jazz has done to him, John "griff das Saxophon und versenkte es wie eine krepierte Katze in den See" (352). Johanna sings a lied which John had once composed in the post-Romantic idiom, and their reunion is complete.

John, having renounced his jazz music and his dissolute life, emerges from the nightmarish experience a better man. But is he a better artist? Will a renewed devotion to the style of the German nineteenth century be artistically profitable in the twentieth? Schickele has begged the question by making jazz, too easily turned into a whipping boy, the sole representative of the modern spirit in music. There are other facets of modern music capable of commanding greater respect. Nevertheless, Schickele must be given credit for his effort to portray, in however unfriendly a fashion, the contemporary musical world. The jazz-hells through which John van Maray wanders are more raffish versions of the Munich musical salons which Mann depicts so cuttingly in *Doktor Faustus*. The candid portraiture of musical circles is a field which the German author, concerned as he often is with plumbing a single artistic personality, has not entered frequently enough.

Novels on the composer from the thirties have less to say about revolutions in music than do works from the preceding decade. Perhaps this is a result of the growing intellectual isolation of Nazi Germany, perhaps of the fact that the twenties, musically speaking, were a more exciting age. A work like Reinhold Konrad Muschler's *Ivola* (1936) deals with a composer who obviously writes in the neo-Romantic vein. (The most popular movement in German music at this time was neo-Romanticism, with Richard Strauss—of whom Muschler has written a biography—as its dean and chief representative.) Muschler's

Abel Kühn has just completed an opera, *Metastasio* (compare the eighteenth century setting of *Der Rosenkavalier*), but all is not well in his world. His wife Antonia, whom he has left on account of her unfaithfulness, wants him back; she claims she needs him in order to continue as a great singer. Abel has fallen in love with the motherly Viola, the wife of a lecherous prince. (Imitating her little boy, Abel calls her Ivola.) The body of the novel is concerned with preparation for *Metastasio* and with the marital entanglements of hero and heroine. Abel plans to divorce Antonia immediately after the premiere; Ivola feels duty-bound to remain with the prince. At the final curtain call on opening night Antonia, who has sung a leading role, tries to shoot Abel; Ivola has got wind of the plan and, aided by her uncle, sees to it that the weapon is unloaded. No one notices Antonia's vain gesture with the pistol, but Ivola is able to compel her by polite blackmail to leave Abel's life. Then the helpful uncle persuades Ivola to abandon her prince and marry Abel.

Even without Ivola, Abel possessed a humble concept of the composer's task: "Wenn diese Arbeit nicht voll im Klang herauskommt, verzichte ich auf alles. Ich bin nur der Vermittler des Werkes, geschrieben hat es ein anderer."[17] Under the influence of Ivola the artist renounces many of the freedoms he might have formerly granted himself. Ivola spends the night at Abel's house; instead of seducing her, he takes pains to save her reputation. If he is at work in his composer's hut, once his most jealously guarded sanctuary (Antonia could not go there), his solitude may be broken by Ivola—and by a little neighbor girl and her kitten. We can foresee an Abel settled down comfortably with wife and children: "Du hast die Kinder, ich mein neues Werk, das dir gehören soll" (78). Abel is no worse a composer for having given up his more extreme attitudes; the musician prospers best, personally and artistically, in the arms of a good woman. Reading Muschler we are reminded of Richard Strauss's "autobiographical" opera, *Intermezzo*, where the composer Storch (Strauss) celebrates the ability of his wife to keep him a good musician and a good paterfamilias. If a great composer can allow himself such sentiments, why not an author considerably less than great?

There are many entertainment novels with a tone like that of *Ivola*: the musician, abandoning a few of his Romantic airs, achieves material success in addition to personal improvement.

In Kurt Kluge's very popular *Die Zaubergeige* (1940)[18] Andreas, a young violinist with ambitions as a composer, is the victim of a Romantically bad temper and an equally Romantic passion for music, a passion which leads him to steal, inadvertently, a Stradivarius from a Leipzig museum. All's well that ends well; in the course of a nation-wide search for the missing instrument a famous violin virtuoso is detained by border police. Andreas fills the virtuoso's shoes at a concert and himself becomes renowned, the Stradivarius is returned to its rightful owners, and the genial miscreant marries the long-suffering Agnes Kegel, who trusts that her beloved has lost at least the more criminal part of his bohemianism. Such false renunciation, another case of both having and eating the artistic cake, is to be expected in the novel designed to entertain a large circle of readers; in a work almost contemporary with Kluge's, by a more serious writer, the musician abandons music, believing that he cannot serve it well enough.

The final part of Jakob Schaffner's Johannes Schattenhold tetralogy, *Kampf und Reife* (1939), comes somewhat later than the main wave of works on renunciation; but the musical ideas it propounds are those of the late nineteenth century, the age which it portrays. (Schaffner was sixty-four years old at the time of the novel's publication.) Johannes Schattenhold, as free of musical knowledge as any incipient composer in German literature, learns about Beethoven and Schubert from a cultured Basel lady; he studies the clarinet under a rural schoolmaster. Armed with these skills he goes to Vienna to become a composer. He finds a job as a street and coffeehouse musician, and the scenes portraying his adventures in this capacity are among the best in the novel. While Schaffner's itinerant musician is evidently drawn from life, Schattenhold's creative activities are less convincing. Mittsbacher, a talented violinist, teaches Schattenhold reverence for the great German masters (a vision of Beethoven saves Schattenhold from the wife of his impresario); the violinst likewise exercises an unmerciful criticism on Schattenhold's oratorio, *Lucifer*, a subject recalling the *Satans* of Schubin and Wolzogen. Burning the manuscript, he tells the baffled composer that one would have to be a Beethoven or a Bruckner to accomplish what he has attempted; his effort was "ungeheuer deutsch im Guten und fast noch mehr im Schlechten."[19] A failure as a musician, Schattenhold returns to

Zürich where a performance of Beethoven's *Eroica* stirs him to new intellectual efforts, this time as a writer. Eventually Schattenhold achieves a philosophy of life in which the freedom-loving man, not the artist, is the central figure.

The fact that the three novels just described were written during the Nazi era is not indicated by a special political bias of their authors, other than the comparatively harmless patriotic rhapsodies of Schaffner or the unobtrusive remarks of Kluge on the sudden success of his hero: ". . . aus Kranichstedt kommt man, heisst irgendwie, und spielt da grosse Konzerte. Deutschland, Deutschland . . ." (172). There does exist, however, a novel in which the musician renounces music for the Nazi cause; Kurt Ziesel's *Verwandlung der Herzen* (1943) can win a minor literary-historical significance by its exposition of renunciation's newest turn. The Austrian violinist Dietrich Vorwerk, for a time a member of an "Arbeitsgemeinschaft" captained by the vital Nazi Seehofer, has gone out to win fame in the concert world. Seehofer is burned to death by Communists; in his last breath he asks for Dietrich, who, giving up both his art and the woman he loves, returns to the "Gemeinschaft" saying: "Wir wollen alles hingeben, was wir vermögen, an dieses Land und seine Not."[20] Music, in Ziesel's unsubtle mind, has no place in the totalitarian state. He is not aware that Thomas Mann, a distinguished lover of the art, has expressed fears in *Der Zauberberg* that music may be precisely the totalitarian state's best spiritual weapon—fears which play a role in the novel which Mann was beginning just as Ziesel published *Verwandlung der Herzen*.

II.

In the post-war period the advances made in the study of music as a matter for critical and historical research began to bear fruit: musicology had developed to a point where it could lay claim to an accuracy corresponding to that of the more established branches of research. The result was a new interest among music-lovers in technical problems, in musical history, and in music's role in the growth and decline of a culture. Closely connected with the development of musicology was the belief among perceptive musicians that the post-Wagnerian age was at an end, that the old concept of harmony was bankrupt, and that the art was perhaps in process of decay. This belief was soon reflected among literary men, who already possessed the tradition of a historical concept of music in certain works of Biedermeier and Poetic Realism. The period from Nietzsche to the First World War had seen little active interest in the musician as a historical figure: there the musicians are contemporary. The revival of the musical past had always had a place in the field of cheap biography, to be sure; the establishment of musical studies as a science and the necessity of reforming the art after the decay of harmony succeeded in interesting literary men of a higher rank in essayistic and biographical treatments of the musical past.

Even the opera is used as a vehicle for the interpretation of the life of an actual musician. Hans Pfitzner's musical legend, *Palestrina*, inspired Thomas Mann to a revealing little essay which contains some of the ideas later expressed in *Doktor Faustus*. The essay was written after Mann had attended the dress rehearsal of the opera and appeared as part of the *Betrachtungen eines Unpolitischen* (1918). Mann calls the opera, which represents Pfitzner's effort to infuse an overripe Romanticism with the austere principles of the polyphonic age, the marriage of "alles Raffinement [des] Vorhalt-Geschiebes" with "Mittelalter, Kargheit, Grabeshauch, Krypta, Totengerippe."[21] Polyphony, redolent of death and decay, especially fascinates Mann. Indeed he treats Pfitzner's work as a musical expression of his own necrolatric urge and allows Pfitzner to express himself concerning the opera in a distinctly Mannian fashion: ". . . im Palestrina neigt alles zum Vergangenen, es herrscht darin Sympathie mit dem Tode" (26). Mann overlooks the chance that musical progress may be present in the return to polyphony; as in the later *Faustus* he takes a pessimistic view of the future of music as an art. In his opinion the opera is the last piece of Romantic art, the glorious but sad conclusion of a period. A further anticipation of the *Faustus* material is the identification of the musician with the political situation. Both *Palestrina* and its creator are regarded as products of a "nationalistic Romanticisim;" the artist "politicizes" himself during the war years into an anti-democratic nationalist (29). The musician, however enlightened he may be, inevitably possesses certain tendencies toward obscurantism and absolutism; he is, Mann implies, by nature the exact opposite of the humanist. In *Die Entstehung des Doktor Faustus* Mann will again ask: "Hat das musikalische Genie überhaupt nichts mit Humanität ... zu tun?"[22]

Mann's next musical effort, the essay *Leiden und Grösse Richard Wagners* (1935),[23] has the general importance of being one of the first lengthy interpretations since Nietzsche of a great musician by a great writer. More specifically, it includes a lengthy discussion of the death theme in Wagner, and a probing into the erotic problems of the operas, a subject which, as we shall see, has an important connection with *Doktor Faustus*. Unlike the works of Nietzsche it is supported by a wealth of factual detail. Nietzsche treated Wagner's personality and music dramas without possessing any intimate knowledge of music and without attempting to support his opinions with evidence, in contrast to his passages on the Greek tragedy, where he was able to draw upon an excellent philological training. Mann approaches Wagner as he does the literary figures in *Leiden und Grösse der Meister*: creative intuition and exact knowledge work hand in hand. Mann's Wagner essay is rather heavily weighted with literary and philosophical information, as opposed to musical detail; yet it is plain that Mann wishes to be taken seriously as an interpreter of Wagner the musician. Music has become a learned matter and the musician a fit subject for the penetrating and careful essay.

In *Palestrina* and *Leiden und Grösse Richard Wagners*, Mann often approaches the line between interpretive and creative literature, frequently taking up the theme of his musical novel, but he does not as yet attempt this latter work nor does he follow the course of Franz Werfel, who united essay and novel in *Verdi*, a fictionalized biography from 1924. The genre of fictionalized biography has been much abused; and it may seem strange to see a work from this class treated in conjunction with creative literature. Yet the fictionalized biography, that uncomfortable mixture of musical and historical fact, psychological and erotic disquisitions, and, often, actual musical criticisms, has found respectable representatives, like Klaus Mann's *Symphonie Pathétique* or Frank Thiess's giant *Caruso*.[24] Not all the laborers in the vineyard have produced entertainment literature of the nature of Robert Hohlbaum's, Hans Watzlik's, or Zdenko von Kraft's efforts. Indeed, in the hands of a discerning and well-informed writer, the *vie romancée* can attempt to propagate new musical ideas. And has not Thomas Mann given *Doktor Faustus* the semblance of a fictionalized biography?

Werfel's *Verdi* is the best of the fictionalized biographies and stands closest to *Doktor Faustus* in seriousness of purpose and validity of musical judgment. Apart from the fact that it gives the Italian musician a fair treatment, it contains a novelty in its glorification of the musician as artisan, and so represents another facet of the renaissance of pre-Romantic musical ideals which accompanies the realization that music stands in the need of reform. In order to accomplish his purpose, Werfel leads us to late nineteenth-century Venice, and in his loving exhumation of the controversies between the supporters of Wagner and Verdi, he sometimes moves us to suspect that he (like Mann) is almost too concerned with the death throes of Romantic music to be a forthright champion of a new attitude. It may be charged that Werfel further obscures his purpose by weaving too many incidents of a sentimental or incredible nature into his plot. An example of the former is Verdi's meeting with a crippled street singer, an example of the latter the story of Marquis Gritti who, more than a hundred years old, has attended the opera every night during his adult life. These and other episodes of a similar nature heighten the contrast between the fictional sections of *Verdi* and those more solid portions based on Verdi's life and work. That part of the book which is fiction is not of the highest quality; that part which concerns itself with the interpretations of Verdi's music is full of discernment, an indication of the strength of the new learned tradition in writing on music.

Wagner and Verdi are placed in opposition, and in them the Romantic and non-Romantic conceptions of the musician. Wagner is the possessor of a magnetic personality; upon seeing him fleetingly, Verdi realizes that not the work but the man captivates even the Italians. Werfel in his sultry fashion uses quasi-sexual imagery: Wagner is like a woman who wishes to conquer, and in his eyes Verdi detects: "Liebeswerben, Einbeziehenwollen, etwas fast Weiblich-Mächtiges."[25] Verdi on the other hand is treated as the musician, not as the personality. A hardworking realist, Verdi's only miracle is his complete naturalness. He regards himself as a sincere artisan but not as a genius, and Werfel, who seldom distinguishes himself by understatement, gives his hero over to relatively little posturing. Resembling in this respect Hoffmann in his treatment of Mozart, Werfel devotes most of his effort to the works rather than the man. The novelist's remarks on the female characters in the Verdi operas are particularly fascinating. Like so many other writers on the musical hero, he sees the woman as at once inspiration and embodiment of music, but Werfel's woman is not the ethereal ideal of Hoffmann or the *hetaera esmeralda* of Mann. It is characteristic of Verdi that a friend, a physician, must reveal to him that he has employed only one feminine type in his operas: "Die Liebende, die vom Manne aufgeopfert wird, oder sich selbst für ihn aufopfert" (237). The doctor then proceeds to name examples, Gilda, Violetta, Leonore, Luise Miller, Aida. Agreeing, Verdi tells a tale from his youth: the screams of a woman in childbirth have left an indelible mark upon him. His great operatic heroines are but expressions of his reverence for the woman as sufferer; often a vision of his dead wife appears to him as he composes. Werfel's feminine ideal of music is more human than either that of Hoffmann or Mann; she is not completely idealized nor is she an instrument of the devil.

However, Werfel cleverly introduces the great feminine voice in the figure of Margherita Dezorzi, a soprano who in her coldness really possesses no sex at all. The ambitious Margherita attempts to seduce the aging Verdi, and he succumbs to the extent of kissing her. That night he is overcome by a feeling of deathly illness, but he recovers from the attack. Suddenly deciding that he is Wagner's friend, he resolves to visit the German; he does so only to find that Wagner has died. The healthy Verdi is attracted by the artificial passion of Margherita and the equally artificial idealism of German art; he conquers the temptation of what for him would be destructive spirits. Wagner, the chief exponent of "idealistic" music, dies during the night while Verdi, a musical Antaeus, lives on. Werfel makes his symbolism even clearer, if more tasteless, by allowing the wife of the doctor who has interpreted Verdi's women characters to bear a child in the midst of the most awful pain. The baby, fathered by a Wagner enthusiast, is accepted by the woman's husband, while the young weakling continues his hopeless pursuit of the soprano Dezorzi. Thus the woman as conceived by Verdi is re-introduced to emphasize the meaning of the composer's work. Margherita Dezorzi, an Italian by birth, is really a representative of German music; Bianca, the wife of the doctor, although only distantly connected with the art, is the representative of Italian music. The concept of the Italian woman presented by Werfel is seemingly different from that in Heine's *Florentinische Nächte*: there Bellini dies as it were from the touch of a woman with the profile of a da Vinci madonna, here the composer survives Dezorzi's touch and is inspired to compose by woman's suffering. Yet in both cases it is the "false" Italian woman who kills or seeks to kill, the French salon beauty, the German-spirited soprano; and Bellini, like Verdi, has created his greatest role in his suffering woman, his Norma. (Only Heinrich Mann—here paradoxically in league with the anti-Italian writers on music—attributes a more destructive role to the bona fide Italian woman, and even his Branzilla, Garlinda, and Alda have something asexual about themselves, in contrast to the passionate Molesin, who saves the little city through her womanhood.)

The association of Verdi with the masters of the polyphonic age in music also suggests a new attitude toward the art: two sections of Werfel's novel are devoted to a return to the age of Claudio Monteverdi: the Monteverdi of 1643 is the ancestor of the Verdi of 1883. Not that Verdi would restore to life the severe glories of a distant past: Verdi (and Werfel) consider the resuscitation of antique forms as artificial pedantry. A young German composer, Fischböck, is befriended by Verdi, but with the best intentions the operatic composer cannot understand the German's frigid works in the style of the Renaissance. Verdi's relationship to the early masters is a question of his mode of work: like them he does not think of himself as a genius and rejects the motto "art for the artist." Thus far Werfel's concept represents a refreshing change from the attitude of the preceding period, in which the artist was granted every privilege without being obligated in the slightest toward society. As the humanistically inclined Senator says in his eulogy on Verdi: "Die romantische Irrlehre hat ein Zerrideal vom Künstler geschaffen: den Zigeuner, den Schmutzigen, den wändebespuckenden Beethoven, den Vergesslichen, den Nervösen, den Unlogischen, den Verantwortungslosen, den Nur-Sensitiven, den Imbezillen!" (545). These words represent a trenchant warning to the musical artist to return to a saner attitude.

Werfel has damaged his case by certain factors. His exclusive praise of the Italian musician makes it appear that he, like the later Nietzsche, put the healthy music of Mediterranean culture into contrast with the effete mysticism of the North; and in celebrating the naiveté of the Italian musical genius and tracing it back to a uterine source he comes dangerously close to a mother-worship as decadent in its own way as the "Sympathie mit dem Tode" of German artists. The connection which Werfel draws between Verdi's inspiration and the woman in labor would degrade the composer to a Corybant. And the re-emphasis of the sensuousness inherent in Italian music, however "normal" this sensuous quality may be, is after all not so very far removed from the attitude to be found in the many musical novels where composition seems to spring solely from a biological urge. While it is gratifying to see a more reasonable attitude toward foreign music and musicians on the part of a German writer, the implied denial of value to the art of the homeland seems an evasion of present problems: German musical culture cannot be saved by the adoption of the Italian style or the Italian philosophy of music.

Verdi, in its combination of fictional elements with musical thought, is related to *Doktor Faustus*, however disparate the two books otherwise may be. Mann's book likewise contains a series of essays on music and musical philosophy, set in a simulated fictionalized biography: not a few of Mann's characters can be shown to have their prototypes among German cultural figures of the first half of the twentieth century. Indeed he stands closer than Werfel to the writers of the usual *vie romancée*, for Werfel interprets only one brief portion of the life of Verdi, while Mann, like a typical author of biography in the novel's guise, pictures the entire career of his hero.

Doktor Faustus (1948) must be regarded as a direct development in the tradition of the classical musical novels and novellas, upon which it draws heavily. Mann's affinity to the Romanticists has long been recognized as a leading feature of his work, and here, in a novel concerning the most Romantic of the arts, his knowledge of the literature of Romanticism appears most extensively. (In *Die Entstehung des Doktor Faustus* Mann notes that he read *Kater Murr* while preparing to work on his novel, 26.) Other periods of German musical literature should not be overlooked, however. The influence of Storm, omnipresent in

Mann's earlier works, continues in *Doktor Faustus*. The interest in psychoanalytical problems (psychoanalysis is a science born of the Romantic movement) is apparent in *Doktor Faustus* as elsewhere in Mann, and it is not unlikely that Mann has more than a passing acquaintance with the works of the preceding period concerning the aberrations of the musician. Contemporary elements are added: in the sections on the latest advances made in music and in the identification of Leverkühn with the decaying German state; yet we have already seen Otto Stoessl's use of the twelve tone scale and Emil Brachvogel's attempt to give the musician historical significance.

Adrian Leverkühn, unlike Berglinger and Kreisler, is the product of a happy home. He spends the greater part of his childhood sheltered from harm, at first on his father's prosperous farm, then at the home of his uncle, a maker of musical instruments. He is a colder and more arrogant child than the nervous Kreisler, and does not manifest an interest in music until he has almost reached maturity, being more engrossed in mathematics and theology. (The Romantic musicians, even as small children, are devoted to music.) A specifically demonic element appears in Leverkühn after he has deserted his religious studies to devote himself to music; the darker and more fantastic side of Leverkühn's nature is released by contact with Mann's art of decay and death. Until his change of interests, Leverkühn has been noted for his extreme clarity of intellect, a condition not generally associated with the composer in literature. Only his inclination toward religious studies gives an inkling of the transformation which is to take place; he and his humanistic friend Zeitblom, the narrator of the novel, attend the lectures of one Eberhard Schleppfuss, a representative of the tendency of theology to become demonology, even though the teacher's demonic conception of God and world is psychologically illuminated and thus made acceptable to the modern scientific intellect.[26] But after Leverkühn has undertaken the study of music at Leipzig he falls prey to hallucinations, which presumably are the results of a venereal infection, yet which, as Mann infers, may also be a part of the torments caused the musician by his art. During a trip to Italy the devil appears before him and tells him what his future will be. There is no such scene in the Kreisler papers of Hoffmann: although Kreisler sees the devil during his improvisations at the piano, the question of a pact with evil does not arise. That theme is present in Hoffmann's works, however; an allusion has already been made to the interview between Klingsohr and Heinrich von Ofterdingen in Hoffmann's *Der Kampf der Sänger*; in this story, as in Mann's novel, use is made of antique German, and, as in the modern work, the representative of evil constantly changes shape. In both cases the hero rejects the advances of the tempter until he realizes that he has already fallen prey to evil through his delving into the secrets of the art, that is, through his attempts to achieve musical progress.

Nevertheless, a basic difference exists between Hoffmann and Mann. Hoffmann occasionally suspects the existence of evil in art; his Heinrich von Ofterdingen and the madness which now and then overcomes Kreisler are examples of his suspicion, but on the whole he regards music as the musician's salvation. Mann, proceeding from his famous assumptions that music possesses a "Sympathie mit dem Tode," and that the state of the artist is a state of sickness, cannot avoid presenting these elements in *Doktor Faustus*, unchanged in their essence and developed to their final extreme. The devil states that music is "Eine hochtheologische Angelegenheit, . . . —wie die Sünde es ist, wie ich es bin" (374). Music is at once knowledge (in the theological sense) and decay. After having stamped music as the "most Christian art," that is, an art begun and developed by Christianity but in its sensual aspects denied and excluded as a demonic sphere by the church, the devil continues to present arguments concerning the relationship between sickness and genius. From Leverkühn's interview with the devil, Mann develops the second half of his novel: the hero is more and more harassed by his disease (or by the demands of his genius), until he at last breaks down at the performance of his Faust cantata for a select group of friends. Before madness takes complete possession of him he delivers an address in the antique German employed in his conversation with the devil. He confesses that he was born for hell (that is, born with genius), studied theology for the sake of evil, and that his adoption of a musical career was but another act by which he sacrificed himself to the devil. At the climax of the passage Leverkühn makes the revealing statement: "Es ist die Zeit, wo auf fromme, nüchterne Weis, mit rechten Dingen, kein Werk mehr zu tun, und die Kunst unmöglich geworden ist ohne Teufelshilf und höllisch Feuer unter dem Kessel" (757). Mann's conception of the composer is still a Romantic one; he may be critical of the theory of the demonically possessed genius, yet he feels that even now it is impossible to return to the concept of the composer as artisan. Leverkühn continues with the statement that art has become too "heavy" for itself and mocks itself—the fault of the times; but if one invites the devil to dinner (if one attempts to create art in such a period) he takes that fault onto his own shoulders and so is damned. The composer cannot create in a natural manner any longer; music is a tired art and those who attempt to bring freshness into the art are doomed to failure. After having delivered himself of this extremely pessimistic thought upon the future of music and its creators, Mann makes the darkness deeper as he tells of the unhappy fate of Leverkühn. The composer goes mad and becomes a child, like Nietzsche and Hugo Wolf.

The wealth of detail used to depict Adrian Leverkühn and his surroundings is drawn in large part from Romanticism. Leverkühn, like Kreisler, often succumbs to fits of wild humor; as in Kreisler's case the affinity with the dark powers is wont to reveal itself as irony, especially in the musician's earlier years; later it takes the form of compositions such as the *Suite for Puppets* which employs sardonic reworkings of legends from the *Gesta Romanorum*. Leverkühn has been accustomed to read these stories aloud before his friends, thus satisfying his "Sinn für Komik . . . diese Begierde nach dem Lachen" (484). The same spirit of irony appears in Leverkühn's use of a baroque style in his letters, and in the disdain he shows even his intimates. Here Mann goes beyond Hoffmann. Kreisler's "scurrility" in the *Kreisleriana* can assume the form of madness, but in *Kater Murr* he exercises his ironic talents more at will, as self-protection. Mann allows Leverkühn to erect a fortification of irony around himself, to be sure, but also causes the irony to appear in Leverkühn's music as an expression of the composer's anti-humanistic and demonic quality. (Werfel, upon hearing certain details from *Faustus,* was quick to seize upon "das . . . alles durchziehende und vielfach abgewandelte Motiv der 'Kälte,' das mit dem des Lachens verwandt ist," *Entstehung,* 66.) Kreisler never degrades music by using it as parody. Leverkühn not only writes his puppet operas but composes such works as the *Apocalipsis cum figuris,* where the voice of the Babylonian whore is parodied by saxophones and muted trumpets, in the use of which Adrian's "Fähigkeit zur spottenden Nachahmung" (573) stands him in good stead.

In *Doktor Faustus* Mann also borrows directly from Storm's *Ein stiller Musikant* and his own *Zauberberg* (Castorp's preference for the "Lindenbaum") to connect music and death with the works of Franz Schubert—and Schubert seen Romantically. Young Leverkühn becomes especially interested in lieder-composition, steeping himself in Schumann, Mendelssohn, Brahms, and Wolf: "Schuberts immer zwielichtiges, vom Tode berührtes Genie aber suchte er dort mit Vorliebe auf, wo es einem gewissen nur halb definierten, aber unabwendbaren Einsamkeitsverhängnis zum höchsten Ausdruck verhilft . . ." (125). The works of Schubert thus are of primary importance in the composition of the group of Brentano poems which Leverkühn undertakes after his meeting with the *hetaera esmeralda*, a meeting given musical form in Leverkühn's composition of "O lieb Mädel, wie schlecht bist du." Likewise, Mann's identification of music with sin and the devil bears a relationship to late Romantic authors (or epigones of Romanticism); Heine's Paganini is in league with the devil, the devil appears as violinist in Lenau's *Faust*, and his Mischka kills by means of music. Mann removes this musical diabolism to a subtler plane, yet his use of music as the instrument of the devil and the call to death remains Romantic in essence and atmosphere.

Mann balances the extreme Romanticism of his musical hero by a dose of humanism, just as Hoffmann's tendency toward a concept of art as evil was more than balanced by his belief in its benefits. Leverkühn is provided with a constant example of serenity in Serenus Zeitblom, professor of classical philology, cultured musical amateur, and performer on the viola d'amore. The contrast between the humanist Zeitblom and the demonically inspired Leverkühn is a transformed version of the relationship (or conflict) between the humanist Settembrini and the obscurantist Naphta in *Der Zauberberg*; in *Faustus*, of course, Leverkühn has Mann's sympathy, while in *Der Zauberberg* "der kleine Herr Naphta" often becomes the object of Mann's scorn. Mann's sympathetic handling of Leverkühn can arise from a number of emotional reactions: the author's own affinity to Romanticism, his love for Romantic music, his feeling for Leverkühn's essentially German nature; yet there is also an intellectual argument for Mann's friendliness to his difficult, even unlovable creation. Leverkühn has destroyed himself by creating works of art in an age which compels the artist to assume the Romantic attitude toward the composition of music, even though that music itself is completely un-Romantic. However, Leverkühn has had humanistic training, and like Settembrini, believes in a better world where such sacrifices as his own will not be necessary. In a conversation with his friends he says: "Die ganze Lebensstimmung der Kunst, glauben Sie mir, wird sich ändern, und zwar ins Heiter-Bescheidenere—es ist unvermeidlich, und es ist ein Glück. Viel melancholische Ambition wird von ihr abfallen und eine neue Unschuld, ja Harmlosigkeit ihr Teil sein" (494-495). The musical art will become the servant of a "Gemeinschaft." The modernity of this statement shocks the humanist Zeitblom, enough the nineteenth-century man to believe in the unassailable rights of the genius, a belief in which he is strengthened by his fear of vulgarization.

Mann has arranged one of his favorite and unsettling shiftings of viewpoint between his contrasting figures. Leverkühn, a final representative of the Romantic concept of the composer, upsets the humanist Zeitblom with the momentary modernity of his thought and the hopeful humanity contained in his concept of art as a servant of society; Zeitblom, on the other hand, is "modern" in that he resents the demonism, the "medieval quality" in Leverkühn—and, a later Settembrini, fears the uses to which music may be put in the service (or slavery?) of the "Gemeinschaft." Admiring Leverkühn, Zeitblom still cannot sympathize with the composer's attempt to return music to a chaotic and animal state through his use of such a technical trick as the glissando ("ein aus tief kulturellen Gründen mit grösster Vorsicht zu behandelndes Mittel," 571); he feels that "howling as a theme" recurs with dangerous frequency in Leverkühn's works. He especially dislikes the glissando's application to the human voice, for the voice was the first musical instrument to liberate music from the primeval state of the animal outcry by clearly defining the tones of the scale. The humanist in Zeitblom (and in Mann) is strong enough to admire the individuality of Leverkühn's personality, yet this same humanism cannot condone the musical efforts of the genius; in them he sees the reduction of the art of music, and perhaps of all culture, to utter primitivity. Zeitblom likewise admires Leverkühn's all too evident pride but he cannot approve the arrogance of intellect which dares to conjure up "die unteren Mächte" (10). Zeitblom's disapprobation of Leverkühn's hybris is stated at the very beginning of the book, before the narrator recounts the composer's life, and we may assume that Mann's intellectual standpoint, not his emotional one, is finally that of Zeitblom, notwithstanding the passages in which he illuminates the foibles and contradictions in Zeitblom's philosophy.

Mann is not distinctly favorable toward the ultramodern musical thoughts expressed by Leverkühn. His rejection of the latest developments of music stems from a twofold source. Intellectually, he is compelled to deny the reactionary elements in an art that on occasion turns to the curious tonal systems of the Middle Ages for its inspiration or that may even go beyond them to explore the jungles of primitivism. Mann's taste for the richness of Romantic harmonies and instrumentation, so often indicated in his works, also causes him to reject the thin, overintellectualized elements in modern music. For all his consciousness of the bankruptcy of Romantic music, he often betrays a yearning for Wagner and Brahms. Zeitblom offers numerous excuses for "Adrians klarer Gleichgültigkeit gegen die Welt der Instrumente" (69) but both he and Mann are disappointed at the lack of instrumental color in modern music. Zeitblom, for example, gives an arresting account of the instruments in the workshop of Nikolaus Leverkühn, Adrian's uncle, but adds that young Adrian took no interest in them whatsoever. In the same way Zeitblom thinks longingly of Wagner's rich modulations; and Mann confesses (*Entstehung*, 86) that he spent a nostalgic evening with Wagner's music during the composition of *Faustus*: "Die Dreiklangwelt des Ringes ist im Grunde meine musikalische Heimat." Of Leverkühn's *Apocalypse* Zeitblom is forced to speak with astonishment, not love; bewildered at its polyphonic harshness, he adds: "... das ganze Werk ist von dem Paradoxon beherrscht (wenn es ein Paradoxon ist), dass die Dissonanz darin für den Ausdruck alles Hohen, Ernsten, Frommen, Geistigen steht, während das Harmonische und Tonale der Welt der Hölle, in diesem Zusammenhang also einer Welt der Banalität und des Gemeinplatzes, vorbehalten ist" (572-573). Even though the Romantic world of harmony has become one of evil and banality, Mann still subconsciously yearns for it.

Mann does not shrink from the problems of modern music, and in this he resembles Hoffmann; yet in his celebrated use of

Schönberg's twelve-tone system, explained to him by Theodor Adorno, he is less the original creator of musical ideas than his predecessor in the musical novel. Like Schönberg, Leverkühn regards the concept of tonality as a means, not an end. Between the twelve notes of the Schönberg-Leverkühn scale no relationship exists other than that of being in the same series. The Romantic theories of chordal and tonal connotations, of tone-painting, of association between chord and emotion are thus removed. Composition can be done by system, although Mann, writing of Leverkühn's works, falls back into the Romantic manner of cataloguing the emotions aroused by the sound, it being impossible to describe music in words without emotional or pictorial expressions. The theory of Schönberg is explained by the devil in the interview with Leverkühn: "Das Prinzip der Tonalität und seine Dynamik verleiht dem Akkord sein spezifisches Gewicht. Er hat es verloren . . ." (370). Each sound has lost its association with its companions, and stands alone, "ganz ohne abstrakte Beziehung aufs technische Gesamtniveau." That Mann places these dicta in the devil's mouth does not altogether imply that he favors them. As it is, Mann, who says in *Die Entstehung* (36) that the Schönbergian system assumes a new character in the sphere of the novel, cannot refrain from adorning Adrian's "Schönbergian" compositions with certain features commonly associated with late Romantic music. His subordination of the monster orchestra to chorus and soloist points to Gustav Mahler or to Schönberg's own Romantic *Gurre-Lieder,* his choice of medieval and ecclesiastical themes recall Wagner and all his progeny. (Yet Leverkühn's late Romantic vestiges are also common to composers who have admittedly "overcome" Romanticism; medievalism and ecclesiasticism have inspired Honegger with *Jeanne d'Arc*, Stravinsky with *Symphonie des Psaumes,* Hindemith with *Mathis der Maler;* and in the *Carmina Burana* of Carl Orff primitivity is combined with the favorite operatic milieu of the Romantics, while Ernst Krenek, for all his inexorable savagery, has never surrendered the lyric aria. The examples of these composers and others like them, not Schönberg alone, stand behind Leverkühn.)

The disassociation of the sound from its emotional connotations and technical surroundings is dealt another blow in Mann's ironical description of the musical system upon which Leverkühn purportedly bases his own work. His German-American teacher, Wendell Kretzschmar, tells the story of Johann Conrad

Beissel, an emigrant from the Palatinate who, living near Philadelphia in the eighteenth century, devised a system of automatic musical composition for his religious sect, the "Anabaptists of the Seventh Day." Beissel decided that there should be "lords" (the tone of the triad) and "servants" (the remaining tones) in each scale. The accented syllables of a text should receive a "lord," the unaccented a "servant." Soon all the Anabaptists of the Seventh Day could compose hymns according to the system (107), which removed every association between the notes except the arbitrary one of textual accent; the emotional content was wholly eliminated. The asceticism inherent in the Beissel system forms a bridge in the mind of Leverkühn to the employment of a mechanical system of composition for religious purposes. The music of Beissel's Anabaptists was noted for its otherworldliness: "Die vom Chore dringenden Töne hätten zarte Instrumental-Musik nachgeahmt und den Eindruck einer himmlischen Sanftmut und Frömmigkeit in dem Hörer hervorgerufen" (108-109). When all sensuous beauty, and all the customary tonal relationships, are removed from music, it is fit to serve religious ends.

The correlation of religious sentiment with the lack of beauty recalls what Zeitblom has had to say of Leverkühn's *Apocalypse*: beauty represents evil, harshness good. Leverkühn's cult of ugliness is then easily related to the element which Zeitblom notes as the basis of his character: the "Kaisersaschern" element, the latent hysteria of the dying Middle Ages, which Zeitblom, once again the humanist-pedagogue, believes to have been implanted into Leverkühn during his boyhood years in the old city. Mann, linking composition by means of a system to asceticism and so to medieval religious fanaticism, stamps modern musical thought as being reactionary in the extreme. Speaking as Zeitblom he has no sympathy with it, and his humanistic sense even rebels at the future "music of the congregation" which Leverkühn suggests as a possible salvation. As for the Romanticism to be found in Leverkühn's conception of the musician as genius and in some of the composer's earlier works, Mann is more than Romantic enough to understand it, feeling that while both the old harmonic system and the new mechanical system are evil in essence, Romanticism seduces by its beauty, modern music by its ugliness. Romanticism held the greater danger for the individual, modern music holds it for the mass. Mann imputes a sinister kind of minor popularity to Leverkühn's music: the composer is not a beloved one, yet Leverkühn festivals are being organized, and wherever his music is played, mass hysteria results among the listeners. Mann's attitude toward modern music is thus unfavorable, in direct contrast to Hoffmann's embracing of the tenets of Romanticism: Mann is too much the Romanticist in emotion to approve its lack of sensuous beauty, and too much the humanist in intellect to overcome a hatred of its tendency toward primitivism. He points out the paradox in his own attitude as well as that in modern music itself; and the double paradox only heightens the pessimism of his opinions.

The religious element in Leverkühn is highly developed, and in this respect he stands close to Wackenroder's Berglinger. The hysteria of Wackenroder's musician has already been indicated, and Mann lets the same quality, well concealed to be sure, warp the character of his composer. Each author gives his composer certain features of the saint, carefully attaching a *sancta vita* to the hero's life. Wackenroder in the *Märchen von einem nackten Heiligen* tells of a saint released from his sufferings by music. Mann gives in detail the plot of one of the puppet operas written by Leverkühn: it is based on Hartmann von Aue's *Gregorius auf dem Steine*. Like Gregory, Leverkühn is a beautiful and talented child; like Gregory, he falls into sin; and like Gregory he is subjected to a long atonement. Finally Gregory is called to Rome to become Pope, Leverkühn goes mad; Gregory is redeemed while Leverkühn is not, despite his efforts to achieve redemption through the *Apocalypse* and the *Dr. Fausti Weheklag*. Likewise both Wackenroder's "naked saint" and his Berglinger are redeemed through the religious power of music; Leverkühn is damned by music, for in it he is lured to his hybris. As Leverkühn says after the first performance of his puppet opera, music is no longer the means of redemption: redemption is a Romantic word, a word of the harmonists, the "word of action" ("Handlungswort") of harmonic music. "Ist es nicht komisch, dass die Musik sich eine Zeitlang als ein Erlösungsmittel empfand, während sie doch selbst, wie alle Kunst, der Erlösung bedarf, nämlich aus einer feierlichen Isolierung, die die Frucht der Kultur-Emanzipation, der Erhebung der Kultur zum Religionsersatz war" (494). Redemption is possible for the Romantic musician of Wackenroder; Mann, again the pessimist, denies it to Leverkühn, despite the fact that the composer has taken the guilt of the age onto his own shoulders.

The hysteria of Berglinger and the hysteria of Leverkühn

are quite different in their nature. Berglinger's religious enthusiasm has taken repose in the arms of the divine as its goal— a goal Berglinger intends to reach. Leverkühn beholds eternal damnation in the offing for himself, and even seems to crave his fall. Although living in a cloister-like peace at a former farm of the Augustinians, Leverkühn is unable to make that peace turn inward as he contemplates eternity. For Berglinger religion is a consolation, for his descendant a torment. Leverkühn has partaken too freely of the demonological Protestantism of the old professor at Halle, who knew the devil "auf Du und Du;" in Leverkühn's magnificently ruinous theological system the devil has assumed an infinitely more important role than God. A self-consciously modern man, Adrian cannot follow the ecstatic but optimistic faith of Berglinger, nor will his almost violent religious impulse allow him to accept the serene, humanistic Catholicism of Zeitblom who, condemning the Christian fascination with Satan, says: "Meinesteils fühle ich mich recht eigentlich in der goldenen Sphäre beheimatet, in der man die Heilige Jungfrau 'Jovis alma parens' nannte" (16). An extreme Protestant, in both the general and the specific senses of the word, Leverkühn makes a lonely search for an answer to the modern dilemma, and finds the devil himself. Like Kreisler he must reject the "sure port" of religion, but Kreisler has a consolation in his art which Leverkühn lacks. For the wretched and yet heroic Leverkühn, music is not a means of salvation but of destruction, and religion becomes an icily frightening cult in which the devil has the leading role.

The religious element in Hoffmann's Kreisler is connected with the figure of the woman in the composer's life: to a great extent Julia replaces religion for Kreisler. The woman in *Doktor Faustus* serves both as musical inspiration and instrument of the devil. In *Leiden und Grösse Richard Wagners* Mann calls attention to the incestuous overtones in Kundry's relationship to Parsifal. During the opera's second act Kundry, attempting to seduce the young Parsifal, kisses him and states that he thus receives the first kiss of love from his mother. (Elsewhere in the essay Mann discusses the scene under the linden tree in *Siegfried*, where the "mother-thoughts" of the hero are slowly transformed into eroticism.) Beginning *Doktor Faustus* in earnest, Mann confesses that he had long called his old plan "Parsifal;" again, nearing the end of the novel, he mentions in his diary that the comparison with the opera *Parsifal* often occurs to him (*Entstehung*, 23, 193). Kundry, seductress and proxy mother, is the ancestress of the two women who direct the life of Parsifal-Leverkühn, his mother and the *hetaera esmeralda*. Frau Leverkühn and the prostitute are but two aspects of the same force—Leverkühn's feelings for his mother and those for his love will be seen upon closer investigation to be identical.

A more immediate source of the mother-incest theme in *Doktor Faustus* might be Huch's *Enzio*. Mann, a close friend and warm admirer of Huch, says that the author of *Enzio* belongs to those few, "welche den deutschen Roman zur Dichtung zu erhöhen, emporzuläutern, ihm als Kunstgattung die Ebenbürtigkeit mit dem Drama, der Lyrik zu erwirken bestrebt waren und sind."[27] It will be recalled that in *Enzio* the mother ambiguously serves as inspiration and ruination of her son, fostering in him the incestuous love which makes him a composer and the sensuality which brings about his downfall. The tortured family relationships of *Enzio* are not indicated in the first chapters of *Doktor Faustus,* and Leverkühn's family life does not seem to have harmed him. Father Leverkühn, apart from a tendency to migraine, has passed an interest in theology and in the natural sciences on to his son. Adrian is of the same physical type as his mother, who would appear to have Italian blood: "Der Dunkelheit ihres Teints, der Schwärze ihres Scheitels und ihrer still und freundlich blickenden Augen nach hätte man sie für eine Welsche halten können . . ." (36). And likewise the boy must have inherited a love for music from his mother, since she possessed both a lovely but untrained mezzo-soprano voice and a charming mode of speech. The mother's influence apparently disappears during Adrian's university years, but when the composer takes up residency on the Bavarian farm, Mann points out the close resemblance between Frau Schweigestill, the wife of the farmer, and Adrian's mother. Once Adrian is finally seized by madness, Elsbeth Leverkühn takes him under her care. Zeitblom remarks that there is nothing sadder than to see an emancipated spirit broken and returned into the realm of the mother, who learns of the son's fall not without satisfaction. In the mother's eyes the Icarus-flight of her offspring is an undertaking as sinful as it is unintelligible, "und den Gestürzten, Vernichteten, das 'arme, liebe Kind' nimmt sie, alles verzeihend, in ihren Schoss zurück, nicht anders meinend, als dass er besser getan hätte, sich nie daraus zu lösen" (767). Some last hidden remnants of pride prompt the mad Adrian to attempt suicide and to attack his mother during the journey from Bavaria to his childhood home. In the outward scheme of things no incestuous relationship is hinted at. The eroticism which Enzio demonstrated toward his mother as a child is not evident here, yet Adrian seeks a milieu resembling that surrounding his mother, and the mother is all too ready to exert her control.

Another woman has ruled Adrian's life during the hiatus in his mother's power. While Adrian is at Leipzig he is led without his knowledge to a house of prostitution. Frightened by the sight of the "Nymphen und Töchter der Wüste" he runs away; but before he does so he strikes a few chords on a piano in the brothel's salon. As he plays, a dark girl with a large mouth and almond-shaped eyes strokes his arm. At this juncture Adrian flees, but he cannot forget the girl; he returns to the house once more, only to find that she has gone. Under the pretext of hearing the first Austrian performance of Strauss's *Salome*, Adrian travels to Graz and from there to Pressburg, where he finally discovers the girl, and despite her warnings, becomes infected with venereal disease. There begins to appear in his compositions again and again the B-modulation which occurred to Adrian in the salon: B, E, A, E, E flat (in German notation H, E, A, E, Es), standing for *hetaera esmeralda*. The theme occurs in the Brentano songs of Adrian's youth and again in the works composed just before his madness. The prostitute, omnipresent in Leverkühn's compositions, also becomes a figure in his fantasies, and in the mad speech held at the performance of the *Faust* score he tells of his union with a mermaid named Hyphialta (a symbol for the venereal infection) whom the devil has brought him; from this union a son has been born. The "son" is actually Leverkühn's little nephew, Nepomuk. Nepomuk's death has affected Leverkühn deeply and he believes that the child has been infected with his own ailment.

After learning these details the true nature of Leverkühn's relationship to his mother becomes apparent, and we see another reason for Mann's detailed recounting of the legend of Gregory. Leverkühn has felt a strong although repressed attachment to his mother. The adventure with the prostitute is but a reflection of the same attachment: the mother and the prostitute are of the same physical type; the one has awakened Leverkühn's senses to music while the other has been the chief element of inspiration in his compositions. Leverkühn also rebels against both attachments, although he seeks them both, following the prostitute to Austria and living on Frau Schweigestill's farm. Mann adds a subtle detail during the scene in the brothel; Leverkühn plays a "Modulation von H- nach C-dur, aufhellender Halbton-Abstand wie im Gebet des Eremiten im Freischütz-Finale" (221). The mention of the hermit just at this point reveals not only Adrian's consciousness of his quasi-religious duty toward music, but his feeling of revulsion at the contact with the sensual. Whether or not Leverkühn is fully conscious of the incestuous element in the attraction which the prostitute exerts upon him, it would seem that a presentiment of incestuous guilt leads him to choose the Gregory text for his puppet opera. Gregory, the child of a liaison between brother and sister, is on a pilgrimage to the Holy Land when he unknowingly meets and marries his mother, an act which leads to his years of atonement on the stone. In *Doktor Faustus*, in contrast to his later *Der Erwählte*, Mann does not develop the first part of the tale, the relation between brother and sister; the story of the mother-son marriage is dwelt upon more lovingly. Zeitblom's conjectures concerning the cause of Adrian's suicide attempt and attack on his mother have not been quite correct. Adrian rebels against the protective nature of the mother, of course, but the rebellion also has another source: Leverkühn, even in his mad state, is repelled by the incestuous element he has felt within himself. What hope is there in a world where music takes the form of a prostitute? Where the prostitute answers the secret love for the mother, who is thus in equal measure an "instrument of the devil"? Where the child Nepomuk, briefly and purely assuming the role of musical inspiration, dies a painful death? Julia has indeed undergone the most hideous of transformations.

Mann has proceeded from a pessimistic premise: by employing the life of the musician, he attempts to illustrate the downfall of the German nation. The weaving of contemporary history into *Doktor Faustus* has not been especially successful; for the most part it seems somehow extraneous, mentioned here and there in order to give the novel a "meaning for our times." Zeitblom refers to the downfall of Poland, the invasion of France, or the advance through the Ukraine, and calls these events the results of the madness of the German people, a madness which he relates on occasion to that of Leverkühn. He likes to point to the "Kaisersaschern-element" in Leverkühn, which has become overt in the composer's increasing artistic atavism—his retreat into chaos. The allusion to similar elements in Nazism is manifest; and the development of Leverkühn's music from a belated Romanticism to apocalyptic visions (conjured up nevertheless by a compositional system of extreme coldness) parallels the trend of German political thought from the Wilhelmian era to the excesses of the Hitler regime. It may be argued that Mann attempts to disclose the seeds of the Nazi-state as they appear in an individual; and the musical genius, serving an art that may well be turned to totalitarian purposes and himself containing elements of "anti-humanity," would seem to be a logical choice for the hero. But the brilliant Leverkühn is so fascinating in his own right that he obscures such an effort, since both author and reader become more concerned with the artistic and personal problems immediately at hand than with the central figure's "historical" implications. The use of lesser individuals: theological students, Jewish Teutophiles, poets of the prophetic strain, degenerate noblemen, and hard-fisted industrialists to illustrate the growth of a milieu favorable to Nazism, is artistically more rewarding than the employment of Leverkühn for the political purpose.

Mann draws upon the musical worlds of Leipzig and Munich for a wealth of minor figures, including descendants of the mentor, the virtuoso, the impresario. Like the figures around Kreisler, they stand in the shadow of the hero, but nevertheless themselves demonstrate single tendencies of modern music present in Leverkühn incidentally or not at all. The most important of them, Wendell Kretzschmar, Leverkühn's teacher, is the representative of progressive musical thought. The other minor musical characters have a less positive quality; they serve to indicate the decadence rife in German musical circles during the first part of the century. Kretzschmar is given a friendlier treatment than they, although he is not altogether spared Mann's satire. The German-American, having come to the land of his ancestors to complete his musical education, takes a position as organist in Kaisersaschern, where he occupies his free hours by composing and lecturing. From his lectures Leverkühn not only learns of Beissel's mechanical system of composition. Kretzschmar seeks to impress the following tenet upon his listeners: "harmonische Subjektivität, polyphonische Sachlichkeit" (82), a combination which, as he admits, is not always correct, especially when applied to the twilight productions of great masters. The late works of Beethoven (like the late works-to-come of

Leverkühn) give polyphonic form to an extreme and lonely subjectivity. Beethoven is further characterized as the master of profane music who by his struggle with the fugal form has tried to find his way back to the liturgical origins of music, a task which Leverkühn assumes when composing his semi-liturgical works. Kretzschmar likewise helps to prepare the coldness so noticeable in Leverkühn's compositions by his often repeated declaration that music has a secret tendency to "Anti-Sinnlichkeit." Music is the most intellectual of the arts since in it, as in no other, form and content are identical: "Man sage wohl, die Musik 'wende sich an das Ohr'; aber das tue sie nur bedingtermassen, nur insofern nämlich, als das Gehör, wie die übrigen Sinne, stellvertretendes Mittel- und Aufnahmeorgan für das Geistige sei" (98). Without Kretzschmar Leverkühn the musician would be impossible.

Kretzschmar acquires an ambiguity similar to that of the mother-figure: while giving Leverkühn inspiration, he encourages him to take the coldly intellectual path which leads to his destruction. In his ambiguity Kretzschmar resembles Meister Abraham who, having taught Kreisler much about music and musical ideals, also curses him with the burden of scurrilous humor. The connotation of evil has not been removed from the mentor-type even in the otherwise comically delineated figure of Kretzschmar. Indeed, Kretzschmar and Abraham are both grotesques, Abraham a twisted little man, Kretzschmar a personage of inconsequential appearance and afflicted with a stutter which can turn his profound lectures into farces. And like Abraham he is associated with the clumsy and grandiose organ.

The virtuoso type in Mann is not so sinister as some of his predecessors. Like Wedekind's Kammersänger he unwittingly creates mischief, but instead of being a party to the destruction of one of his admirers, he brings about his own downfall. The apple-cheeked violinist Rudi Schwerdtfeger possesses great technical dexterity and little intelligence: applause for his whistling pleases him more than that granted him in the concert hall. There is no description of Schwerdtfeger's performance in the fashion of Heine's Paganini-passage. Even when Rudi plays Leverkühn's violin concerto, Mann is careful first to give a detailed description of the music itself (indicative of music's position as a learned matter, quite separate from its emotional effect), and then sets down the following vignette of Rudi's performance: "**Der Schweiss perlte jedesmal, wenn er die Aufgabe** durchgeführt, unter seinem lockig aufstrebenden Blondhaar, und das Weisse seiner hübschen zyanenblauen Augen war von rotem Geäder durchzogen" (625). The age of the great demonic virtuoso has long since ended; the music has become the primary matter once more. The virtuoso is now regarded as a comically self-important individual who has enough to do when rendering a work with technical accuracy. Modern music has so increased in its difficulty that the virtuoso cannot play it competently and still have opportunity to create dramatic effects. Even the concerto, the genre of the virtuoso, is regarded with an ironic smile; when Zeitblom has the courage to call Leverkühn's violin concerto "die Apotheose der Salonmusik" (625) in the composer's presence, Adrian receives the blame without anger, realizing full well that the concerto, essentially a show-piece, should not be included among the serious works of a master. Mann, no more respectful than Zeitblom, names the concerto "Adrians hybrides Geschenk an die Zutraulichkeit" (*Entstehung*, 180). In this respect, at least, Mann takes a bright view of the development of music; the virtuoso-cult, the bane of the nineteenth-century concert stage, has vanished as a serious threat to musical culture.

Yet Mann cannot resist hinting that the virtuoso may still do harm through his personality. Women, old and young, make up a large portion of Schwerdtfeger's audiences, which he, like every other virtuoso, seeks to control through his personality. In addition, he attempts to overcome a more difficult public, Leverkühn himself. Like a child he feels he must make a special claim on the love of those who reject him, as Adrian has done through his cold aloofness, and like a child he demands the concerto from Adrian as a concrete proof of his love. The tendency to homosexuality in Rudi's nature gives his relationship to Leverkühn a character somewhat like the suspect friendships we find in Hesse's early novels. In Mann the relationship can be explained for the most part by the innocent appeal which Rudi's childish naiveté makes to Leverkühn; only once is the matter presented in another light. Rudi visits the migraine sufferer Leverkühn in his darkened room, and after confessing his profoundly regretted liaison with the wife of an art professor, he begs the composer for a concerto: "Einverleiben wollt' ich es mir, dass ich's im Schlafe spielen könnte und es hegen und pflegen in jeder Note wie eine Mutter, denn Mutter wäre ich ihm, und Sie wären der Vater,—es wäre zwischen uns wie ein Kind, ein platonisches Kind" (538). The homosexual trait is not developed further, and when Leverkühn decides to marry a girl much younger than he, he dispatches Schwerdtfeger as his John Alden. Schwerdtfeger wins the girl for himself but is shot by his former mistress. Mann thus probes into the psychological background of the virtuoso type; he has long since determined the virtuoso's value as a musician. The virtuoso is an ambisexual individual, possessed by the desire to overcome everyone's resistance to his personality. He still possesses a certain demonic aura, yet his demonism has been weakened into "kindische Dämonie" (538). In the end he does not cause destruction but is himself destroyed.

The impresario in Mann has been purified of the evil characterizing his predecessors, Hauff's de Planto and Bahr's Amschl. Mann's chapter concerning Saul Fitelberg is an objective effort to get at the core of the impresario's profession. One day a limousine pulls up before the Schweigestill house, and a fat, clean-shaven man appears. Saul Fitelberg has heard of the growing interest in Leverkühn's music and wishes to capitalize on it. Speaking in French and German he attempts to persuade the composer to direct a series of concerts of his works; when Leverkühn refuses, Fitelberg asks him merely to present himself at the concerts and at certain Parisian salons. Leverkühn remains adamant. A mentor of sorts, since he seeks to control others, Fitelberg's motivation is financial rather than personal. Fitelberg is a Polish Jew who made his way to Paris and there established a *théâtre des fourberies gracieuses*, a gathering place for the intellectual lights of the day. From this occupation to the impresario's office was an easy step for a man knowing how to employ the snobbery of the public. Fitelberg understands "das Deutschtum" as well as Parisian intellectual circles; he realizes that the German thinks that abroad there is nothing but *valse brilliante*, while earnestness dwells in Germany alone (619). As a Jew Fitelberg has a great sympathy for Germany: the Jews and the Germans are the only groups conscious of their roles as priests (621). Thus, he says, he can fathom the German conception of the composer, a conception which we have seen underlying every serious work on the creative musician: "Man ist ein einfaches, kindliches Gemüt, aber die Musik ist einem die geheimnisvolle Offenbarung höchster Erkenntnisse, ein Gottesdienst, und der musikalische Lehrberuf ein priesterliches Amt" (621). The statement is made with particular reference to Bruckner, but its second part may be applied to all German composers. Fitelberg is an instructive new figure in the field of the musical novel, a mentor interested in making money for himself through his skillful handling of the artist, whom for a price he is willing to defend against the world. There is no harm but much wisdom in Mann's modern impresario.

Leverkühn is aided or tormented, as the case may be, by a host of women, who manage to overlook his coldness. Usually of a mannish nature, they have taken the burdens of practical life from Leverkühn's shoulders. The most entrancing personage among them is the Frau von Tolna, a mysterious noblewoman who faithfully attends the concerts of Leverkühn's works, and takes up residence near him, without ever meeting him face to face. Leverkühn is invited to spend a vacation at the lady's Hungarian castle during her absence. At the composer's funeral a veiled figure appears, only to slip away as the earth is tossed upon the casket. Mann makes use of the well-known "soul-friendship" between Tschaikowsky and the Frau von Meck; according to legend, the lady likewise appeared incognito at Tschaikowsky's burial. We wonder at Mann's decision to borrow so openly from the life of an actual composer; the incident momentarily lowers the tone of *Doktor Faustus* to that of the ordinary *vie romancée*. Perhaps this was Mann's sardonic intention.

Leverkühn's friendship with the poet and Anglophile, Rüdiger Schildknapp, bears some features of the collaboration between Strauss and Hofmannsthal; but Schildknapp, an industrious toiler in the field of belles-lettres, is hardly a genius of Hofmannsthal's rank. Schildknapp likes to think of himself as the equal of Leverkühn, and Leverkühn does recognize the value of his talents, but no real inspiration passes from the artist in one genre to that in another. Schildknapp is interesting rather in that he illuminates the extremely literary nature of Leverkühn's talent, another trait betraying Leverkühn's Romantic heritage. When Leverkühn is composing the work of a foreign poet, he insists upon using the original text. A masterful translator, especially of English, Schildknapp is full of hints for Leverkühn. The *littérateur* also serves as a foil to the collection of decadent artists who inhabit the Munich musical world, people whose relationship to music or literature is that of the dilettante, but who nevertheless demand the prerogatives of the actual artist. The second half of the novel is set in the midst of these individuals, and their presence contributes substantially to the atmosphere of despair permeating the last years of Leverkühn's sane life.

Characteristically, the assemblage at the reading of the Faust-score melts away as Leverkühn makes his long confession concerning the nature of his fate; only the most faithful remain. The dilettantes have contributed much to the downfall of musical culture, but refuse to be present at the destruction of the composer who has sacrificed himself in an effort to save music.

Mann's conclusion is therefore appallingly tragic. The art of music is worn out and cannot be saved through any of the measures taken by Leverkühn, through a new association with theology, through a removal of Romantic elements, or through the reduction of the art to a chaotic ugliness. The character of the composer has remained Romantic; he still regards himself as the chosen individual, the higher type of priest. This conception has not led to a new humility but rather to an ever increasing hybris: the composer, attempting to escape the old traditions and to establish new ones by his intellect alone, must devote such tremendous effort to the compositions of each measure that he cannot possibly regard himself as a simple artisan. Leverkühn is the logical conclusion to the development which began, literarily, with Berglinger and Kreisler: the musical expression of the individual personality has been exhausted, yet the personality is forced to remain as a part of the creative process; in order to retain some sort of ideal the musician must continue to associate himself with religion and the priest's office, while lacking any actual belief in the divine power that presumably inspires him. Thus Berglinger finds salvation while Leverkühn does not. And the depressing fact must be added that an investigation of the psyche has removed all possibility of belief in the ideal and in inspiration as such; Leverkühn's music is shown to stem from sexual sources, and by applying Mann's techniques to Hoffmann's Kreisler, we might easily discover the same about the Romantic hero.

There is no solution in *Doktor Faustus*; Leverkühn merely dreams of an answer to the problem when he speaks of the music of the congregation, an art without melancholy ambition, possessing a new innocence, "eine Kunst ohne Leiden, seelisch gesund, unfeierlich, untraurig-zutraulich, eine Kunst mit der Menschheit auf Du und Du" (495). Hermann Hesse has also conceived such a future for music and has depicted it in *Das Glasperlenspiel*, published in 1943; Mann received the novel while at work on *Doktor Faustus*, and he notes, among other resemblances, "dieselbe Idee der fingierten Biographie—mit den Einschlägen

von Parodie, die diese Form mit sich bringt" (*Entstehung*, 68).
Hesse does not employ the Romantic background, but turns to
the familiar tradition of the "Pedagogical Province." Music is
an aid to the achievement of an Apollonic equilibrium, the musician becoming the teacher whose value lies in his ability to provide an edifying example. The "pedagogical novel" does not
necessarily imply a rejection of the personality: the development
of the personality is its primary aim. Paradoxically it would
seem to be a more egocentric movement than Romanticism in
music, for the Romantic presumably creates music, while the
pedagogue does not and must teach by means of his personality.
However Romanticism fostered the formation of an unusual
personality to be expressed in the creative works of the artist;
the "Glasperlenspieler" of Hesse's novel have as their object the
formation of harmonious natures representative of the highest
culture and in close sympathy with one another. A process of
"normalization" to a high standard takes place.

Hesse leads us into the future. After the "period of the
feuilleton" (our own age) and an ensuing time of devastating
wars, an era of peace has come. This era has seen the flowering of an organization composed of "Glasperlenspieler," initiates
in the great intellectual game which constitutes the basic ceremony of the monk-like order. The players live in a little state,
Castalia, set aside for them; it maintains schools where prospective candidates for the "Glasperlenspiel" are instructed.
Following years of apprenticeship the young men are admitted
directly into the order, some becoming adepts of the *ludus*
itself, others becoming scholars. The favorite subjects for research are music and mathematics, since they have so large a
part in the "Glasperlenspiel" itself. Music is no longer regarded as a creative art, but as a matter of pure learning, much
like the classical languages. The "players" do not consider their
cultural age creative, and this "ebenso heitere wie resignierte,
tapfere Stellungnahme zum Problem der Kulturlebensalter"[28]
has led to the cultivation of musical history. Special enthusiasm is evinced for the period of music from the Renaissance to Bach, and this music is performed (shades of Johann
Körrer) "ohne Schwellungen und Abschwellungen . . . mit der
Naivität und Keuschheit einer andern Zeit und Welt" (I, 39).
The Romantic age of music is ignored; music is a contemplative
exercise, refining spirit and intellect. Since composition is not

undertaken, the mechanical systems of writing music described by Mann are not employed by the "players;" nevertheless the relationship between musician and mathematician hinted at in *Doktor Faustus* flowers here: mathematics innoculates the "players" against the sensuality of harmonic music. In its capacity as a leading part of the "Glasperlenspiel" music also fulfills another important duty; it keeps concord among the people of the state, and indeed the prosperity of music is identified with that of culture and morality. The prototype for this conception of music as socially healthful is to be found in ancient China, where ". . . die Musikmeister hatten streng über der Wahrung und Reinhaltung der 'alten Tonarten' zu wachen" (I, 42).

Therefore the position of the music teacher in the world of Castalia is of extreme importance; he is an example of the entirely good mentor, whose influence is not confined to single pupils but permeates Castalia's whole organization. When little Josef Knecht meets his music teacher, it is evident that Knecht is not the first student to pass under the teacher's conrol, although the old man takes an extraordinary interest in the subsequent development of the talented boy. Hesse's musician, "von einer nicht lachenden oder lächelnden, sondern stillglänzenden, ruhigen Heiterkeit" (I, 76), is neither tormented and ironic like Kreisler and Leverkühn, nor a grotesque like Abraham and Kretzschmar. In his quiet dignity he reminds us of a Stifterian character, and his method of teaching corresponds to the impression he makes. Knecht is not asked to perform a show-piece on his violin (there is no virtuosity in Castalia); it is suggested that he play a simple song. Then the master begins to accompany him, and step by step the melody is turned into an entire polyphonic web; polyphony, not harmony, is the musical form preferred by the "Glasperlenspieler." Thereupon Knecht is selected as a candidate for the group. In later life the *magister musicae* continues to form the personality of his student by his example. Knecht, visiting the master just before the latter's death, finds his former teacher as if in another world; he tries to question him but fails, and the old man says simply "Du ermüdest dich, Josef . . ." (I, 403). Knecht is thankful for the statement, bald as it may seem; he realizes that the teacher's spirit has been completely transfigured, and silently draws inspiration from his saintly presence. The musician in *Das Glasperlenspiel* inspires by example, not by his compositions or by his performance; he succeeds in approaching blessedness, not through musical creation like Berglinger, but by achieving an extreme purity of soul. Grillparzer's Spielmann is one of the master's ancestors. The saintliness of the Spielmann springs from a source of which he is unconscious, while the teacher has evidently made a conscious exertion to mold himself into such perfection, yet the two have attained an equal degree of purification. The music teacher is however a wise saint of the Confucian type (the oriental studies of Hesse have influenced his conception) while the Spielmann remains a profoundly Christian figure, one of the "poor in spirit."

The music teacher may be an admirable product of the Castalian system; on the other hand, in the course of the narrative it becomes apparent that Hesse does not wholly approve of the "province," and his disapproval is expressed by Josef Knecht. At an early age Knecht has become a *ludi magister*, a leader of the great festival games held at regular intervals in the pedagogical province. He soon becomes dissatisfied with the "Glasperlenspieler," believing that, failing their pedagogical mission, they have turned themselves into an intellectual elite with contempt for the outside world. Knecht is supported in his views by Carlo Ferromonte, a musicologist. Carlo himself is an excellent representative of what the Castalian could become; while a scholar, an investigator, and a "man of categories," he realizes that his talents should be applied to the understanding of beautiful phenomena (such as the art of music or the death of the music teacher) so that these phenomena can be preserved as edifying examples for a larger public. Discussing the last days of the music teacher with Knecht, Carlo says: "Es klingt schulmeisterlich, aber wir Kastalier sind nun einmal Schulmeister, und wenn ich Euer und unser Erlebnis einzuordnen und zu benennen wünsche, so wünsche ich das nicht, weil ich seine Wirklichkeit und Wahrheit durch Abstraktion und Verallgemeinerung auflösen, sondern weil ich sie möglichst bestimmt und deutlich aufzeichnen und festhalten möchte" (I, 407). Knecht realizes that not every member of the order views the use of scholarship in Ferromonte's fashion, and despairing of transforming the nature of what he believes to be an already decadent organization, he resigns from his position, an unheard-of procedure, and becomes the tutor of a problem-child, the son of an old friend who has left Castalia. He takes but one possession with him, a simple wooden flute, a symbol of his realization that the learned tradition in music, the study of music as a science, is approaching an impoverishment similar to that of the earlier creative tradition. A new beginning must be made with the most humble of means. Taking up his task as tutor, he tries to swim in a mountain lake, so that his charge will not lose respect for him, and is drowned. The youth feels a guilt at his teacher's death, but then he is seized by "die Ahnung, dass diese Schuld ihn selbst und sein Leben umgestalten und viel Grösseres von ihm fordern werde, als er bisher je von sich verlangt hatte" (II, 237).

Das Glasperlenspiel is not a musical novel in the usual sense of the word; its second volume, except for the renunciation of "Musik als exakte Wissenschaft" by Knecht, is entirely concerned with problems of pedagogy. In effect the novel skips a stage of the development of music: the consideration of the art as a matter of learning forms only the background of Mann's *Doktor Faustus*, the important character still being the composer. While the "age of musicology" is treated in the historical sections of *Das Glasperlenspiel*, the novel itself does not depict the flowering of this age, which Mann predicts and whose decay Hesse portrays. For music Hesse offers no solution save that rather naive one of a new beginning at a most primitive stage; the musician himself has a possibility of salvation in his capacity as pedagogue. A negative attitude is taken toward the creative musician; the musician as priest is excluded together with the Romantic concept of genius; the musician as monk, the member of a select and isolated body of "beautiful spirits," all dedicated to a serene but passive cultivation of the art, is likewise denied by Knecht's return to the world. The musician can be "religious" only by his saintly example, to which he must however give active force in his teaching. Hesse's rejection of music both as a means of personal expression and as a kind of learning arises from his pedagogical aims; Mann's fears about music are primarily aesthetic. Both Mann and Hesse have sought to make their "musical" novels a general criticism of culture. The day of the artistic novel, where the problems of art are treated without reference to other questions, has drawn to a close.

The development of the musician from Romanticism to the present has come almost full circle. The writers of Romanticism, Hoffmann in particular, had stood in close connection with contemporary musical thought, just as Thomas Mann has endeavored to do. Hoffmann has created in his Kreisler an archetype of the creative musician, the majority of whose characteristics Mann has seen fit to use in his portrayal of Leverkühn. The other types of the musician, the virtuoso, the mentor, the Spielmann, the woman musician, have one by one ceased to be of interest or value for the literary man; only the figure of the composer, at once demonic and idealistic, remains essentially unchanged. The negation of this figure by Biedermeier and Poetic Realism, its transformation to melodrama by the Weltschmerzler and to sensationalism by the writers of the *fin-de-siècle*, have not been able to detract from its value. The creative musician remains a Romantic figure in German literature, an individual saved or destroyed by his unswerving devotion to the art. This difference between the Romantics and Mann has appeared: that the Romantics tend toward an affirmative answer, one of salvation through music, while Mann is pessimistic, seeing nothing but destruction for the Romantic composer. Nevertheless Mann cannot conceive of a composer who is not a Romanticist, however much his Leverkühn may deny music which in its technique remains Romantic.

Parallel to this principal line of development of the Romantic musician with his many variations, there runs the quieter theme of music as a means of pedagogy and the musician as the supreme example of the pedagogue. Despite the fact that this conception has been the inspiration of Goethe, Stifter, and Hesse, it is not entirely satisfactory, for it does not concern itself with the main issue at hand: what is the future of the creative musician to be in a world where the Romantic attitude is becoming increasingly difficult to maintain and where the artisan-composer bears the taint of artificiality? The pedagogical approach does not consider music as a living art or the musician as a creative artist; noble in itself, it represents in effect an evasion, not a solution. Mann offers an answer, if not precisely a solution; the musician must sacrifice himself to the art, in return for ever decreasing results.

Certain general conclusions then may be drawn from the foregoing investigation. Literary men have demonstrated a relatively insensitive attitude toward the problems of the musician, choosing to accentuate some particular feature of his personality rather than to treat him as a complete individual. They have likewise lagged behind in their knowledge of musical developments, thus rendering their judgments on music and the musician less valuable than they might otherwise have been. There have been exceptions to the rule, and these major ones. In Kreisler Hoffmann has delineated one of the great original figures of German literature, and Mann's Leverkühn, if not a Kreisler, is surely one of the most important creations in the modern novel.

NOTES

INTRODUCTION

1. Hans Friedrich Menck, *Der Musiker im Roman: ein Beitrag zur Geschichte der vorromantischen Erzählliteratur* in *Beiträge zur neueren Literaturgeschichte*, XVIII (Heidelberg 1931), has discussed at length the novels of Beer, Printz, Kuhnau, and Heinse.
2. Adolf Knigge, *Die Reise nach Braunschweig* (Leipzig, 1868), 30-31.
3. Wilhelm Heinse, *Sämmtliche Werke*, herausgegeben von Carl Schüddekopf (Leipzig, 1902-1925), VI, 154.

CHAPTER I

1. Wilhelm Wackenroder, *Werke und Briefe*, herausgegeben von Friedrich von der Leyen (Jena, 1910), II, 2.
2. J. N. Forkel, *Über Johann Sebastian Bachs Leben, Kunst, und Kunstwerke*, herausgegeben von Max F. Schneider (Basel, [1948]).
3. Johann Mattheson, *Grundlagen einer musikalischen Ehrenpforte*, herausgegeben von M. Schneider (Berlin, 1910).
4. Friedrich Rochlitz, *Auswahl aus den Sämmtlichen Schriften* (Züllichau, 1821-1822), V, 327.
5. Ernst Theodor Amadeus Hoffmann, *Dichtungen und Schriften*, herausgegeben von Walther Harich (Weimar, 1924), I, 13.
6. Heinrich von Kleist, *Werke*, im Verein mit Georg Minde-Pouet und Reinhold Steig herausgegeben von Erich Schmidt (Leipzig und Wien, 1904-05), III, 377-390.
7. Robert Schumann, *Gesammelte Schriften über Musik und Musiker* (Leipzig, 1854).
8. Ludwig Tieck, *Schriften* (Berlin, 1828-1854), XVII, 288.
9. Wilhelm Hauff, *Werke*, herausgegeben von Max Drescher (Berlin, Leipzig, Wien, 1907), V, 220.
10. Heinrich Heine, *Werke*, unter Mitwirkung von Jonas Fränkel, Ludwig Krähe, Albert Leitzmann, und Julius Petersen herausgegeben von Oskar Walzel (Leipzig, 1910-1915), VIII, 101.
11. Daniel Elster, *Die Irrfahrten des Daniel Elster, Student, Philhellene, Musikant*, neubearbeitet und herausgegeben von Hans Martin Elster (Stuttgart, 1912); Karl Ditters von Dittersdorf, *Lebensbeschreibung*, herausgegeben von Eugen Schmitz (Regensburg, 1940).
12. Clemens Brentano, *Ausgewählte Werke*, herausgegeben und mit einer Einleitung versehen von Max Morris (Leipzig, [1904]), III, 137.
13. Achim von Arnim, *Werke*, herausgegeben von Monty Jacobs (Leipzig, Wien, Stuttgart, 1908), IV, 171.
14. Joseph von Eichendorff, *Sämtliche Werke*, in Verbindung mit Philip August Becker herausgegeben von Wilhelm Kosch und August Sauer, (Regensburg, 1908-   ), X, 434.
15. Joseph von Eichendorff, *Werke*, herausgegeben von Rudolf von Gottschall (Leipzig, 1907), II, 4. For *Die Freier*, not included in Gottschall's edition, see *Lustspiele*, herausgegeben von Paul Kluckhohn, in *Deutsche Literatur ... in Entwicklungsreihen: Reihe Romantik*, (Leipzig, 1938), XXIII, 253-306.
16. Karl Maria von Weber, *Sämtliche Schriften*, kritische Ausgabe von Georg Kaiser (Berlin und Leipzig, 1908), 437-510.
17. Wilhelm Müller, *Diary and Letters*, edited by Philip Schuyler Allen and James Taft Hatfield (Chicago, 1903), 5.
18. Wilhelm Müller, *Gedichte*, vollständige kritische Ausgabe bearbeitet von James Taft Hatfield (Berlin, 1905), 43.
19. *Dramen von Clemens Brentano und Ludwig Achim von Arnim*, herausgegeben von Paul Kluckhohn, in *Deutsche Literatur ... in Entwicklungsreihen: Reihe Romantik* (Leipzig, 1938), XXI, 20.

CHAPTER II

1. Franz Grillparzer, *Sämtliche Werke*, herausgegeben von August Sauer, fortgeführt von Reinhold Bachmann (Wien, 1909-), Abt. I, Bd. X, 194.
2. Theodor Mundt, *Das Duett* (Berlin, 1831), 54-55.
3. Karl Gutzkow, *Novellen* (Hamburg, 1834), II, 66-67.
4. Karl Gutzkow, *Novellenbuch* (Frankfurt a.M., 1846), 198.
5. Ferdinand Kürnberger, *Novellen* (Prag, 1857), 162.
6. Gottfried und Johanna Kinkel, *Erzählungen* (Tübingen und Stuttgart, 1849), 139.
7. Johanna Kinkel, *Hans Ibeles in London: ein Familienbild aus dem Flüchtlingsleben* (Stuttgart, 1860), I, 353.
8. Ludwig Spohr, *Selbstbiographie* (Kassel und Göttingen, 1860-61), II, 94 ff.
9. Alfred Meissner, *Gesammelte Schriften* (Leipzig, 1872), XV, 115.
10. Adalbert Stifter, *Sämtliche Werke*, herausgegeben von Franz Hüller u.a. (Prag, 1904-1939), IV, I, 80-81.
11. Johann Wolfgang Goethe, *Sämtliche Werke*: Jubiläumsausgabe (Stuttgart und Berlin, 1902-07), XIX, 177.
12. Theodor Storm, *Sämtliche Werke*, herausgegeben von Albert Köster (Leipzig, 1939), II, 85.
13. Ferdinand Tönnies, "Karl Storm: ein Gedenkblatt" in *Deutsche Rundschau*, XCIX (April-June, 1899), 461-463.
14. Thomas Mann, *Buddenbrooks*: Verfall einer Familie (Berlin, 1911), II, 471.
15. Nikolaus Lenau, *Werke und Briefe*, herausgegeben von Eduard Castle (Leipzig, 1910-1923), II, 31.
16. Emil Ermatinger, *Gottfried Kellers Leben, Briefe, und Tagebücher* (Stuttgart und Berlin, 1916), I, 347ff.
17. Gottfried Keller, *Sämtliche Werke*, herausgegeben von Jonas Fränkel (Erlenbach-Zürich und München, 1926-1948), VII, 130-131.
18. Richard Wagner, *Sämtliche Schriften und Dichtungen* (Leipzig, 1912-14), IV, 269; XIII, 287-288.
19. Joseph Viktor von Scheffel, *Sämtliche Werke*, herausgegeben von Johannes Franke (Leipzig, 1916), I, 47.
20. Wilhelm Heinrich Riehl, *Geschichten und Novellen* (Stuttgart und Berlin, 1899-1901), I.
21. Albert Emil Brachvogel, *Dramatische Schriften* (Jena, [1883]), 318.
22. Wilhelm Raabe, *Das Horn von Wanza* (Braunschweig, 1881), 128.
23. Albert Emil Brachvogel, *Friedemann Bach*, vollständige Ausgabe mit Einleitung von Arno Holst (Berlin, [1909]), 157-158.
24. Eduard Mörike, *Briefe*, ausgewählt und herausgegeben von Karl Fischer und Rudolf Krauss (Berlin, 1903), I, 212-213.
25. Eduard Mörike, *Werke*, herausgegeben von Harry Maync (Leipzig und Wien, 1909), I, 108.
26. Ferdinand Kürnberger, *Novellen* (München, 1861), II, 50.
27. Friedrich Nietzsche, *Werke*, herausgegeben von Elisabeth Förster-Nietzsche (Leipzig, 1921-1926, I, 147.

CHAPTER III

1. Ossip Schubin, *Die Geschichte eines Genies* in *Neuer deutscher Novellenschatz*, herausgegeben von P. Heyse und L. Laistner (München und Leipzig, 1885), XI, 161.
2. Ernst von Wolzogen, *Der Kraft-Mayr: ein humoristischer Musikanten-Roman, dem Andenken Franz Liszts gewidmet* (Stuttgart, [1897]), I, 10.
3. Emil Strauss, *Freund Hein* (Berlin, 1905), 239.
4. Friedrich Huch, *Enzio: ein musikalischer Roman* (München, 1911), 211.
5. Hermann Bahr, *Der arme Narr* (Wien, 1906), 92.

6. Richard Schaukal, *Kapellmeister Kreisler: ein imaginäres Porträt* (München und Leipzig, 1906), 80.
7. Arthur Schnitzler, *Gesammelte Werke: Theaterstücke* (Berlin, 1913), III, 114.
8. Jakob Wassermann, *Das Gänsemännchen* (Berlin, 1915), 595.
9. Ferdinand von Saar, *Sämtliche Werke*, herausgegeben von Jakob Minor (Leipzig, 1908), VII, 196.
10. Hermann Sudermann, *Heimat* (Stuttgart, 1893).
11. Arthur Schnitzler, *Gesammelte Werke: Erzählungen* (Berlin, 1913), II, 180-181.
12. Hermann Bahr, *Die Andere* (Berlin, 1906), 81.
13. Frank Wedekind, *Gesammelte Werke* (München und Leipzig, 1919-1920), V, 98.
14. Max Dauthendey, *Gesammelte Werke* (München, 1925), III, 444.
15. Hugo von Hofmannsthal, *Theater in Versen* (Berlin, 1899), 188.
16. Heinrich Mann, *Gesammelte Romane und Novellen* (Leipzig, 1917), I, 250.
17. Thomas Mann, *Ausgewählte Erzählungen* (Stockholm, 1945), 80.
18. Max Halbe, *Die Tat des Dietrich Stobäus* (München, 1911), 516-517.
19. Hermann Hesse, *Gertrud* (München, 1910).
20. Joseph Friedrich Perkonig, *Der Guslaspieler* (Leipzig, 1944).
21. Ernst Zahn, *Helden des Alltags* (Stuttgart und Berlin, 1922), 139.
22. Carl Sternheim, *Bürger Schippel* (Leipzig, 1913), 93.
23. Adolf Stern, *Ausgewählte Werke* (Dresden und Leipzig, 1906), III, 108.
24. Hermann Bahr, *Das Konzert* (Berlin, 1909), 129.
25. Carl Sternheim, *Schuhlin* (Berlin, 1915), 32.
26. Hermann Sudermann, *Das hohe Lied* (Stuttgart und Berlin, 1924).
27. Hermann Hesse, *Peter Camenzind* (Berlin, 1920), 66.

CHAPTER IV

1. Jakob Wassermann, *Laudin und die Seinen* (Berlin, 1925).
2. Gerhart Hauptmann, *Die Hochzeit auf Buchenhorst* (Berlin, 1932), 25.
3. Wilhelm Schäfer, *Die Anekdoten* (München, 1928), 319.
4. Albrecht Schaeffer, *Das Prisma* (Leipzig, 1925), 63.
5. Martin Borrmann, *Der Don Juan der halben Dinge* (Berlin, 1925), 133.
6. Martin Borrmann, *Venus mit dem Orgelspieler* (Berlin, 1922), 105.
7. Alfred Neumann, *Rugge*, (München, 1920), 13.
8. Ludwig Winder, *Die jüdische Orgel* (Wien, München, Leipzig, 1922).
9. See note 5 above.
10. Robert Neumann, *Karriere* (Stuttgart, 1931).
11. Emil Strauss, *Der Spiegel* (Berlin, 1919), 225-226.
12. Hermann Stehr, *Der Geigenmacher* (Berlin-Grunewald, 1926).
13. Hermann Hesse, *Der Steppenwolf* (Zürich, 1946), 305.
14. Max Brod, *Ausgewählte Romane und Novellen* (Wien und Leipzig, 1918), VI, 205.
15. Otto Stoessl, *Sonnenmelodie: eine Lebensgeschichte* (Stuttgart, Berlin, und Leipzig, 1923), 165-166.
16. René Schickele, *Symphonie für Jazz* (Berlin, 1929), 21.
17. Reinhold Konrad Muschler, *Ivola* (Dresden, 1936), 60-61.
18. Kurt Kluge, *Die Zaubergeige* (Stuttgart, 1940).
19. Jakob Schaffner, *Kampf und Reife* (Stuttgart und Berlin, 1939), 323.
20. Kurt Ziesel, *Verwandlung der Herzen* (Wien, 1943), 359.
21. Thomas Mann, *Palestrina: Sonderdruck aus den Betrachtungen eines Unpolitischen* (Berlin, 1919), 7.
22. Thomas Mann, *Die Entstehung des Doktor Faustus* (Amsterdam, 1949), 189.
23. Thomas Mann, *Leiden und Grösse der Meister* (Berlin, 1935).
24. Klaus Mann, *Symphonie Pathétique* (Amsterdam, 1935); Frank Thiess, *Caruso* (Wien, 1952), first published as *Neapolitanische Legende* (Wien, 1942) and *Caruso in Sorrent* (Hamburg, 1946).

25. Franz Werfel, *Verdi: Roman der Oper* (Berlin, Leipzig, Wien, 1925), 23.
26. Thomas Mann, *Doktor Faustus: das Leben des deutschen Tonsetzers Adrian Leverkühn, erzählt von einem Freunde* (Stockholm, 1948), 157-158.
27. Thomas Mann, *Rede und Antwort* (Berlin, 1922), 278.
28. Hermann Hesse, *Das Glasperlenspiel* (Zürich, 1943), I, 39.

INDEX

A

Adorno, Theodor, 178.
Arnim, Ludwig Achim v., viii, 47, 48, 197.
Aue, Hartmann v., see Hartmann v. Aue.

B

Bach, Johann Sebastian, 6, 10, 12, 43, 48, 63, 64, 122, 162, 191.
Bach, Wilhelm Friedemann, ix, 84, 90, 92, 93, 95, 120, 198.
Bahr, Hermann, x, xi, 2, 38, 95, 116, 117, 118, 123, 125, 126, 127, 134, 141, 142, 143, 144, 146, 188, 198, 199.
Beer, Johann, vii, 2, 197.
Beethoven, Ludwig van, 19, 20, 39, 48, 59, 60, 61, 63, 82, 96, 105, 115, 164, 165, 170, 185, 186.
Beissel, Johann Conrad, 178, 179, 185.
Bellini, Vincenzo, viii, 39, 40, 41, 42, 106, 112, 146, 170.
Berlioz, Hector, 39, 105.
Bizet, Georges, 105, 106, 146.
Borrmann, Martin, xi, 153, 154, 155, 199.
Brachvogel, Albert Emil, ix, 70, 84, 90, 92, 93, 94, 95, 96, 107, 120, 172, 198.
Brahms, Johannes, 107, 121, 175, 177.
Brentano, Clemens, viii, 46, 47, 48, 55, 81, 82, 85, 175, 183, 197.
Brod, Max, xi, 158, 159, 199.
Bruckner, Anton, 106, 107, 164, 188.
Bürger, Gottfried August, 121.
Byron, George Gordon, 60.

C

Caruso, Enrico, 167, 199.
Chopin, Frédéric, 69, 105, 139.
Clementi, Muzio, 78.
Colloredo, Hieronymus v. (archbishop of Salzburg), 5.

D

Dante Alighieri, 103.
Dauthendey, Max, x, 127, 128, 129, 130, 160, 199.
Diderot, Denis, 93.
Dittersdorf, Karl Ditters v., 43, 197.
Donizetti, Gaetano, 106.

Dürer, Albrecht, 10, 11, 12.

E

Eichendorff, Joseph v., viii, 42, 46, 47, 48, 49, 50, 51, 52, 53, 54, 66, 77, 87, 197.
Elster, Daniel, 43, 197.
Ermatinger, Emil, 85, 198.
Eschenbach, Wolfram v., see Wolfram v. Eschenbach.
Esterházy, Prince Paul Anton, 5.

F

Forkel, Johann Nikolaus, 10, 12, 13, 43, 93, 197.
Fouqué, Friedrich de la Motte-, xiii.
Friedrich Wilhelm III (king of Prussia), 16.

G

Gluck, Christoph Willibald, vii, 7, 8, 14, 18, 20, 22, 28, 39, 48, 56, 65, 95, 97.
Goethe, Johann Wolfgang v., vii, 3, 4, 29, 76, 77, 87, 121, 128, 129, 160, 191, 195, 198.
Gottfried v. Strassburg, vii, 1.
Graun, Karl Heinrich, 14.
Grillparzer, Franz, viii, 15, 49, 58, 59, 60, 61, 62, 63, 64, 78, 79, 82, 147, 193, 198.
Grimmelshausen, Hans Jakob Christoffel v., vii, xiii, 2, 155.
Gröpel, 21.
Gutzkow, Karl, viii, ix, 64, 66, 67, 122, 198.

H

Hadlaub, Johannes, ix, 87.
Händel, Georg Friedrich, 7, 12, 15, 48, 158.
Halbe, Max, x, 133, 134, 135, 199.
Hardenberg, Friedrich v., see Novalis.
Harich, Walther, 118.
Hartmann v. Aue, 180, 183, 184.
Hasse, Johann Adolph, 14.
Hassler, Hans Leo, 1.
Hauff, Wilhelm, viii, 29, 31, 32, 37, 38, 122, 188, 197.
Hauptmann, Gerhart, xi, 148, 151, 152, 199.
Haydn, Franz Joseph, 15, 20, 25, 65, 96, 97.
Heine, Heinrich, viii, 38, 39, 40, 41, 42, 51, 81, 82, 83, 89, 95, 96, 102, 111, 112, 146, 170, 175, 186, 197.

Heinse, Wilhelm, vii, xiii, 4, 5, 6, 7, 8, 9, 197.
Herz, Henri (Heinrich), 69.
Hesse, Hermann, x, xi, xii, 13, 27, 51, 77, 114, 129, 130, 136, 137, 146, 147, 148, 149, 150, 151, 156, 157, 158, 159, 161, 187, 190, 191, 192, 193, 194, 195, 199, 200.
Hindemith, Paul, 178.
Hölderlin, Friedrich, 142, 160.
Hoffmann, Ernst Theodor Amadeus, vii, viii, ix, 1, 3, 5, 7, 8, 11, 13, 15-38, 41, 43, 44, 45, 47, 48, 49, 51, 53, 54, 56, 57, 58, 59, 61, 62, 64-67, 68, 70, 71, 72, 74, 77, 78, 81, 82, 85, 87-91, 94, 95, 97, 99, 100-103, 104, 112, 113, 118, 119, 120, 128, 132, 133, 144, 147, 150, 154, 169, 171-174, 175, 177, 181, 184, 185, 186, 190, 192, 195, 196, 197.
Hofmannsthal, Hugo v., x, 123, 130, 131, 132, 134, 135, 189, 199.
Hohlbaum, Robert, 167.
Honegger, Arthur, 178.
Hucbaldus, 69.
Huch, Friedrich, x, xiv, 51, 80, 105, 114, 115, 116, 134, 146, 148, 149, 151, 182, 183, 198.

I

Iomelli (Iommelli), Niccolò, 6, 7, 8.

K

Keller, Gottfried, ix, 45, 84-88, 103, 198.
Kierkegaard, Søren, xv.
Kinkel, Gottfried, 68, 198.
Kinkel, Johanna, ix, xiv, 68-71, 84, 92, 94, 103, 122, 198.
Kirschner, Lola, see Schubin, Ossip.
Kleist, Heinrich v., vii, 26, 197.
Kluge, Kurt, xi, 164, 165, 199.
Knigge, Adolf, vii, 3, 197.
Köpke, Rudolf, 58.
Kraft, Zdenko v., 167.
Křenek, Ernst, 178.
Kürnberger, Ferdinand, ix, 67, 68, 103, 128, 198.
Kuhnau, Johann, vii, 2, 3, 43, 197.

L

Lenau, Nikolaus (*i.e.*, Nikolaus Niembsch, Edler v. Strehlenau), ix, 25, 51, 81-84, 89, 91, 175, 198.
Lessing, Gotthold Ephraim, 15.

Leutgeb (Leitgeb), Ignaz, 43.
Lind, Jenny, 72.
Liszt, Franz, x, 109, 110, 111, 118, 134, 138, 152, 198.
Lyser, Johann Peter, xiii.

M

Mahler, Gustav, 106, 107, 178.
Majo, Francesco di, 7.
Mann, Heinrich, x, xi, 39, 48, 106, 124, 131-135, 136, 144, 145, 146, 153, 154, 170, 199.
Mann, Klaus, 167, 199.
Mann, Thomas, x, xi xii, xiii, xiv, 13, 24, 27, 29, 51, 58, 70, 79, 80, 88, 90, 92, 94, 95, 104, 106, 111, 113, 114, 116, 117, 119, 120, 121, 130, 133, 135, 136, 137, 145-148, 159-162, 165-169, 171, 172, 173, 174, 175-192, 194, 195, 196, 198, 199.
Marc, Julia, 17, 18, 21, 22.
Matthe3on, Johann, 10, 197.
Meck, Nadejda v., 189.
Meissner, Alfred, ix, 71, 72, 198.
Menck, Hans Friedrich, xiii, 197.
Mendelssohn, Felix, 69, 175.
Metastasio, Pietro Antonio Domenico, 163.
Meyerbeer, Giacomo, 39.
Michelangelo Buonarroti, 10.
Milanollo sisters (Theresa and Maria), 73, 76.
Mörike, Eduard, ix, xiv, 1, 11, 84, 92, 93, 96-103, 107, 119, 120, 198.
Monteverdi, Claudio, 170.
Moritz, Karl Philipp, vii, 4, 55.
Mozart, Wolfgang Amadeus, ix, xi, 1, 7, 14, 18, 19, 20, 22, 23, 28, 30, 39, 43, 48, 59, 60, 62-67, 79, 84, 92, 96-104, 113, 114, 119, 149, 155, 157, 158, 161, 169.
Müller, Wilhelm, viii, 54, 55, 197.
Mundt, Theodor, viii, 64, 65, 66, 122, 134, 198.
Muschler, Reinhold Conrad, xi, 162, 163, 199.

N

Neumann, Alfred, xi, 154, 155, 199.
Neumann, Robert, xi, 155, 199.
Niembsch, Edler v. Strehlenau, Nikolaus, see Lenau, Nikolaus.
Nietzsche, Friedrich, ix, 103-107, 117, 146, 148, 166, 167, 171, 174, 198.
Novalis (*i.e.*, Friedrich v. Harden-

berg), ix, 51, 58, 87, 89, 90, 173.

O

Orff, Carl, 178.

P

Paganini, Nicolò, viii, 39, 40, 41, 42, 73, 81, 82, 89, 102, 112, 138, 175, 186.
Palestrina, Giovanni Pierluigi da, xii, 166, 167, 199.
Pergolesi, Giovanni Battista, 47.
Perkonig, Joseph Friedrich, 137, 199.
Pfitzner, Hans Erich, 106, 166, 167.
Ponte, Lorenzo da, ix, 103.
Praetorius, Michael, 1.
Printz, Wolfgang Caspar, vii, 2, 197.
Puccini, Giacomo, 106.
Pucitta (Puccitta), Vincenzo, 20.

R

Raabe, Wilhelm, ix, 94, 95, 198.
Rameau, Jean François (Narcisse), ix, 70, 84, 92, 93, 94.
Raphael, 10.
Reger, Max, 106.
Reichardt, Johann Friedrich, 29.
Riehl, Wilhelm, xiii, 92, 198.
Rochlitz, Friedrich, vii, 7, 14-17, 56, 58, 95, 128, 147, 197.
Rossini, Gioacchino, 20, 22, 39, 65, 69.

S

Saar, Ferdinand v., x, 123-127, 134, 199.
Sachs, Hans, 89.
Scarlatti, Alessandro, 43.
Schäfer, Wilhelm, xi, 152, 199.
Schaeffer, Albrecht, xi, 152, 153, 199.
Schaffner, Jakob, xi, xii, 164, 165, 199.
Schaukal, Richard v., x, 118, 199.
Scheffel, Joseph Viktor v., ix, 90, 91, 198.
Schickele, René, xi, 119, 158, 161, 162, 199.
Schiller, Friedrich v., vii, 3, 4, 42, 55.
Schnitzler, Arthur, x, 118, 119, 120, 125, 127, 131, 133, 146, 199.
Schönberg, Arnold, 160, 178.
Schubert, Franz, 54, 79, 96, 105, 164, 175.

Schubin, Ossip (i.e., Lola Kirschner), x, 108, 109, 152, 164, 198.
Schumann, Klara, 72.
Schumann, Robert, 29, 72, 77, 175, 197.
Sophocles, 8.
Spohr, Ludwig, 65, 69, 70, 198.
Spontini, Gasparo Luigi Pacifico, 69.
Stadler, Anton, 43.
Stehr, Hermann, xi, 155-158, 199.
Stern, Adolf, x, 138, 139, 199.
Sternheim, Carl, x, xi, 137, 138, 142, 143, 199.
Stifter, Adalbert, ix, 72-77, 128, 155, 156, 192, 195, 198.
Stoessl, Otto, xi, 158-161, 172, 191, 199.
Storm, Karl, 78, 198.
Storm, Theodor, ix, 77-81, 84, 95, 100, 112, 153, 171, 172, 175, 198.
Strassburg, Gottfried v., see Gottfried v. Strassburg.
Strauss, Emil, x, xi, 12, 51, 111-114, 116, 146, 147, 148, 155, 156, 159, 198, 199.
Strauss, Richard, 107, 162, 163, 183, 189.
Stravinsky, Igor, 178.
Strindberg, August, xv.
Sudermann, Hermann, x, xi, 105, 124, 127, 143, 144, 199.

T

Tannhäuser, ix, 51, 87, 89, 90.
Tchaikovsky, Pëtr Ilich, 167, 189, 199.
Thiess, Frank, 167, 199.
Tieck, Ludwig, viii, 10, 11, 13, 24, 29-32, 36, 37, 44-47, 56, 58, 59, 61, 79, 85, 89, 197.
Tönnies, Ferdinand, 78, 198.
Traetta, Tommaso, 7.
Turner, Joseph Mallord William, 70.

V

Vasari, Giorgio, 10.
Verdi, Giuseppe, xii, 106, 146, 151, 167-171, 200.
Vinci, Leonardo da, 170.

W

Wackenroder, Wilhelm, vii, xiii, 6, 10-14, 16, 17, 19, 25, 26, 28, 29, 31, 32, 38, 49, 56, 65, 81, 88, 95, 132, 154, 172, 180, 181, 190, 193, 197.

Wagner, Richard, ix, xii, xv, 23, 38, 51, 56, 59, 69, 84, 87-91, 103-107, 114, 115, 121, 126, 133, 138, 140, 143, 146, 147, 148, 151, 159, 167, 168, 169, 177, 178, 181, 182, 198.
Wassermann, Jakob, x, xi, 113, 119-122, 134, 146, 148-151, 159, 199.
Watzlik, Hans, 167.
Weber, Karl Maria v., 48, 51, 59, 60, 62, 69, 184, 197.
Wedekind, Frank, x, xiv, 2, 38, 123, 125, 126, 127, 139-144, 152, 153, 186, 199.

Werfel, Franz, xii, 39, 106, 130, 146, 151, 167-171, 174, 200.
Wesendonck, Otto, 88.
Winder, Ludwig, xi, 154, 155, 199.
Wittenweiler, Heinrich, vii, 1.
Wolf, Hugo, 107, 117, 174, 175.
Wolfram v. Eschenbach, ix, 51, 89, 90.
Wolzogen, Ernst v., x, 109, 110, 111, 118, 134, 138, 146, 164, 198.

Z

Zahn, Ernst, x, 137, 142, 199.
Ziesel, Kurt, xii, 165, 199.

www.ingramcontent.com/pod-product-compliance
Lightning Source LLC
Chambersburg PA
CBHW020756160426
43192CB00006B/346